The Left Strikes Back

Latin American Perspectives Series
Ronald H. Chilcote, Series Editor

The Left Strikes Back

Class Conflict in Latin America in the Age of Neoliberalism

James Petras

with

Todd Cavaluzzi, Morris Morley, and Steve Vieux

Routledge
Taylor & Francis Group

NEW YORK AND LONDON

To Stefan and Anthippy

Latin American Perspectives Series, number 19

First published 1999 by Westview Press

Published 2018 by Routledge
605 Third Avenue, New York, NY 10017
4 Park Square, Milton Park, Abingdon, Oxon OX14 4RN

Routledge is an imprint of the Taylor & Francis Group, an informa business

Library of Congress Cataloging-in-Publication Data
Petras, James F., 1937–
  The left strikes back : class conflict in Latin America in the age
of neoliberalism / James Petras.
     p. cm. — (Latin American perspectives series)
  Includes bibliographical references and index.
  ISBN 0-8133-3554-X (hc) —ISBN 0-8133-3892-1 (pb)
  1. Social conflict—Latin America. 2. Latin America—Economic
policy. 3. Latin America—Politics and government—1980– 4. Latin
America—Relations—United States. 5. United States—Relations—
Latin America. I. Title. II. Series.
HN110.5.A8P458 1999
303.6'098—dc21   98-20772
                                                                                              CIP

ISBN 13: 978-0-8133-3892-7 (pbk)

Contents

Part 2
Elections and Extraparliamentary Politics   111

Tables

Acronyms

APRA	American Popular Revolutionary Alliance
ARENA	National Republican Alliance
ASP	Assembly for the Sovereignty of the Peoples
BANACCI	Banco Nacional de Mexico
CANF	Cuban-American National Foundation
CARICOM	Caribbean Community
CDA	Cuban Democracy Act
CGT	General Confederation of Workers
CLOC	Confederation of Latin American Peasant Organizations
CND	National Democratic Convention
COB	Bolivian Workers' Confederation
CP	Communist Party
CTA	Argentine Workers Confederation
CTM	Mexican Labor Confederation
CUT	National Labor Confederation
DEA	Drug Enforcement Administration
DIESSE	statistical department of Brazil's trade union
EC	European Community
ELN	National Liberation Army
EPR	Popular Revolutionary Army
ERP	People's Revolutionary Army
EU	European Union
EZLN	Zapatista National Liberation Army
FARC	Colombian Revolutionary Armed Forces
FMLN	Farabundo Martí National Liberation Front
FSLN	Sandinista Front for National Liberation
FZLN	National Zapatista Liberation Front
GAM	Guatemalan Mothers Group
GATT	General Agreement on Tariffs and Trade
GDP	gross domestic product
GNP	gross national product
IBGE	Brazil's national statistical institute
IDB	Inter-American Development Bank
IMF	International Monetary Fund

INDEC	National Statistics Institution
MAS	Movement to Socialism Party
MIR	Movement of the Revolutionary Left
MNCs	multinational corporations
MST	Landless Workers Movement
NAFTA	North American Free Trade Agreement
NAM	nonalignment movement
NBC	National Broadcasting Company
NGOs	nongovernmental organizations
NSC	National Security Council
OAS	Organization of American States
PAN	National Action Party
PEMEX	Mexico's state-owned petrochemical industry
PFL	Liberal Front Party
PIT-CNT	National Confederation of Labor
PMDB	Brazilian Democratic Movement Party
PRD	Revolutionary Democratic Party
PRI	Institutional Revolutionary Party
PSDB	Brazilian Social Democratic Party
PT	Partido de los Trabajadores
RN	National Renovation
SAPs	structural adjustment policies
WP	Workers Party
YPFB	Bolivian Petroleum Company

Foreword

Over the past generation, James Petras has incessantly awakened us to the essential issues of struggle in Latin America. He is the author of dozens of scholarly books and hundreds of journal articles and polemical and informative pieces in the Left press. In the present work he challenges us to resist the temptation of assuming all is well or that the Left in Latin America has faded into oblivion. In *The Left Strikes Back* he argues that there is indeed a future for the revolutionary Left in Latin America. He not only takes exception to the pervasive neoliberal model that dominates thinking and practice today but also demolishes the argument articulated by Mexican political observer Jorge Castañeda that the demise of the Left is a reality today. As a close observer of political happenings in the area, Petras shows that whereas traditional Left political parties, urban labor, and some social movements have suffered in the face of the global reorganization of capital and capitalism, newly emerging popular organizations have appeared. Deeply disillusioned over the failure of electoral politics to solve problems, and generally found in the countryside and active in local arenas, these organizations nevertheless have evolved with an international consciousness and a resistance to the neoliberal policies that pervade contemporary Latin America.

This volume should be a welcome addition to the classrooms and libraries of academics, students, and even community activists in the fields of social sciences and modern history. It should also be in demand among journalists, opinion makers, and the broad progressive movement in church groups and in nongovernmental organizations that are concerned about poverty and exploitation in the Third World and who search for understanding of the complexities of Latin America. It not only fills a gap in the literature but also serves as a text on popular resistance to neoliberal policies. It elaborates on an alternative to the danger of military intervention and authoritarianism, long obscured since the democratic openings and fall of dictatorships in the early 1980s. In this task, it recognizes the rise of a new Left in Latin America, and it touches on important issues such as why many Left groups and intellectuals have moved rightward in recent years and how the reorganization of capitalism undermines the militancy of organized labor and pressures Left political movements to take up social democracy and participate pragmatically in the electoral process, although minimal social programs are abandoned by governments.

This is another book in Westview Press's Latin American Perspectives Series, which over the past fifteen years has produced nearly twenty volumes on various themes, beginning initially with the debates on dependency and its relevancy to Marxism as well as to analyses of class and class struggle.

Ronald H. Chilcote
Series Editor for the Collective of
Coordinating Editors of Latin American Perspectives

1

Introduction:
Ten Theses on Latin America

A great debate is taking place in Latin America over the appropriate development model for Latin America: On the one hand, there are the advocates of
the free market promoted by the United States and its allies among the Latin
American political and economic elite, and on the other, there are the conti-
nent-wide sociopolitical movements in large part rooted in the countryside.
These two dynamic poles of social action have established the groundwork
within which academics, intellectuals, journalists, policymakers, and party
leaders are debating whether to continue on the neoliberal path or to seek
alternatives to neoliberalism.

This book is about the opposition to neoliberalism—a significant political
movement that has voice, numbers, and increasing influence, particularly
among the popular classes. U.S. hegemony and the ascendancy of neoliberalism are being challenged and questioned by the most dynamic political and
social movements in Latin America: in Brazil, by the Landless Workers
Movement; in Mexico, by the Zapatista peasant communities, guerrilla
movements, and their urban allies; in Colombia, by peasant and guerrilla
movements influential in half the rural municipalities of the countryside.

The triumphalist rhetoric emanating from Washington that celebrates the
victory of "free markets and free elections" is premature. There is another
reality, found in the growing electoral and extraparliamentary opposition demanding participatory democracy and social equality. In Brazil, Mexico, Argentina, and elsewhere, new pragmatic Center-Left political alliances have
emerged to challenge the incumbent neoliberal regimes. In some cases, their
coalitions are supported by the growing extraparliamentary movements; in
other cases, they go their separate ways. The different opposition groups in
turn have opened a political debate over programs, tactics, and strategy. In
many cases, the critics of neoliberalism appeal to different social constituencies. Extraparliamentary movements draw political sustenance from intellec-

tuals who combine ideas drawn from Marxism and from theology of liberation, national-ethnic, and feminist ideologies. The Center-Left electoral
coalitions are advised and influenced by pragmatic Social Democratic and social liberal ideologists. The ideas and debates among the intellectuals are frequently linked to political leaders and often have political consequences. In
many cases, the intellectuals interpret and reinterpret the past to fit the particular strategies of the moment. For example, the pragmatic ideologue
Jorge Castañeda argues (see Chapter 5) that the military defeats of the guerrilla Left in the 1960s and 1970s have resulted in the demise of utopias and
the ascendency of "possibilism"—piecemeal "reform mongering" within the
interstices of U.S. hegemony. However, Marxists argue that revolutionary
ideas are far from dead. They point to the rich mosaic of radical ideas and
practices in the 1960s and 1970s that were not associated merely with guerrilla groups but found expression in a wide gamut of popular movements. In
the contemporary world, they point to the new revolutionary social movements that have resurfaced today, headed by young leaders who have renewed the revolutionary tradition.

Contrary to the mass media and conventional academia's view of Latin
America as having consummated a democratic transition and having become
an "emerging market," the leaders and activists of the new revolutionary
movements point to the authoritarian and elitist nature of the political system and to the social exclusion endemic to the economic model as justifications for the primacy of extraparliamentary activity. Their opposition to neoliberalism takes the form of hundreds of land occupations in Brazil,
expansion of guerrilla influence across a wide swath of rural municipalities in
Colombia, and general strikes in Bolivia and Ecuador involving peasants, Indians, trade unionists, and urban street vendors.

The reality of extraparliamentary opposition and its increasing presence
contrasts with the meager social reforms and progressive changes that have
emerged from the electoral process and electoral politicians who promise
populist reforms in their campaigns but pursue a virulent neoliberal agenda
once they are elected. For a growing number of Latin Americans, the *electoral regimes* today have become the sources of authoritarian practices and
poverty-inducing strategies. Their compromises with generals and bankers
and their facile acceptance of International Monetary Fund (IMF) austerity
programs have engendered a cycle of increased militarization of regions of
social conflict and a downward spiral of incomes for wageworkers and peasants.

The intersection of rising authoritarian civilian rule and declining living
standards marks the point of departure for the new extraparliamentary social
movements. Today, there are 70,000 soldiers surrounding the Indian communities of Chiapas; the peasants of Guerrero and elsewhere in South Mexico are living in virtually military-occupied territory. The military-police re-

pression in Brazil has resulted in the assassination, injury, and arrest of scores of peasant activists. In Colombia, thousands of peasant activists have been assassinated by military-sponsored right-wing paramilitary groups, while over 1 million have been forcibly displaced by the counterinsurgency strategy. Washington has increasingly been drawn into this conflict, providing arms to the Mexican and Colombian armies under the pretext of an antidrug campaign. But the Huey helicopters that daily fly over Zapatista villages and transport Colombian commandos to firefights with the peasant guerrillas make it clear that Washington is deeply implicated.

Although the struggles and debates take place in Latin America, many of the key beneficiaries and supporters of the status quo are in Washington, Wall Street, the City of London, and elsewhere. The issues involve not only social justice and equitable development but national sovereignty. The United States is not an "external actor"; its representatives in the international financial agencies design the macroeconomic policies that promote the privatizations, free trade, and debt payments agenda of Latin regimes. U.S. government officials promote and negotiate the openings for the multinational corporations. Officials from the Drug Enforcement Administration (DEA), CIA, and FBI are present, enforcing U.S. drug laws within Latin America. Cultural commodities and media products are ubiquitous in Latin America, influencing the values and outlook of Latin consumers and providing lucrative returns, in accord with U.S. business interests.

Yet the very system of exploitation and hegemonic control has provoked widespread opposition. Power is a two-way relationship, and the Latin American Left is striking back with diverse voices, programs, and strategies. As resistance increases, a coherent systemic alternative is beginning to take shape. For example, there has been massive popular rejection of the austerity measures and structural adjustment programs. The glaring contrast of a hundred or so new multibillionaires amid 200 million new and old poor reflects the growing polarization. Further, the Left is debating the question of incremental reform versus radical structural change. The majority of the opposition favors reform, but a growing number of the poor are openly expressing support for a radical social transformation. The relationship between reformist and radical opposition may be reversed. President John F. Kennedy once said, "Those who make reform impossible make revolution inevitable." All the indications to date point to the likelihood that the current neoliberal regimes will deepen and extend their "exclusive" strategies, despite mounting popular resistance. For this reason, it is worthwhile to give careful and reasoned attention to the new extraparliamentary opposition that is emerging.

The chapters in this book are organized around ten interrelated theses that link the growth of oppositional movements to the intellectual political debates and strategies occurring in Latin America. These debates are contextualized within the broader framework and constraints imposed by Washington's policies and strategies toward Latin America. The book concludes with a perspective on political change in Latin America that rescues state and class analysis from the tyranny of "globaloney" doctrine and provides some solutions to these dilemmas of change.

At the core of the discussion here is a single question: Is neoliberalism the only viable economic system? One would think so if one listened only to World Bank officials, IMF directors, and many of our leading academics and journalists. This book disputes this assertion. Neoliberalism is at the moment the hegemonic paradigm—but it is *not the only approach,* at least in the eyes of the leaders and activists in the burgeoning peasant movements in Latin America. Increasingly, the neoliberal ascendancy is showing signs of decay. After a decade and a half, the pain resulting from the implementation of neoliberal economic doctrine should be giving way to plenty, but the pain persists and the prosperity has failed to materialize. There are more landless peasants than ever, and living standards of wage and salaried workers have failed to recover from the "lost decade" of the 1980s. Rather than a linear trajectory in which neoliberalism is seen as the "end of history," we are experiencing a more familiar cycle of ascendancy, consolidation, and decay. Instead of the harmony of interest between producers, smallholders, and labor in North and South, we are witnessing the reemergence of political, social, and economic contradictions and conflicts among classes, states, and ethnic groups.

Thesis One

The uneven and unequal development and crises provoked by neoliberal policies have narrowed the social base of support for such policies. The integration of the economic elites with the state creates a formidable basis of institutional power but opens the elites to sociopolitical opposition from the majority of the labor force, which is marginalized by the decisionmaking process and excluded from the economic expansion generated by the economic enclaves in the export and financial sectors.

Marginalization of young job seekers in the working class and displacement of millions of peasants and rural laborers has generated mass opposition, which has found expression in the growth of popular resistance in the countryside and among sectors of the unemployed young in the cities. In Chapter 2, the two phenomena of resistance and marginality are discussed, looking at the burgeoning peasant movements in Latin America. The challenge of these new movements calls into question the premises of globalization theorists who argue that we are entering a new phase of globalized capitalism in which class divisions and struggles have been transcended by an integrated and interdependent world. This study argues that globalized capitalism represents a continuation of history, in which historical exploitative relations between states and classes have been extended and have intensified the rates of exploitation of wealth from producers and labor in the form of rents, interest, profits, and royalties. This exploitative system is institutionalized throughout the world in the form of free trade agreements such as the General Agreement on Tariffs and Trade (GATT) and the North American Free Trade Association (NAFTA).

Thesis Two

There are several lines of debate that influence the political alignments: the debates between neoliberals and their intellectual adversaries; between Marxists and pragmatic critics of neoliberalism; and between the past and the present generation of opponents of neoliberalism. These debates are discussed in Part 1, "Resistance, Pragmatism, and Alternatives."

The neoliberal opposition essentially pits intellectual advocates of self-help and community-based projects against those intellectuals who favor reforms and others who propose fundamental systemic changes at the national and even international level. Among the intellectuals who discuss structural change, there is a further debate between the pragmatists, who essentially advocate piecemeal redistributive reforms within the parameters of neoliberalism, and the Marxists, who propose transforming the structures of property ownership and the role of the market.

The variety of responses to neoliberalism can be conceptualized as occurring among the following: intellectuals who propose adaptive strategies to bring about change in the interstices of the system; policy advisers who advocate measures to increase social spending without changing the neoliberal foundations; and revolutionary writers who propose to change underlying property relations. These different perspectives appeal to different political constituencies. The "adapters" work through nongovernmental organizations (NGOs), frequently collaborate with overseas banks and local regimes, and focus on local projects. The pragmatic reformers are largely oriented toward building cross-class coalitions and focus on capturing voters. The Marxists, or transformative intellectuals, collaborate with extraparliamentary movements and focus on linking local struggles with national structural changes.

Thesis Three

Small-scale projects and reforms are neither viable nor effective in dealing with the systemic imperatives of neoliberalism: The problems are rooted in the market and the neoliberal state. The current regimes have eliminated the social welfare pact between labor and capital, which produced the minimalist welfare state that existed in Latin America between 1950 and 1980. The choice today is between neoliberalism or a highly regulated economy in which the market is subordinated to socialized enterprises.

Thesis Four

Electoral politics have been ineffectual as a vehicle for realizing progressive social changes. Political parties and groups that have relied on electoral styles of politics have drifted to the right and have accommodated themselves to the neoliberal political and economic elites. This thesis is discussed in Part 2, "Elections and Extraparliamentary Politics." A corollary to this thesis is the argument that although extraparliamentary movements have suffered severe state repression (and thus the cost and risk of participation is higher) and occasional setbacks, they have been more effective in blocking, limiting, or challenging neoliberal initiatives than Center-Left electoral coalitions.

Thesis Five

Political parties that were on the Left in the 1970s and 1980s have moved to the Right in the 1990s. This shift was induced in part by the repression and terror employed by the military and civilian regimes of the period and in part by the co-opting of the intellectuals through overseas funding of NGOs. This right turn was influenced by the bureaucratization of the trade unions and the decline in union membership, due to the growth of the informal sector. A comparison of the leaders and followers of the Left parties reveals sharp social differences. Most leaders of the Center-Left parties are upwardly mobile middle-class professionals who temporarily "detoured" toward the revolutionary Left and then returned to their original middle-class milieux. Their followers, however, are mostly peasants, urban poor, and workers, who have no such possibility of social mobility. The drift toward the center by the ex-leftist parties and leaders (like the Chilean Socialists, the Workers Party in Brazil, the Sandinistas of Nicaragua, the Farabundo Martí National Liberation Front (FMLN) in El Salvador, and so forth) in one sense is "irrational." The possibilities of social reform under neoliberalism are minimal. The few remaining social programs that do exist are being dismantled. Rather than reform the system, the Social Democrats are being converted to social liberalism.

Thesis Six

The right-wing drift of the Left does not respond to the needs of their original lower-class constituents. The shift reflects the social interests of the leaders of the Left parties (upward mobility) and the hegemony of the neoliberal doctrine over the intellectuals, leaders, and opinion makers of the Left (see Chapter 7). This hegemony of ideas influences the "material reality" that shapes the form and direction of political competition.

Thesis Seven

The establishment of neoliberal hegemony is directly related to the role of international actors, that is, to the strategy of the U.S. state and multinational corporations operating in Latin America. This is discussed in Part 3, "The United States and Latin America."

Thesis Eight

In pursuit of strategic economic interests, the U.S. government has played a major role in promoting the ascendancy of neoliberalism. Washington and Wall Street have opposed the emergence of any alternative to neoliberalism, past or present. In the 1970s, Washington collaborated in the overthrow of the Democratic Socialist president of Chile, Salvador Allende. In the 1980s, Washington organized and financed the contra war in Nicaragua. And in the 1990s, Washington is tightening the blockade of Cuba (see Chapter 9). In none of these cases of U.S. intervention were strategic national security interests seriously threatened. Nor, for that matter, were narrowly defined private economic interests of great importance. Rather, the threat, as perceived by Washington, was found in the fact that these regimes represented a challenge to U.S. multinational corporations and the neoliberal doctrine. In the discussion of U.S.-Latin American relations in this book, several issues related to the conflict between the neoliberal Washington consensus and the Left are confronted. The U.S.-Cuba conflict is central to the ongoing debate on neoliberalism and its alternatives. The enactment of the Helms-Burton Act and President Bill Clinton's embargo policy is Washington's effort to change Cuba's mixed economy. This conflict of paradigms is discussed and elaborated in Chapter 9, "Clinton's Cuba Policy." Contrary to pundits, Clinton's hostile policy toward Cuba is not merely electoral pandering to the Miami exiles but is based on a larger policy of eliminating the only regime that has a consequential critique of the inequitable consequences of U.S. hegemony in the hemisphere. Cuba is part of the ongoing challenge to globalist thinking and still represents an alternative to neoliberalism, despite market reforms.

The state creates the framework for the expansion and consolidation of U.S. multinationals in Latin America. The state also provides material support for Latin regimes for the repression of opponents of neoliberalism. This continued and even expanded role of the state argues against the doctrinal assumptions of globalist and neoliberal theorists and practitioners. The latter argue that the global world order is a new phenomenon that transcends nation-states and narrow class interests. They argue that globalization is the product of irresistible market forces, which makes national integration into the world market inevitable and social transformations at the national level impossible or anachronistic. Neoliberals and not an insignificant number of pragmatic critics argue that governments, movements, and parties should seek ways to "adjust" to the inevitable and seek the best terms for integration in the new globalized market.

Thesis Nine

The state—in this case the U.S. government—plays an essential role in the increasing flow of investments and loans of U.S. multinationals in Latin America and plays a powerful enforcer role in securing the prompt and effective outflow of profits, interest payments, and royalties from Latin America to the United States. Far from being transcended by the emergence of a global "market," the U.S. state continues to play an influential role through its intervention. The market depends heavily on the continued role of state institutions in preventing market collapse through bailouts (see Chapter 10, "Mexico and the United States: The Political Economy of Early Debt Payment").

Thesis Ten

U.S. promotion throughout Latin America of the neoliberal doctrine has strategic importance in the worldwide competition of economic blocs. The only major region with which the United States has favorable external accounts is Latin America. The positive balances compensate for the negative trade and service accounts that the United States has with Asia and Germany. The greater the openness of Latin America to U.S. buyouts of lucrative firms, the greater the profits remitted. The greater the number of loans and speculative ventures, the greater the interest payments transferred to the United States. The greater the number of subsidiaries and the greater the circulation of U.S. cultural commodities, the greater the transfer of royalty payments. The greater the accumulation of these surpluses in the favor of Washington, the stronger the international position of the United States. The neoliberal doctrine thus benefits Washington's global hegemonic aspirations while increasing the profits for multinational corporations and banks. As an ideology, globalization and neoliberalism serve specific state and class interests. Although these ideologies have little analytical value for understanding the nature of socioeconomic systems, the emerging conflicts, and the growing opposition, they do have political value in legitimating U.S. hegemony and neutralizing potential political and intellectual critics.

Chapter 12 sums up the principal inadequacy of globalist neoliberal doctrine and presents an analysis of the contradictions that propelled the reemergence of the Left.

This book goes beyond an intellectual critique of neoliberalism to describe and analyze the emergence of a new Left grounded in the new social forces in the countryside and in the urban slums. It does not slight the role of urban trade unions and the downwardly mobile lower-middle-class. Rather, it highlights the first phase of an expanding process of the accumulation of forces on the Left that takes place in the countryside. These new rural movements that blend class, gender, ethnic, and ecological issues are working toward the formulation of a coherent political project. They are directing their attention to building urban coalitions, reaching out to the cities and the more strategic sectors of the economy. The new rural movements are strategic political catalysts even as they are economically marginal producers. The new thinkers among these movements seek to link up with the politically weak but strategic economic sectors of the working class in the energy, transport, manufacturing, and agro-industrial sectors. The new class conflicts are only at their beginning stage, and it will not be an easy road. Already with the support of U.S. military aid, the neoliberal regimes are militarizing the countryside, criminalizing the legitimate demands of peasants for land, protected markets, and credits. What is new and promising is that we are dealing with a new generation of activists—and that is not surprising, since it is a new generation of workers and peasants that has experienced the full brunt of the neoliberal austerity programs. Generational politics, however, are played out in class terms. In Latin America today, the principal opposition to neoliberalism has its source in the rural areas and spreads to the cities, led by a new generation of landless workers and peasants who have education but not land, political savvy without being seduced by the financial emoluments of a parliamentary seat.

The questions raised in this book are not only of academic interest in the United States but are part of a vital ongoing political debate in Latin America and, it is hoped, in the United States.

PART ONE

Resistance, Pragmatism, and Alternatives

The opposition to neoliberalism has taken diverse political, economic, and social forms. Essentially, three distinct tendencies can be identified: the "alternative local projects" approach proposed by intellectuals working with nongovernmental organizations; the reform-pragmatic approach, which proposes a return of state intervention to curb the excesses of the free market; and the radical, or revolutionary, approach, which opposes the free trade, privatization, and austerity agenda and argues for collective forms of property, greater social equality, and more emphasis on developing the internal market.

Part 1 describes and analyzes the growth of revolutionary opposition to the neoliberal regimes and policies. The principal protagonists of change are found in the countryside, among a new generation of landless men and women who have developed a sophisticated vision of the world and who share a lifestyle and mode of conducting politics based on equality of conditions and direct participation in popular assemblies.

The opposition is continental in scope, growing in support, and eclectic in ideology, and it draws intellectual sustenance from Marxist, Christian, feminist, and indigenous traditions of thought. The movements have developed a variety of strategies, but most are independent of political parties and states and have their own styles of autonomous direct action politics. These movements and their advances provide an alternative pole to U.S.-sponsored neoliberal doctrines and regimes.

2

Latin America:
The Left Strikes Back

The Left in Latin America is staging a major comeback. While most publicists, journalists, government, and World Bank officials and academics either celebrate or bemoan the triumph of "neoliberalism," a vast movement of opposition is growing that in time could challenge the dominance of the whole free market power structure. As yet, this new oppositional force is only loosely associated, appearing in forums, seminars, and international gatherings, but it has solid roots in a number of countries and is extending its support from specific regions and classes to the construction of a national counterhegemonic bloc.

The term "the Left" is a misnomer. In Latin America, using the description "the Left" is misleading because there is an overhang from the past that remains like a parasitic vine, blocking from view the emergence of the new sociopolitical movements. Many casual observers and not a few journalists and academics refer frequently to "the Left," but their reference is largely out of date or even misleading. Many of these "referents" have long abandoned the class struggle and in a large part been assimilated into the liberal political establishment or its NGO periphery. What perhaps explains the confusion is the way in which the conversion has taken place: The ex-leftists frequently resort to a kind of intellectual posturing in which they label the earlier positions as "conservative," "outmoded," and "orthodox" and present themselves as the up-to-date, renovated, modern, post-something, democratic Left.

In order to come to terms with the emergence of a new revolutionary Left in Latin America, it is important first to identify the different waves of the Left and to differentiate them; second, to discuss their spatial-economic focus, social base, style of political action, and political perspective; third, to present data documenting the growth, contradictions, and political challenges that confront these burgeoning sociopolitical movements. The concluding section will focus on systematizing the relations between this new Left with past experiences, the present confrontations with the U.S.-led neoliberal power bloc, and the future potentialities for a socialist transformation.

The Signs and Substance of Leftist Resurgence

The centerpiece for the resurgence of the Left is found in the countryside: The 1990s have been characterized by the massive land occupation movement by landless peasantry, in a number of countries. The most important movement for size and political significance is the Landless Rural Workers Movement, or MST, in Brazil. With hundreds of peasant organizers and hundreds of thousands of active supporters in the countryside, it has forced a national debate among all the political parties on the issue of agrarian reform.[1] Most political observers of Brazilian politics agree that the MST is the most dynamic, best organized, and most effective social movement in Brazil today. In Bolivia, the closing of most of the tin mines and the heavy influx of cheap imports and government-condoned contraband have weakened the mining and industrial unions. In their place, the peasant confederations, particularly the coca-growing farmers, have led major confrontations with the state and their U.S. patrons, cutting highways and spearheading general strikes that have paralyzed the country.[2] In Paraguay, the National Peasant Federation is in the center of the political mobilizations blocking the return of the military and forcing agrarian issues into the center of debate. Together with other peasant organizations, the group led an unprecedented number of peasants—50,000—through the streets of Asunción to the presidential palace and national Congress.[3] In Mexico, the major popular struggles have taken place in the countryside: In Guerrero, Chiapas, Oaxaca, and other locations, there have been large-scale confrontations between peasants and the state.[4] In Ecuador, Colombia, and El Salvador, similar processes of peasant mobilization have come to the forefront to define the national political agenda.

Not all the instances of Left resurgence are located in the countryside: There is a resurgence of civic unions in Colombia, the growing influence of the Chilean Communist Party in the trade unions, explosive urban movements in Venezuela and Argentina. There has been the emergence of a growing independent "class-oriented" trade unionism in Mexico City and in the North among the autoworkers; of dissident and combative sectors of the National Labor Confederation (CUT) in Brazil; and of militant teachers' unions, increasingly led by Marxists in Bolivia, Paraguay, Chile, Mexico, and Brazil. Although organized urban working-class movements are not absent from the struggle and in some instances may take center stage, the truly revolutionary action and movements in this resurgence of the Left are in the countryside.

The epitaph on the peasantry written by commentator Eric Hobsbawm, among others, was not only premature but wrongheaded and misinformed. The "demographic" arguments about the shrinking size of the rural labor force do not translate into a serious political analysis—at least in the bulk of the Latin American countries.[5] First, percentages do not nullify the fact that tens of millions of families continue to live in the countryside. Second, the urban industrial crises and growing urban unemployment and poverty resulting from free market policies has not created an encouraging outlet for young peasants. Third, there is a movement from provincial towns and cities back to the countryside when land occupations are on the agenda—the "repeasantization" effect. Fourth, the liberal economy has battered the small producers, driving down prices of staples and increasing indebtedness, creating family and social bonds with mostly young landless sons and daughters involved in land invasions. Fifth, "structural" considerations apart, a new generation of "educated" (primary or secondary school) peasant leaders has emerged over the last decade, with strong organizational capabilities, a sophisticated understanding of national and international politics, and a profound commitment to creating a highly politically educated set of cadres. Regional and local leaders and organizers of both sexes have intervened in conflictual regions and converted previously spontaneous and easily defeated occupations into well-planned and executed mass political actions. The combination of structural conditions and the growth of a new "subjectivity"—revolutionary leadership of a new kind that is built around "every member an organizer"—has been instrumental in catapulting the "peasant movements" in an upward trajectory.

It should be noted first, however, that these are not peasant movements in the traditional sense, nor are the rural cultivators divorced from urban life or activities. In some instances, the new peasants are former workers or miners who have been displaced or fired because of plant or mine closures;[6] in some cases, they were peasants one generation earlier.[7] In other cases, they are the "excess" sons and daughters of peasants, who joined religious-sponsored social movements, became involved in the rural struggles, then abandoned the church to lead the struggle for land reform as leaders in the peasant movements.[8] Often, they are small peasants' daughters with primary or secondary education, who join and sometimes lead land occupations rather than migrate to the cities to work as domestic servants.[9] The "new peasantry," especially those who are leading the struggle travel to the cities, participate in seminars and leadership training schools and engage in political debates.[10] In a word, they have a cosmopolitan vision—even as they are rooted in the rural struggle, live in land settlements, and engage in agricultural cultivation. The quantity and quality of these new "peasant intellectuals" varies from country to country depending on the resources and maturity of the movement. In Brazil, the MST is well known for its heavy investment in leadership training, with hundreds of its members passing every year through different levels of sociopolitical and technical training.[11] Other movements such as those in Paraguay and Bolivia still rely on a reduced number of savvy leaders.

The second point about the "new peasantry" is that it is politically autonomous of any of the existing electoral or sectarian Left parties. The MST in Brazil has "fraternal" relations with the Workers Party (WP); it generally supports WP candidates and occasionally presents its own candidate within the party.[12] But the main strength of the MST lies in its extraparliamentary struggles, land invasions, highway blocking, and sit-ins at the Agrarian Reform Institutes. The MST tactics, strategy, and ideological debates are decided *within* the movement and are not subordinated to the party or its parliamentary representatives. On the contrary, it is the MST through its action that has shaped the commitment of the leadership to the agrarian struggle. The recent massacre in Pará is a case in point. When the state governor sent the army to dislodge peaceful protesters marching on the state capital, which led to the massacre of nineteen peasants (and four disappeared), the MST mounted a national campaign that drew on the support of the Partido de los Trabajadores (PT) congresspeople, who formed an investigatory committee, and the CUT, which launched a series of national demonstrations.[13] The MST was the catalyst in the protest and followed up with a new wave of land occupations, while President Fernando Cardoso's popularity plummeted to its lowest level—support ratings below 30 percent. The repressive governor belonged to Cardoso's party. Similarly, in Bolivia, the militant peasant organizations have largely broken past ties with the Nationalist parties and Socialist sects and have been engaging in internal debates about forming their own political movement. In Paraguay, many of the federation leaders recently launched a new revolutionary socialist political movement—in an attempt to provide a national political referent for the peasantry.

Third, the new peasantry is largely engaged in direct action and extraparliamentary activity, land occupations, and so forth rather than electoral processes. These activists negotiate with the state and work with parties and other trade unions on determinate actions like coordinating general strikes or specific pieces of legislation but retain control over the rhythm and direction of the "main struggle"—mass mobilizations.

Fourth, the new peasant movements are strongly influenced by a blend of classical Marxism and, in differing contexts, ethnic, gender, and ecological influences. In Paraguay and particularly in Bolivia, the questions of social liberation and the rural struggle are strongly infused with a revindication of ethnic, linguistic, cultural, and even national claims.[14] In Brazil and Bolivia, there are organized groups of peasant women within the movements pressuring for greater influence and representation in the decisionmaking structure of the movements, cooperatives, and other organizations.[15]

Fifth, the new peasant movements are linked together in a Latin American regional organization, the Confederation of Latin American Peasant Organizations (CLOC), and are increasingly involved in the international formation called Via Campesina, which discusses, debates, and exchanges ideas and experience pertaining to the rural struggles. Through these links and others, an internationalist consciousness and practice is emerging. For example, the militants of the Brazilian MST work across the borders with their counterparts in Paraguay and, to a lesser degree, in Argentina and Uruguay.

In summary, the resurgence of the peasant movements of the 1990s is not a simple replay of the movements of the 1960s. In many cases, the successes and failures of the earlier movements have been studied and discussed. Although there is a certain continuity through the presence of a handful of older militants in the new movements and though some of the leaders are children of the past generation, there are important differences at the tactical, strategic, political, and organizational levels that define the new movements as a promising and creative political force capable of challenging the existing free market order: The village base that can bring down the global empire has little in common with the traditional peasantry.

The Political Context for Peasant Resurgence

The reemergence of revolutionary peasant movements takes place in a complex and changing political context. In the first instance, the neoliberal political regimes have been implementing policies that have had a negative impact on a vast array of social forces—including segments of the bourgeoisie.[16] At the same time, the urban movements and trade unions have been in decline in most countries since the late 1980s. In this context, the eruption of the peasant movements has been looked upon favorably by the adversely affected groups as a mechanism to delegitimize or weaken the application of neoliberal policies, hence the favorable press and media accounts that have on occasion appeared—particularly in Brazil.

The support for the MST by sectors of the bourgeoisie was graphically illustrated while I was in Brazil in May 1996. A group of entrepreneurs organized a luncheon with the MST to express support for agrarian reform.[17] The peasant movements as opposition to neoliberalism have filled the political space abandoned by the Center-Left electoral coalitions. The Center-Left either failed to win elections or turned toward assimilating liberal politics, in some cases joining neoliberal regimes. The ebbing of the electoral expression of Center-Left opposition was accompanied in many cases by the weakening of the trade unions, partly as a result of antilabor legislation, mass firings, and high unemployment and in part because of the accommodationist atti-

tudes of the trade union leadership. The end result was a kind of general im-
mobilism in the cities and stagnation of the electoral parties. Under these
circumstances, the eruption of class warfare in the countryside became the
"spark" that ignited public debate and called into question the overall political project of the regime.

The Left: The Three Waves

Over the last twenty-five years, the Left emerged in three distinct waves. To
understand the significance and the nature of the current sociopolitical
movements, it is important to place it in the context of its predecessors.

The first wave of the contemporary Left began in the 1960s and continued to the mid-1970s. It included mass social movements, guerrilla armies,
and electoral parties. In some instances, class and military activities
merged;[18] in others, electoral and trade union politics combined.[19] This was
a period of the New Left—of movements and parties that challenged the
dominance of the pro-Moscow Communist parties. Some were Maoist or
Fidelista; some were influenced by Trotskyist ideas. Others grew out of the
Christian and Populist movements. The dictatorships decimated this wave;
many activists were killed, jailed, or forced into exile. As a result of the repression and overseas relations with Social Democratic foundations, the
great majority that returned to politics did so as Social Democrats at best
and, more often than not, as neoliberals.

The second wave of leftists emerged in the postdictatorial period, first in
opposition to the authoritarian regime and later against the neoliberal
agenda. This wave found expression in the Foro of São Paulo and included
the FMLN of El Salvador, the Sandinistas (FSLN), the Workers Party of
Brazil, the Broad Front of Uruguay, Causa R of Venezuela, the Revolutionary Democratic Party of Mexico, the Frente Grande of Argentina, and so
on.[20] However, these parties, coalitions, and ex-guerrilla movements became
deeply entrenched in electoral politics and began to assimilate neoliberal
policies on privatization, globalization, and free trade. With time, they lost a
good part of their identity, as parties of the Left became more and more divorced from the mass popular struggles in the shantytowns, countryside, and
factories. Some were assimilated into the NGO framework—working in the
niches of the World Bank's free market and antistatist politics.

Overlapping with the latter group but emerging with greater resiliency
and force, the third wave of the movement is today coming to the forefront.
In large part made up leaders in their early twenties to mid-thirties, it draws
its leadership heavily from peasants, provincial trade union leaders, and
schoolteachers.

This wave of sociopolitical movements differs in significant ways from the
earlier ones.[21] First, many are not anchored in universities; in fact, the intel-

lectuals are still largely oriented to the Center-Left electoral machines or their professional careers. Most movement members are of peasant or work-ing-class background. Second, the new movements have few financial re-sources but do have tremendous élan and mystique. Members travel by bus (thirty- or forty-hour trips to meetings), live on their wages or farm income, and have spartanlike offices. There are very few full-time paid officials—and virtually no bureaucracy. There are no privileges, such as cars, office equip-ment, and staff. The members are moral—honest and scrupulous in terms of financial affairs and personal relations. Very few are "personalist" leaders, that is, they debate in assemblies and are part of collective leaderships. The idea of their organization is that each member should be an organizer. To a greater or lesser extent, the movements are highly critical of the oppor-tunism of the electoral Left and NGO intellectuals, whom they have experi-enced as manipulative outsiders serving external patrons. They have strong personal relationships with many of the activist militants. Those who were part of guerrilla struggles are today highly critical of the vertical style of lead-ership and their use as "transmission belts." They have rejected the call to become the new cogs in the electoral machines—choosing instead to deepen their ties to their social base.

Brazil: The MST

The resurgence of the Left takes place in distinct settings and cannot be eas-ily pigeonholed. For example, the MST in Brazil has grown from a regional movement largely based in South Central Brazil to a national movement with organizers increasingly active in the northern, northeastern, and west-ern regions of the country.[22] The MST struggle increasingly draws support from the cities, among trade unions, and from sectors of the church. The MST is viewed with respect and sympathy by the bulk of the *favelados* (slum dwellers) of Rio and São Paulo. In early 1996, the MST shifted toward orga-nizing large-scale land occupations near provincial cities, both to facilitate support and to form urban alliances.[23] As the organization moves into the inner heartland of uncultivated large estates, it faces increasing violence and in some cases has been forced to engage in self-defense committees to pre-vent marauding by *pistoleros* (armed guards) hired by landowners to drive out the land settlers. The MST has organized over 139,000 families into productive cooperatives, some of whom are engaged in export agriculture. They have "expropriated" a total of 7.2 million hectares of land. They have organized 55 rural cooperatives in 12 states and have established 880 schools with 38,000 pupils.[24] Successful cooperatives usually free activists to participate in support of landless peasants occupying land, and they con-tribute food to the land occupants who are waiting for government expro-priation and credits. The MST Congress in July 1995 drew over 5,000 delegates, who represented several hundred thousand peasants;[25] each state hired its own buses and brought its own food and bedding. The leadership training school in Santa Catarina houses about eighty people in bunk beds and provides bread, cheese, and coffee breakfast, cold-water showers, and rudimentary classrooms. Despite the austere conditions, it all comes together. Today, the countryside in Brazil is a tinderbox. The problem is not organizing land occupations, for hundreds of thousands of hungry families are ready and would respond to an MST appeal: *The issue is organizing to win.* For that, there needs to be political support prior to the occupation, political organization to resist displacement, and logistical support (food, supplies, tents) while the movement negotiates with the government expropriation and raises funds to finance production.

The MST works within the Constitution, which stipulates that "uncultivated land can be expropriated for social use." Thus, the organization is both "legalist" and direct-action oriented. The politics of direct action are inserted in the gap between the democratic ideology (and progressive clauses of the Constitution) and the ruling-class socioeconomic ties of the liberal regime.

In 1995, the MST led 92 land occupations. By June 1996, 120 land occupations had taken place, with a total of 168 *campamentos* (sites of occupation) and 40,000 families awaiting government expropriation.[26] The rightward shift of the PT in 1995, following its electoral defeat in the presidential elections, set the stage for the current land occupation offensive of the MST.

There were four reasons for the MST offensive. First, it resulted from a recognition that newly elected president Cardoso was closely tied to the right-wing landlord parties (the Liberal Front Party (PFL) and the Brazilian Democratic Movement Party (PMDB) as well as reactionary sectors of his own party, the Brazilian Social Democratic Party (PSDB). His links with the World Bank and overseas multinational corporations deepened his commitment to privatize strategic industries, to promote agro-export sectors and to entice large-scale investors under favorable "rules of the game."

Second, the MST offensive was also a response to the demoralization within the Left due to the electoral defeat. It served to boost morale among the militants as well as to fill the political vacuum resulting from the retreat of much of the PT leadership.

The third reason for the offensive was the growing pressure exerted by a number of militants in the MST who were pushing for a more aggressive policy outside of and independent of the PT, which was correctly perceived as an increasingly electoral party in which sectors were moving beyond classical Social Democratic politics toward "social liberal" policies.[27]

The final reason for the offensive was recognition that "objective" conditions and "subjective factors" in the countryside were increasingly "maturing" for an offensive. The initial response to the first occupations was eminently positive in areas adjoining successful land occupations. Spontaneous land occupations began to take place. The MST decided to move and provide organizational leadership and conscious organization in turning the spontaneous local activities into a national movement. Toward the end of 1995 and into early 1996, land invasions became everyday affairs in regions that were previously bulwarks of the Right. Cardoso responded by threatening forceful repression and making empty promises to settle squatters in exchange for a moratorium on new occupations. The MST negotiated but pointedly refused to stop the land occupation movement—knowing that a truce would eliminate its main negotiating card, weaken its appeal to the landless, and demobilize hundreds of its young leaders and activists.[28] Thus, the struggle deepened and extended to the most dangerous and conflictual regions. The overall climate in Brazil, particularly in São Paulo, is (or was, at least until mid-1996) quite favorable to the MST. Following the massacre of nineteen landless workers on April 19, 1996, polls in São Paulo showed huge majorities in favor of agrarian reform (over 65 percent) and an absolute majority in favor of the MST (including its land-occupation strategy).

The MST is developing an effective counterhegemonic strategy and powerful political bloc integrating city and countryside. How durable the bloc will be, particularly if the MST moves beyond its agenda of land reform to a socialist transformation is open to debate. MST leader João Pedro Stedile provides a useful analysis of the national conjunctures that favor the activities of the MST.[29] He identifies three moments in recent history: the final stages in the struggle against the military dictatorship (late 1970s through early 1980s), the mass struggle to impeach ex-president Fernando Collor, and the current phase in which President Cardoso is implementing the neoliberal agenda. During each period, important sectors of the bourgeoisie and their allies in the mass media and the major political parties were interested in weakening the incumbent power holders and thus gave "tactical support" to the struggles of the MST. When their ends were accomplished, they withdrew support. Thus, from the point of view of the MST, the points of internal division within the ruling bloc are propitious moments to launch activities that at least have the tacit backing of sectors of the elite and the press.

Bolivia: The Triangle of Popular Power

The particularities of the contemporary upsurge of peasant revolutionaries can also be seen in the case of Bolivia, where the dialectic of capitalist exploitation and restructuring confronts a labor force that resisted, then was displaced and reorganized to become, in a different site, a formidable opposition to imperialism and its local political spokespeople.

There are at least three distinct centers of popular mobilization: the peasant movements in the South, the mining regions, and the trade unions in La

Paz. Although formally coordinated by the Bolivian Workers' Confederation (COB), each regional movement has demonstrated varying capacity for struggle. In the past, the miners were both strategically and organizationally the decisive force. And this was expressed in the statutes of the confederation: The first secretary had to be a mining leader. Strictly speaking, the COB, unlike other labor confederations, is not a wageworkers' organization: Street vendors, professionals, and students, as well as peasants and small producers, women, and ecologists, are members, but each is given a proportion of delegates.[30]

Today, the miners' unions, particularly those in the state sector, have declined substantially; over 50,000 were fired under the restructuring project designed by the IMF-World Bank and U.S. academic advisers. Despite the reduced number of miners (approximately 15,000), most of whom are now employed by foreign-owned multinationals, the mining sector still generates close to 75 percent of legal foreign exchange.[31] Thus, the miners still represent a strategic sector of the economy, even as their numerical weight in popular mobilizations has declined.

As the miners have receded, the peasants, including a contingent of over 30,000 former miners, have emerged as the most dynamic and influential sector in direct confrontation with the neoliberal regime. One can distinguish for analytical purposes two sectors: the coca farmers, made up of peasants who are ex-miners; and traditional peasant producers. The break of the peasants with the traditional nationalist parties was in part a product of the shift by the Center-Left toward neoliberal policies and outright subordination to U.S. policymakers, particularly the military, the DEA, and the embassy. The political rupture and independence of the peasant movement was strengthened by the influx of former miners, led by Filomen Escobar, who have brought a high degree of organization and political experience to the movement. Young innovative leaders like Evo Morales and Alejo Velez Lazo have brought new ideas and political projects from the countryside to the larger Bolivian public. The fusion of two distinct political cultures has created a movement that combines organizational forms, tactics, and strategies of confrontation that are derived from the advanced sectors of the class-conscious working class with demands for land, Indian cultural autonomy, and respect for traditional spiritual values rooted in Indian peasant communities.

Like the Zapatistas, the "new peasant movement" has harnessed the struggle for land and cultural autonomy to the incursions of U.S. imperialism—in this case, its military and political agencies. Unlike in Mexico, however, the public spokespeople are the Indian peasant leaders themselves: sophisticated, self-taught militant-intellectuals who share the hardships and failings of the everyday life of the rank and file. Their offices are rudimentary, containing a few old chairs, battered desks, and posters of past mobilizations and revolutionary leaders.

First, the peasant movements, particularly those of the coca farmers, have engaged in the largest and most sustained struggle with the neoliberal regime and its U.S. overseers. The result has been a heightening of national consciousness: The concept of an "Indian nation" has become common currency.[32]

The second major shift is the struggle for greater recognition and influence in the COB as a leading, if not hegemonic, force in the movement. This became evident in the COB Congress in June 1996, where the challenge to miners' hegemony was forcefully raised.

Third, important sectors of the peasant movement have taken a serious step toward combining direct action with electoral politics through independent political organization. This has raised a debate on the relation between social movements and parties. The historic position was that they were distinct elements in the social and political struggles.

The peasant movement, frustrated by the deception and betrayal of nationalist and leftist parties, has launched a new political formation, the Assembly for the Sovereignty of the Peoples (ASP), has won a dozen local elections in the coca-growing regions, and has elected two peasant leaders to the national Congress. Today the *cocaleros* (coca growers) are proposing the ASP as a national alternative, hoping to give the peasantry a decisive voice in shaping class politics at the national level. The politics of the coca growers involves harnessing ancestral spiritual beliefs to modern forms of class and anti-imperial struggle. Marxist historical materialist analysis is linked to a pre-European set of values. The cosmology of the past is evoked in support of earning a living in the interstices of a world dominated by multinational capital and overseas banks.[33]

Although the land issue continues to be relevant for many of the coca growers who possess land, the current struggle is for free trade against the U.S.-directed attempts at state eradication. The paradox of a neoliberal regime promoting state intervention and peasant rebels fighting for unrestricted production of traditional crops highlights the heterodox nature of the peasant movement in Bolivia.[34]

The Indian/peasant movements face a dual challenge: (1) a U.S. directed counterinsurgency strategy using Bolivian military personnel directed at eradicating coca production, and (2) the neoliberal regime's use of "culturalist" strategies that pay lip service to Indian demands—largely symbolic gratification that focuses on token representation (a vice president was an Indian) and bilingual education. Although the *cocaleros* have made cogent critiques of class-reductionist leftist parties, their critiques and rejection of cultural manipulation are based more on "empirical factors": The vice president, they told me, is not really an Indian once he serves the neoliberal elite.[35] As in Mexico, anti-imperialism is emerging as a driving force in the new peasant struggles: at the macro level, fixing economic policy; at the micro level, directing the military effort to destroy the only crop that generates sufficient income to sustain a family.

The first major change in modern Bolivian history began with the 1952 revolution, in which armed worker and peasant militias expropriated the mines, lands, and factories under the government of the Revolutionary Nationalist Movement. By 1996, every revolutionary change had been reversed or was under challenge. The decisive turning point was 1985, when the government of Jaime Paz Zamora, under IMF tutelage, decided to close most of the state tin mines, firing 30,000 miners and effectively undermining the traditional centers of trade union power.

The subsequent reconversion of miners into coca farmers marked the second major change, shifting the axis of social power back to the countryside but toward a totally different type of peasantry. There have always been a variety of peasantries based on cultural, regional, and market opportunities. However, small-scale producers who are linked to the mining struggles are clearly different from the traditional peasantry. Distinctive in background, the highly class-conscious miners-turned-peasants have been able to disseminate a class-conscious ideology and forms of leadership among the peasantry that provide a qualitatively different perspective on the struggle. At the same time, the settlement of the miners in peasant areas, in particular in Indian coca-growing communities, has been accompanied by an acculturation into the traditional spiritual discourses and practices associated with the coca leaf and the demands for greater Indian autonomy.

The deepening involvement of the U.S. government—military advisers and DEA agents—in making basic political decisions (through a nominally Bolivian president who speaks Spanish with an Ivy League accent) that adversely affect the coca farmers has deepened the nationalist, or anti-imperialist, nature of the struggle. "Coca cultivators versus the Empire" is not a far cry from the reality of Bolivian politics. As the Bolivian Workers' Confederation becomes entwined in internal conflicts and its leaders in government negotiations, the initiative for political action has passed to sectoral movements and, more specifically, to the militant peasant movement.[36]

The proposal by the coca unions to form their own Assembly for the Sovereignty of the Peoples reflects the growing estrangement between the La Paz intellectual Left and the new sociopolitical movements in the countryside—a dissociation that in all likelihood will continue.

At the center of the political debate is not the question of land reform per se as much as the issue of the freedom to cultivate coca, a demand embedded in a traditionalist ideology yet linked to the modern global market and defended by Marxist leaders. The traditional defense of coca in turn revolves around the revindication of the historical Indian nation, a concept that subsumes class into nation and links nation with a defense of sovereignty. The interpenetration of modern forms of class warfare and traditional crop production, material demands for a livable income through market production, and a return to pre-Colombian spiritual belief reflects the reality of a movement that is building from the bottom up and from the inside is working outward.

The third element revolves around the linkages and relations with other classes and social organizations. To date, the COB has given support to the coca farmers while reserving exclusive control of the leading positions for the mining leaders—a position increasingly contested by the leadership of the peasantry.[37] The miners argue that although they are numerically weaker, they still produce the bulk of foreign exchange earnings and are thus in a strategic position to overthrow the neoliberal regime. The problem is that the strategic positions are not backed up by a "subjectivity" capable of sustaining opposition. To date, the cooperation of miners and peasants continues, but the new peasants have lost their deference and defensiveness: They feel they have the power, leadership, and ideological cohesion to lead.

Finally, within the revival of economic and cultural politics of the Indian nation is a struggle to define "nationality"—which is not an academic exercise, given the fact that the neoliberal regime co-opted a leading Indian politician as vice president and passed a series of laws legalizing bilingual education.

Bourgeois culturalism, in its attempt to manipulate symbols of Indian identity, is flatly rejected by the coca farmers; and the vice president is denied Indianhood on the basis of his politics, not his affinity for Aymara. The issue, however, of defining the relation between nation and class is still in the process of reformulation. But the prognosis is that the space for political negotiation is shrinking as the U.S. increases its pressure for immediate and massive eradication. An armed confrontation is not to be excluded.

In Bolivia, among the principal political opponents of the neoliberal regimes of President Sánchez de Lozada and President Banzer are the coca farmers of Chaparé—over 40,000 family farmers. The free market policies led to cheap food imports, lowering the price of traditional crops like corn below the level of subsistence. As a result, many of the ex-miners (and also ex-factory workers) turned to cultivating the coca leaf, which provided enough income for an adequate diet, clothes, and basic family needs. The U.S. government, because of its close ties to the banking and financial elites that launder most of the drug profits, chose to press its drug campaign against the peasant cultivators of a legal crop, coca. Under the operational leadership of the DEA, the Bolivian regime has periodically launched eradication campaigns against the peasant producers, jailing hundreds and killing or injuring scores during marches, general strikes, and highway blockages. The much-vaunted U.S. funding for alternative crops, estimated at $15 million, ends up in the pockets of government officials, according to peasant leaders.[38] In early May 1996, the government announced a plan to totally eradicate coca production (in excess of medicinal uses). The Bolivian Rural Workers Confederation responded by calling the plan "crazy" and "irrational" and warned the government that if the eradication plan were put into practice, the peasants would rise up in arms "in defense of our families, our lives, and our survival."[39] The peasant leader Evo Morales warned that "Chaparé will be a new version of the Mexican state of Chiapas in the heart of South America."[40] The coca farmers are determined to avoid, by any means necessary, the total eradication of coca, which means, as they put it, the eradication of their families. In early 1998, a major confrontation took place, resulting in scores of deaths and injuries as the government pushed ahead with eradication against bitter resistance.

The coca farmers' movement is strongly infused with a strong "national" ideology: The concept of an Indian nation based on spiritual and traditional linguistic and territorial claims has gained strength. In debates and discussions, it is clear that many of the Indian peasants feel defrauded by both nationalist and leftist parties and groupings. There is a process underfoot to organize a new peasant-Indian-based movement to provide direct political representation from the trade union to the political process.

Paraguay: Recovering the Past to Change the Future

The transition from the Stroessner dictatorship to a conservative electoral regime in the early 1990s has been accompanied by a growing mobilization of peasants and workers.[41] In the immediate aftermath of the overthrow of the dictator, a wave of peasant invasions was followed by a counterattack from the landlord class; paramilitary forces and then the army intervened to dislodge many of the families.[42] This pattern of invasions and dislodgement has continued under the Wasmosy regime. Nevertheless, the cumulative effect of peasant pressure on the land has created a positive outcome: permanent settlement of occupying families in some cases and a growing sympathy for the peasant struggle in Asunción. The center of the counterhegemonic bloc is increasingly located in the peasant movement, which demonstrates a capacity for sustained confrontation.

The influence of militant peasant movement in Asunción was brought home during my stay in Paraguay in July 1996. In interviews in the mass media (radio, TV, and press), in restaurants, taxis, and in the streets, the peasant leaders accompanying me were greeted warmly and were encouraged and openly supported. Major demonstrations critical of government policy were led first and foremost by peasant groups. The agrarian issue has become a major point of contention. And the blunt-speaking peasant leaders are in no mood to be put off. In a recent meeting with President Juan Carlos Wasmosy, Albert Areco began the interview in the following fashion: "Three months ago you told us that you would immediately deal with the issue of agrarian reform. Nothing has happened. Either you are a liar or incompetent."[43] Wasmosy flushed, got entangled in the telephone cord as he sought to get up, tipping the phone off the desk, walked out and came back ten minutes later.

As in the rest of Latin America, the electoral transition is premised on the continuation in power of the economic elite, impunity of the military, the deepening of liberalization, and the repression of social mobilization. A key support for the transition is the U.S. embassy, with its five-block-long installations the size of a military base. When Wasmosy was threatened by a military coup, his first reaction was to run to the U.S. embassy, even as thousands of Paraguayan prodemocracy demonstrators filled the streets. The U.S. strategy is to maintain the alliance between the civilian regime and the right-wing military in order to promote and protect the deepening of liberalization from trade union and peasant movement opposition.

The current peasant movement had its roots in the 1970s, when blossoming peasant leagues were crushed by military repression.[44] Those activists who survived began the slow process of clandestine organizing throughout the early 1980s; by the end of that decade, regional organizations had been formed to coordinate activities.[45] The fall of Stroessner and the splits in the elite were the signal for a large-scale land occupation movement that, with ups and downs, has continued to this day. The major outcome today is the growing recognition that the peasant movement is no longer a "rural issue" but rather a major actor in national politics. Despite the shift to an electoral regime, scores of peasants are arrested each month, violent military intervention dislodging peasants from working unused land is a routine procedure, and dozens of peasants are beaten and killed by paramilitary forces working with the state.[46] While in Asunción the progressive middle class and public employees debate the scope and depth of liberalization, the crucial rural struggle has gathered steam, held back only by physical force.

Within the countryside, peasant militancy is an uneven process, with some regions (San Pedro in the North) more prone to direct action than others. Likewise, there is not always a direct correlation between social activism and political loyalty: Many peasants active in the radical National Peasant Federation also continue to vote for Stroessner's Colorado Party.[47] The appeal of direct action does not obliterate the clientelistic ties of the past and present.

The appeals of the landless peasants against neoliberal free market concentration of land also resonate strongly with small farmers, and frequently, they collaborate in joint struggles. A major problem in such efforts, however, is the immediate direct involvement of the state, namely, the army. Rapid military intervention reflects the structural interlock between generals and landownership: Often, fallow land occupied by peasants has been appropriated (frequently illegally) by high military officers. This was brought home to me in a visit to a land squatter settlement in eastern Paraguay.[48] The peasants had sought an out-of-the-way plot of land in the *monte* (hills). Unbeknownst to them, a general had illegally acquired title to the land. Initially, private gunmen and bulldozers were sent in, but they were successfully repulsed by the peasant community. Local small farmers contributed food and seeds in support. Organized in a semicircle of collectives, the land settlers were prepared to resist the paramilitary but not the military. Shortly after, 200 soldiers with armored carriers destroyed the houses and crops and killed the farm animals, driving out 100 families, beating men, women, and children in the process. The electoral regime has much more democratic content in U.S. press fliers than in the Paraguayan countryside.

In this community, national peasant leaders and I engaged in an informal discussion of neoliberalism and socialism, in which local issues were linked to broader social transformations. Apparently, in the hills of Paraguay, socialism is a live issue in confronting militarized capitalism.

The current struggle in Paraguay is against the clientelistic-statist legacy of the Stroessner dictatorship and U.S.-promoted free market capitalism, both of which seriously undermine small-scale producers and autonomous class-based peasant movements.

To date, the peasant movement is developing on two fronts: through the formation of local and regional organizations and through their growing affiliation with national federated structures. In 1996, the National Peasant Federation was made up of thirty regional groups, loosely associated and without formal "membership cards," a practice common throughout Latin America.[49] The leaders are themselves working peasants. There are no "full-time" paid functionaries, no vehicles (they travel by bus), and few, if any, voluntary professional advisers. Yet such associations are growing, despite (or perhaps because of) the lack of any paid staff. The secret is the "virtuous" nature of the leaders: They organize, discuss, and share the jails and struggles in direct everyday contact.

Apart from the land issue, there are three discernible strands that are embedded in the appeal and growth of the peasant movement. First, there is the incorporation, conscious or not, of Indian traditions (Guarani is the common language): Paraguay is the only country in which the "country" conquered the city. In the countryside, there is a fusion of "Indian" and peasant styles of cultivation: community-based farming and "market" activity. The cohesion, urban orientation, and political sophistication of the peasant leaders is combined with a desire to farm in the *monte,* to be left alone close to nature, and to produce for self-consumption and secondarily for the market.

Second, among some peasant leaders, socialism has become an important political tendency—ironically, while the urban intellectuals move toward postmodern doctrines. This means a socialism that is dissociated from theoretical elaboration, rooted in a common opposition to capitalist depredation, and embedded in traditional peasant communitarianism.

Third, nationalism in the countryside is based on the opposition between Guarani speaking small cultivators and landless workers and the wealthy European settlers who own vast tracts of fertile lands. Tens of thousands of acres of irrigated lands are owned by Mennonites, as well as by German, Dutch, and U.S. corporate farmers who employ seasonal Guarani-speaking peasants. The national-ethnic question is linked to the nineteenth-century nationalist experience. Successful state-directed industrialization was pioneered in Paraguay and was destroyed through external intervention during the War of the Triple Alliance. The historical memory remains, in part because of the valor of the fighters and the success of the experiment.

Extensive discussions, seminars, and participation in activities with the National Peasant Federation brought out several important features of this cutting-edge organization. First, there is the growing responsiveness of the peasants to militant organization and mobilization. It is increasingly common to find scores of land occupations, organized with a minimum of economic resources and with no paid staff and virtually no support from NGOs.[50] Second, the struggle for land reform is increasingly seen as a political struggle in which the peasant movement is organizing its own revolutionary socialist political instrument. Third, in Paraguay, the small and fragmented nature of the industrial working class has catapulted the militant peasantry into the center of action. Fourth, although the number of formal affiliates is small, the number of peasants capable of being activated in general strikes and direct action land occupations is far greater. Fifth, as in Brazil and Bolivia, Marxism is the main ideological, analytical, and theoretical influence shaping the outlook of the peasant leaders.

During the March days when there was a threat of a military coup and President Wasmosy shamefully sought refuge in the U.S. embassy, the peasants paralyzed highways and mobilized to march on the capital. Although students received most of the publicity, it was largely young workers and peasants who stood ready to paralyze the country if the military made its move. A few days after the coup threat dissipated, Paraguay experienced the most powerful general strike in over half a century, an effort that shut down all major activities. Tens of thousands of peasants filled the streets, and the land issue was one of the centerpieces of the struggle.

In Paraguay as in Brazil and Bolivia, there is a deep estrangement between intellectuals and peasant activists. In part, the intellectuals are increasingly tied to NGOs and projects that are fundable and responsive to overseas donors and not relevant to peasant leaders. And the peasants are increasingly suspicious, if not hostile, to the organizational competition and manipulation by the NGOs, "who use the movement to secure overseas funding," as one Paraguayan peasant leader spelled it out.

The Marxist revolutionary outlook of the peasant militants is in direct conflict with the varieties of "post-Marxism" embraced by the intellectuals. Very few intellectuals are willing and able to work as subordinate resource people for the peasant movements. Although the peasant leaders are eager and deeply interested in working with committed intellectuals, they reject working together through the "institutes" of the intellectuals.

Colombia: The Revolution Advances

Colombia possesses the most developed guerrilla movement in Latin America, and most likely in the world. Unlike what has happened in the rest of Latin America, where guerrilla movements were defeated or assimilated into liberal electoral politics, in Columbia the guerrilla movement has increased its influence in new regions, gaining significant popular support among the peasantry while at the same time increasing its military firepower. Despite international neglect or disinterest, the guerrillas can count on a high degree of legitimation at the local and regional level. In large part, the guerrillas, more particularly the Colombian Revolutionary Armed Forces (FARC), offer peasants protection against military and landlord depredation and support food cultivation and social services. Although the FARC was historically influenced by Soviet Marxism, today it is principally engaged in an agrarian struggle for land reform and a democratic transformation. The FARC leadership continues to be strongly influenced by Marxist ideology and is still led by its legendary leader Manuel Marulanda. The FARC number approximately 15,000 armed[51] guerrillas and several hundred thousand civilian activists, overwhelmingly peasants. The other three guerrilla groups are much smaller and number about 4,000 armed fighters. Informed observers estimate that the guerrillas have a presence in 800 of the 1,500 municipalities in the country and are strongly established in the nation's principal productive regions, including the coffee, banana, and petroleum regions.[52] The FARC has built its power base patiently over time with a precise strategic plan: the accumulation of local power. The FARC guerrillas initiated their struggles as early as the late 1950s and have continued advancing to this day.

Like the other peasant-based movements, the Colombian guerrillas have little or no support from university students or intellectuals, many of whom originally joined a disbanded ex-guerrilla group called MR-19 in an electoral coalition. The strength of the alliance, which captured an initial vote of nearly 20 percent, was dissipated when the MR-19 entered the neoliberal Gaviria regime. The MR-19 is now an insignificant political force, and its ex-candidate for president, Antonio Navarro Wolf, is a mayor in a small city near the Ecuador border.

In September 1996, the guerrillas inflicted the greatest defeat on the Colombian army in thirty years: A military post (ironically called Las Delicias) in the jungle province of Putumayo was overrun; 27 soldiers were killed, 19 were injured, and 67 were taken prisoner. The FARC and its allies in the National Liberation Army (ELN) organized in the Simon Bolivar

Guerrilla Coordinating Movement is in daily combat with the military in fifteen of the thirty-two departments (provinces) of the country. The guerrillas, armed with automatic rifles, grenade launchers, and rockets, are attacking military garrisons and air bases; so far, the government concedes that almost 500 soldiers have been killed or wounded. A press release from the FARC announced the first liberated zone in the departments of Guavaire, Meta, Caqueta, Putumayo, and Amazonas. Increasingly, a dual-power situation is emerging. Over the past six years, the FARC has increased its military fronts from 10 to 105. The FARC program of agrarian reform and social transformation is informed by its Marxist commitments. The spread of the guerrilla struggle from the countryside to the city is evident in the recent attack in Bogotá itself upon the military school, Escuela de Artilleria Francisco Aguilar.

Manuel (Tirofijo-Sureshot) Marulanda is still the undisputed leader, but the guerrilla leader in charge of the current offensive and Tirofijo's likely successor is Jorge Briceño. Son of a guerrilla and raised with the FARC from birth, Briceño is a protégé of Marulanda. He commands the most powerful guerrilla front, Bloque Oriental, in the eastern *cordillera* (mountain range). Briceño's headquarters in Sumarpaz is virtually the doorway to Bogotá.

Faced with a devastating attack on traditional crops via cheap U.S. imports of grains and under an intense campaign of eradication of coca, the only money-earning crop for *campesinos,* thousands of peasants are joining the FARC. To counteract peasant organization, over 100 paramilitary groups with over 2,000 members have been formed and financed by the military and landowners. Operating in the areas of peasant militancy, they have murdered hundreds of activists. The principal target of the paramilitary and military is Urabá: In the past year, more than 500 workers have been killed, including entire executive committees of rural workers' unions. In this context, in which the government and its landowner allies resolve labor disputes with bullets, it is not surprising that Urabá has also become a center of guerrilla recruitment. It is not so farfetched to believe that Briceño's goal of "entering triumphantly into Plaza Bolivar" (the center of Bogotá) could happen in the near future.

By early 1998, the FARC had begun to gain significant adherents and increasingly encroached upon the major urban centers.[53] This resulted from several factors. To begin with, profound divisions have arisen within the ruling elite and between President Ernesto Samper and the United States. Washington has launched a full-scale diplomatic and political campaign to force Samper to resign, alleging drug ties with the cocaine cartels. This has divided the Congress, the ruling Liberal Party, and the executive branch, politically weakening the regime, and has led Samper to launch a coca-eradication campaign against hundreds of thousands of coca-growing farmers. This in turn has radicalized the peasantry and increased ties between the FARC and the peasantry, thus augmenting the number of political and military supporters.

Another important factor is the tendency of the petroleum companies to "rent" military units, paying fees to commanding officers to protect oil pipelines from guerrilla attacks.[54] The result is that fewer elite army units are available to confront the guerrillas. Finally, the breakup of the old cartels has led to increased competition between new traffickers, the military, and political officers over payoffs. Under these optimal conditions for new guerrilla growth, the FARC, operating a scant thirty miles from the capital, has been successful in cutting off the highway transport that provides the food supply to Bogotá. This is the closest guerrilla penetration in the thirty-year war and reflects the growing political and social power of the peasant guerrillas. It is possible that if this process of fragmentation and division at the top continues and if antipeasant eradication policies are pursued, the neoliberal regime will be severely tested in the immediate future. Colombia could become the first successful peasant revolution since the Vietnam War.

Chile: The Resurgent Left

Besides these new revolutionary peasant forces, there are also other positive developments emerging on the Latin American Left. In Chile, after a series of setbacks resulting from the dictatorship, following the isolation imposed by the collaboration of the Socialists with the ultraliberal "Concertación" regime, and in the wake of the disorientation and defections resulting from the collapse of former Soviet Union, the Communist Party (CP) is once again the major force in the trade union movement. In the recent CUT elections, despite desperate last-minute maneuvers by the Christian Democrats and Socialists to manipulate voting procedures, the Communists emerged with the most delegates, even as they agreed to vote for a dissident Socialist as the new president to democratize the union.[55] The Communists won elections in three major unions—health, education, and coal. They increased their influence in a number of other unions and won the presidency of the student federation. Under the dynamic leadership of Gladys Marin, the CP has opened itself to new debates on the working class and social movements; it has critically analyzed the Soviet past, while retaining a basic Marxist class analysis.

Chile, despite appearances, is one of the most tightly controlled military-political societies in Latin America. It is evident in the lifetime senators, Pinochet's direct and indirect control of the military and intelligence, the authoritarian Constitution, and the restrictive and unjust electoral laws. Control emanates from the tightly integrated relationships between the government and big business. The result is the virtual absence of any institution or outlet of the mass media open to public criticism of neoliberal strategy. Closure of public space is a product of civilian politicians, namely Christian

Democrats and Socialists who control state funds, manage enterprises, and direct research institutions and important sectors of the mass media. They are obsessed with gaining the confidence of the corporate directorates.[56] They have opposed efforts to investigate the responsibility of notorious military officials identified as murderers by survivors and human rights groups. A majority in the judiciary are holdovers from the military or are beholden to the new civilian power holders. The bulk of the Chilean academics and upwardly mobile professionals are embedded in the middle levels of power and are deeply conformist.[57] Individuals promoting public debate on military atrocities are subject to judicial proceedings. Television is wholly given over to debating the fine-tuning of "the model." Ministerial "Socialists" celebrate the miracle of the model, even though it has produced the worst inequalities in recent Chilean history and among the most lopsided income patterns in Latin America.

The Christian Democratic and Socialist regime and the right-wing opposition together totally control the electoral system, campaign financing, and the media in order to promote their candidates and uphold the electoral laws perpetuating biparty rule.

Yet there are signs of a Left revival, particularly in the growth of Communist Party influence in the trade unions, in working-class neighborhoods, and in the universities. Despite efforts at electoral manipulation, the Communists increased their trade union representation in the National Confederation by 41 percent, whereas the Christian Democrats and Socialists declined. The growing influence of the Left reflects the growing dissatisfaction of rank-and-file trade unionists with union officials who have been mere transmission belts of neoliberal policy. As "outsiders," the Communists have been active in defending worker interests against the harsh Pinochet labor laws enforced by Socialist and Christian Democratic officials. Virtual exclusion from Parliament has favored Communist activism in the social movements. A new generation of autonomous trade union and student leaders have joined in forging the growth of CP influence.

Gladys Marin, the party secretary, is a popular and consequential leader, frequently found in the front lines of demonstrations. She has spoken of efforts to renovate the party, to rid it of its dogmatic and authoritarian past.[58]

Several questions, however, confront the CP. One is the flight and absence of intellectuals. Most of its economists left for lucrative salaries in the government; others resigned for political reasons, claiming the lack of open debate. The challenge to the party is to make room for internal debate and provide autonomy for the new popular leaders. The problem of the intellectuals can only be solved with the emergence of a new generation that is attracted to an open party.

Second, the continued growth of the party depends on accepting the autonomy of action of the new trade union and student leaders; centralist attempts to impose a political line inimical to movement interests will quickly alienate those leaders who were not formed in the previous Communist culture.

Finally, the party needs to develop an analysis of the new conditions of factory work and a better understanding of the class and state relations behind the globalization rhetoric, which is circulating freely and uncriticized in Chile. There are other leftist groups like the network of independent trade unions (*co-ordinadores*) that are gaining influence in the industrial zones around Santiago. The Democratic Forum (a group of Center-Left professionals), a small group of independent political economists, and a burgeoning anticorporate ecology movement could, if they converge, provide the impetus for a significant left-wing political presence in Chile.

Argentina: Between Stagnation and Rebellion

The political struggles in Argentina have been cyclical. There was widespread mobilization in the transition from the military regime (following the Malvinas defeat) and during the subsequent attempted military coups. There were six general strikes against the Radical government in the mid- to late 1980s. In the 1990s, there have been widespread provincial riots. In August 1996, the first successful general strike against the faltering Carlos Menem regime could be symptomatic of a new cycle of class conflict. The crucial issue in Argentina is not the periodic outbursts of mass popular protest but the national dissociation from an alternative political project. Where politics has been joined to the social struggle, as in the general strikes of the General Confederation of Workers (CGT) in the 1980s and the urban protests in the early 1990s,[59] that energy has been channeled into political projects that have been assimilated into the neoliberal project. The CGT helped bring down Alfonsín in order to become the transmission belt for the ultraliberal policies of the Menem regime. The dissident trade unionists (Argentine Workers Confederation, or CTA) of the early 1990s were instrumental in the creation of the Big Front (Frente Grande), which later supported the neoliberal stabilization policies. The organized social movements have thus far not been able to create a political instrument expressive of their own social bases.

Another feature of the Left in Argentina is its dissociation from the major spontaneous uprisings in the provinces, with some notable exceptions in the province of Jujuy. This was brought home to me while I was in Neuquén, speaking for a group of trade unionists, academics, and professionals. Just fifty miles away, over 20,000 people had blocked a major highway in protest over the governor's policies. When I questioned the local organizers of the meeting in Neuquén about the nature of the leadership of this mass action, they told me that none of the leftist or other organized groups were involved. Similar uprisings have taken place in Salta, Rosario, Córdoba, San Juan, Mendoza, and Tierra del Fuego. In some cases, the riots led to the burning of public buildings and large-scale street confrontations, with very little to show in the way of building a national or regional political alternative. Not infrequently, the demonstrators return to previous clientelistic political relations with one or the other of the traditional parties.

The revolt of the provinces has not yet been theorized by any of the many Buenos Aires intellectuals—which is a brand of their own provincialism, though they are well-versed in the latest nuances of postmodern discourse. This is yet another example of cultural alienation and political dissociation.

On the surface, the Left is divided between the Center-Left electoral front in Buenos Aires and the provincial movements involved in direct action. In practice, these differences are subject to severe qualification. The Madres del Plaza de Mayo, the human rights group, has become an important reference point for popular mobilization of young people, dissident trade unionists, and neighborhood organizations, as well as forming a nucleus of university students and academics. Hebe Bonafini, the principal spokesperson, described to me her conception of building a national inclusive sociopolitical movement, independent of the existing Center-Left coalitions.[60] There is no question that the Madres have become a political reference point, based on their intransigent insistence on bringing to justice the military responsible for the deaths of 30,000 people. Beyond that, they have been able to convoke over 50,000 people, mostly the young, in militant demonstrations. The problem of moving from protest to politics, however, remains to be resolved.

The Marxist Left remains very small, internally divided, and socially isolated, though individual militants are found in some of the major trade unions (those for teachers, public employees, and municipal employees). What is lacking is a Left sociopolitical movement that has political credibility among the participants in the urban social struggles and that retains an intransigent opposition to the neoliberal project. Electoral politics can only have meaning as part of a growing political identity that comes out of the social struggles and polarizations of the direct action movements. The new leaders, insofar as they have emerged, are likely to come out of the provinces, whether or not that is to the liking of the Buenos Aires Left.

In the meantime, the social decomposition of the corrupt and inept Menem regime is accompanied by a growing militarization of politics.[61] During the August 1996 general strike, the military packed the streets and blocked public protests to avoid demonstrations of popular power in public spaces.

The general strike of August itself has an ambiguous character: On the one hand, it was important in defining the further decline of Menem support and the growing pressure on the CGT bureaucracy; on the other hand, the trade union officials saw it as an escape valve to deflect internal opposition, and they have no intention of deepening the struggle. In other words, the Argentine Left is marginalized by the conflict between the Center Left and the rightist Menem regime. The promising politicization of provincial rebellion remains as a source of political renewal, but without political leadership, it will return to clientelistic politics.

Mexico

In Mexico, the internationally famous Zapatista movement—and its leader, Marcos—is only one of several important peasant movements located in other states, including Guerrero, Oaxaca, and elsewhere. Nonetheless, what is crucial about the Zapatista movement is the blend of Marxist analysis and Indian practices: the linkage of national or international strategic thinking and local community-based rank-and-file support. Since the Center-Left party, the Revolutionary Democratic Party (PRD), continues to be marginalized from any legislative role, the peasant movement is equally important, in particular the Zapatista National Liberation Army (EZLN), which has established the basis for a national political debate on the crucial issues of NAFTA, democratization, land reform, and social justice. Like its more powerful and numerical counterparts in Latin America, the EZLN combines social struggle with efforts to forge a political instrument to transform the larger society.[62]

EZLN and the Intellectuals

The relationship between the EZLN and the intellectuals, both in Mexico and overseas, is complex and changing. Initially, only a small group of Mexican intellectuals supported the EZLN uprising, most notably Pablo Gonzalez Casanova. Most of the others expressed outright hostility or reservations on the "methods" (which were armed uprising).

Octavio Paz, the late poet of solitude and peace, supported the Salinas government's violent repression and condemned the uprising. Political pundits Carlos Fuentes and Jorge Castañeda expressed "support" for the goals but condemned the Indians' resort to armed struggle, a posture later adopted by the so-called Nexus Group and then eventually adopted by most of the other traditional politicos.

The division among the local intelligentsia was manifested later on when the cease-fire took hold and peace negotiations began. A substantial group of intellectuals became advisers to the EZLN in formulating alternative economic, political, and cultural proposals, though others stayed on the sidelines, raising questions about the issue of "internal" democracy in the Zapatista movement. As the peace process progressed, the bulk of the sympathetic intellectuals pressed the EZLN toward a political solution and renunciation of armed struggle. By the end of the second year of the uprising, with most progressive overseas intellectuals expressing support for the EZLN, the reticent intellectuals jumped on the bandwagon, praising the personal qualities of Marcos. The major weakness of the intellectual support was its "inorganic" quality: sporadic activity; occasional cultural meetings; signed statements, letters, and newspaper columns; but almost no success in organizing a national grassroots organization capable of sustained struggle and active solidarity.

A similar pattern is evident with regard to progressive overseas intellectuals. Most of the mobilizations are organized by young activists and progressive professionals active in the solidarity movements. Although they expressed support and occasionally signed letters condemning the Mexican government, the bulk of the progressive intellectuals have not taken an active role in the defense of the EZLN uprising. This was evident in the Encounter Against Neo-Liberalism and for Humanity in 1996, for which only a handful of the invited intellectuals bothered to interrupt their summer vacations. Among the foreign intellectuals, two distinct and contrasting participants emerge—Eduardo Galeano and Regis Debray: The former is a committed supporter linked to the Indian struggle who actively engaged in the meeting; the latter, a former speechwriter for the right-wing Social Democrat François Mitterand, whose lifetime career has been based on vicarious prestige, on rubbing shoulders with political leaders of many political stripes. In his reportage, the defender of the French nuclear bomb and European Great Power politics reverted to rhetorical questions about the pitfalls of armed struggle and revolutionary politics.[63]

As in the rest of Latin America (and in the world), many of the Mexican intellectuals are largely divorced from the popular struggles as they occur. Movements are at best objects of reportage, not of engagement. The small, committed minorities in turn are divided between those who provide intellectual resources for the natural leaders and those who see themselves as potential leaders.

In the case of the EZLN in Mexico, the fact that the public spokesman Marcos is a committed intellectual who listens, takes notes, and is open to criticism and suggestions has not prevented some from raising doubts about his "manipulative" leadership. This is a case of "political transference"—attributing to Marcos behavior largely found in university faculties. Marcos is a serious challenge to the world intelligentsia to measure up: He has integrated revolutionary democratic values into his everyday life. He lives the austere life of his Indian comrades. He discusses and "rules by obeying."[64] He lives a difficult existential situation, reflecting on the profound consequences of a turn to civilian politics or the continuation of armed struggle. He has courageously resisted the criticism and hostility of the other Central American ex-guerrillas who have embraced electoral politics and largely abandoned the peasant struggle for land. He speaks quietly, without charisma. He attempts to come to terms with realities that provide difficult choices. He takes ideas seriously. At one point as I interviewed him, he mentioned that he has read several of my books and had profuse notes, agreeing with many ideas and differing with others. If ever there was a movement and a moment for intellectual commitment, this is it. The defeat of neoliberalism in Mexico will have massive repercussions not only in the rest of Latin America, but it will shake the major banks and multinationals in North America.

Beyond Zapatismo

It would be a mistake in discussing the perspectives for revolution in Mexico to focus exclusively on the EZLN, first of all, because of the limits of the EZLN, and second, because of the substantial growth of other oppositional forces. The potential for radical change is located in several areas: the eruption of new guerrilla groups, the proliferation of local and regional peasant movements, the radical social base of the Revolutionary Democratic Party, or PRD, and the emergence of significant splits in the official trade unions, parallel to the emergence of autonomous "class-oriented unions" such as Ruta 100. Each component has some overlap: For example, it is clear that the Popular Revolutionary Army (EPR) has substantial support among at least some peasant communities in Guerrero.[65] The radical social activists in the peasant struggle are also part of the left wing of the PRD, and so on. These movements are not responding to political space opened by President Ernesto Zedillo's "electoral reform." On the contrary, they are creating political space under the growing militarization of the country. Mexico's political rulers are the product of a marriage between Mexican trustees for Wall Street, narco-capitalists and viceroys from the World Bank and the IMF. The growth of the political-social movements is in part a result of the transition from a kind of authoritarian state capitalism to a police-state kleptocracy that dubs itself free market liberalism and describes its electoral reforms and assassination of opponents as a transition to democracy.

The fundamental point of the extension and deepening of radical opposition, however, is that it lacks a political axis. The movement's diverse and local character attracts a substantial following in search of immediate solutions but has thus far inhibited the creation of a national movement capable of challenging the party-state. What is clear, however, is that the decomposition of the Institutional Revolutionary Party (PRI) and its internal intrigues, power struggles, and violent vendettas have loosened the hold of the PRI's political tentacles on the popular classes in civil society.

At the electoral level, the right-wing National Action Party (PAN) is the main beneficiary, having almost doubled its electoral power over the past six years to almost 15 million voters. The left-of-center PRD is torn between its leftist social base, which has been pressuring for more active intervention and support of direct action struggles, and its parliamentary leaders, who are pressuring to convert the PRD into an electoral machine catering to middle-class voters in the northern big cities. With the election of Obregon Lopez as party president, the PRD has promised to try to ride both horses without falling between them—a difficult exercise. In any case, basic social change will not take place through the electoral process, least of all under a militarized party-state.

The growth of revolutionary politics in Mexico should not be any surprise to students of revolution. Vice President Gore compares NAFTA to the nineteenth-century Louisiana Purchase. As John Saxe Fernandez has pointed out, it is easy to speak of U.S. policy in the late twentieth century as the "Mexico Purchase."[66] With the financial squeeze by the banks on the Mexican debtor, the 40-cent-per-hour exploitative wages of wageworkers, and the massive displacement of peasants via agribusiness, it is a revolution waiting to be made. The fissures in the trade unions and the public expressions such as Ruta 100, the transport workers' union, quickly attract a vast array of supporting groups that extend far beyond the workplace.

The EZLN: Arms and Politics

The Zapatista National Liberation Army and its public spokesperson, sub-commandant Marcos, have captured the imagination, sympathy, and support of a very substantial part of the Left throughout the world. This was brought home in the international meeting organized by the Zapatistas in the jungles of Chiapas (July 27–August 3), at which over 4,000 participants gathered from 41 countries. From interviews and discussion, including one session with Marcos, a complex picture emerges of the evolution and current situation of the EZLN.

As Marcos has commented, the EZLN has gone through substantial shifts in political perspective since the January 1, 1994, uprising.[67] In telegraphic form, I will list the changes and analyze their broader political significance. But before doing so, it is important to note that these changes and the policies of the Zapatistas have world-historic significance far beyond the twenty-five communities in Chiapas influenced by the EZLN. As has happened in the past, the EZLN has become a political reference point for a significant part of the Left, and thus the pronouncements, perspectives, and policies have significance throughout the region.

It is clear from conversations with Marcos and other EZLN leaders, as well as from published speeches, communiqués, and interviews, that the EZLN has narrowed its goals. At the beginning, the broad focus was on basic socioeconomic transformation (concerning which Zapatista militants even spoke of a Socialist transformation), but the overwhelming emphasis today is on "democratization," "demilitarization," and a "political transition." In part, this is because of the tightening military encirclement, the failure of previous attempts to extend the revolutionary process through other instruments (the National Democratic Convention, or CND), and the growing influence of the Center-Left on the political process. The intransigence of the government and its "salami tactics"—isolating, starving, and subsidizing Indian communities to break with the EZLN—have heightened the prospects for a direct military assault on the remaining communities. The result would be the displacement of Marcos's political discourse, the so-called *adios de las armas,* and the return to armed struggle. To sign a political deal under these circumstances is suicide for the EZLN and in particular for Marcos. In the meantime, the *pressures* are building *for* a political settlement: the need to achieve political space to organize what is perceived to be a "ripe public," especially in the countryside and Mexico City. However, the decomposition of the PRI and the growth of opposition is resulting in the militarization of the countryside (particularly the regions with strong peasant organization) and the spectacular electoral growth of the right-wing PAN. The question for the Zapatistas is how to reach out to the growing popular opposition and convert diffuse sympathy into an organized political force. To do this, the Zapatistas need to elaborate a program that challenges the deep structural linkages between Mexican capitalism and political institutions and the U.S. imperial state, banks, and multinational corporations. A critique of neoliberalism that does not put U.S. imperialism (both its military state and its economic actors) at the center is doomed to promoting a liberal-electoral transition not dissimilar to what has occurred in Latin America. Without transforming land tenure and socializing the highly concentrated industrial banking structure, the democratic discourse of Marcos will become a lyrical exercise.

The proposed transformation from a military to a political structure and the introduction of democratic norms is a problematic issue. First and foremost, there is the problem of the immediate and direct military intervention in many of the Zapatista communities.[68] To prematurely put assembly-type structures in the center of decisionmaking is to ignore the lightning invasion of February 1995 and to increase the vulnerability of the leadership who support democratic values. The culture of community solidarity and survival is a necessary prerequisite for the construction of democracy. The continuance in present circumstances of the Zapatista army is one guarantee. Marcos is of course aware of the centralist tendency in guerrilla formations and anguishes over the issue. The tension between military defense and democracy cannot be resolved by issuing democratic directives: It can only be dealt with in the concrete context of an occupied Chiapas, with helicopters hovering overhead and special airborne troops awaiting orders to strike.[69] The question of war or peace cannot be resolved by unilateral concessions from Marcos. The Zapatistas prefer to go the road of open political struggle but will return to warfare if forced. The war, if it breaks out, however, will be decided in the larger political struggle in which the forces outside of Chiapas will play a major role. Can the Mexican regime wage a multifront struggle with guerrillas in Guerrero, peasant mobilization in Tabasco, growing trade union discontent in Oaxaca? On May Day 1998, over 300,000 marched against the PRI regime. The PRI has suffered a precipitous decline in voter support in the North, and the economy is heavily dependent on liquid "flight capital"—capital that is ready to fly at the least sign of instability. The Zapatistas are tactically weak and strategically strong.

In the event of a government attack, the EZLN would be separated from its social base, and the public image projected by the media would shift from a struggle between Indian communities and the one-party state to a military conflict between guerrillas and the armed forces, a polarization that would weaken progressive urban support.

The EZLN's narrowing of goals is accompanied by the broadening of international support. The indefinition or uncertainty of the EZLN leadership regarding its overarching political program results in each group reading into the EZLN its own political program. For example, some French intellectuals praise the Zapatistas as the reincarnation of nineteenth-century republican citizens.[70] Spanish anarchists see them in terms of Durrutti's peasant armies during the Spanish Civil War. Mexican progressives see the EZLN as a wedge opening the political system. Indefinition has its advantages, but it also has limitations in terms of building a coherent national movement beyond Chiapas. Moreover, it is not clear that the narrowing of goals is not a reflection of an internal shift among the political currents that make up the EZLN. Marcos has pointed out that there is a diversity of political perspectives within the movement.[71]

In 1996, however, as Marcos described it, the best protection against a military blitz is the continuing support from with international public opinion. The Mexican neoliberal regime is deeply dependent on foreign financing and hence on its political image as a "stable" regime. A prolonged guerrilla war and large-scale demonstrations could lead to another massive flight of capital, particularly if prominent foreigners figure among the victims.

The EZLN has modified its approach, shifting away from diffuse appeals to "civil society" (which has not led to "self-organization") and toward increasing collaboration and coordination with specific active organized groups in Mexico that have a demonstrated capacity to resist the Mexican government. In June and July 1996, the debtors' organization Barzon, which claims 1 million affiliates, held a national conference in Zapatista territory and established links. Shortly thereafter, a number of national and regional Indian organizations met in the same terrain. In the same period, the EZLN leadership participated in a weeklong seminar with Mexican intellectuals on reforming the state. These ties with ongoing organized groups hold greater promise for building a national political alternative and serve notice to the government that the encirclement strategy is not working. More important, this begins to give substance to the social character of the movement that Marcos envisions.

The third shift in the Zapatista policy is the preponderance of nonexclusive emphasis on a political solution and the quasi-renunciation of armed struggle. In his speech to the encounter seminar, Marcos placed the armed struggle in the context of an early "phase" in the struggle—meant as a means of achieving societal recognition, opening a political dialogue with the regime, and advancing toward (the current phase), which is a political solution. This is particularly highlighted by the strong overtures to liberal-democratic public opinion and the distant, if not hostile, relation to the new guerrilla movement in Guerrero, the ERP, which emerged in June 1996.[72]

In our interview in 1996, Marcos articulated the dilemma in choosing between military and political struggle. Although he was clearly intent on moving toward insertion into legal political activity, the regime was tightening the military circle, increasing the repression of peasants in Chiapas via support for paramilitary groups and offering no concessions in ending the stranglehold that the PRI state has over all aspects of political and social life. The real political conditions in Mexico are deeply repressive; an average of two PRD (the legal Left electoral opposition) leaders or activists are killed every week—bringing the total to over 250 since the election of President Zedillo. One could imagine what would happen to the Zapatistas if they came out of the jungles and began serious organizing.

Marcos is keenly aware of the pitfalls of the peace accords in Central America and the limited nature of "democratization" under the auspices of the military and the IMF in Latin America.[73] In the interview, he emphasized that agrarian reform and cultural autonomy were essential to any peace settlement. For Marcos and the EZLN, the issue of land distribution is linked to the self-government of the Indian communities. The Mexican government, like its counterparts in Bolivia, Guatemala, and Ecuador, attempts to dissociate Indian cultural issues (bilingualism) from socioeconomic changes (land reform) and autonomous political power. In any case, the government negotiators are putting no meaningful concessions on the table, hoping through time and a war of attrition to tire outside supporters, wear down the communities through deprivation, and then deal a quick military blow.

Marcos: A New Style of Leadership

Marcos, the best-known leader of the EZLN, personifies a new type of leadership in Latin America. The differences are obvious: Marcos is an intellectual of urban origin with a literary flair that is unmatched among his counterparts in Latin America.

Yet despite these surface differences, there are important similarities among them. Marcos is a quiet speaker who listens and is open to new ideas. He searches for new insights and analysis to deepen his understanding of the evolving structure of capitalism ("neoliberalism") and its political implications. Like his counterparts, he is equally concerned with cultural, subjective, and historical dimensions of social revolution. Furthermore, while thinking "internationally," Marcos and the new leadership are deeply grounded in "national" and regional realities, sensitive to the nuances of local customs, traditions, and norms. None of the leaders today follow a "model" extrapolated from other countries, past or present.

While profoundly immersed in day-to-day activities, the new leaders are reflective. Marcos spends long nights reading, taking notes, writing in the margins of books and essays. Similarly, the leaders of the MST on their bus rides in the interior of the country do not object to the long travel time. As João Pedro Stedile told me, it is the best time to read, think, and mull over perplexing issues.

To a lesser or greater degree, most leaders today are very conscious of the need to avoid personality cults and to be responsive to the rank and file. They consciously encourage various spokespersons, listen to rank-and-file assemblies, avoid differentiating themselves through material privileges from their bases, and take the same personal risks as their followers.

Almost all the leaders come out of a religious background, either directly or through their association with the militant rank and file. The Zapatistas drew heavily on the consciousness-raising of the progressive Catholics of Chiapas, particularly Bishop Samuel Ruiz. Most of the original organizers of the MST came out of seminaries and rural pastoral movements. Some of the Paraguayan peasant leaders are sons and daughters of earlier militants who were organized in the Ligas Campesinas promoted by progressive churchpeople; the Bolivian leadership draws on the spiritual traditions of the Indian communities. Popular religiosity fuses with Marxism in a syncretic fashion, a process that does not seem to pose any contradictions among the new leaders.

Although the new leaders are excellent organizers and effective leaders, they are neither charismatic spellbinders nor apparatchiks. They rule by obeying—to some degree. They do not force their ideas on the militants through emotional fervor, instead convincing them through discussions and interchanges. Like most of us, they do not always appreciate criticism and are at times evasive when they do not have the answer in difficult situations. However, it is evident that they live the difficult problems of the militants as part of their own problems: The social and existential are not distinct realities. Despite the widely circulated democratic rhetoric and current electoral system, the new leaders are aware of the ongoing physical risks of assassinations directed by the governments through a variety of extrajudicial paramilitary groups that function with impunity. Marcos, for example, expressed his awareness of the Mexican government's intent to assassinate him. Although this sense of death surfaces occasionally, it is not an obsession, nor does it lessen or modify the leaders' activity. They are always present at the meetings and demonstrations and in many cases have been beaten, arrested, and exiled to remote prisons. Taking the same risks as the rank and file is the only style of leadership to retain loyalty and support. To direct from a bunker would be a sign of weakness or even cowardice. The militants respect those leaders who share their fight: "Showing face" gives courage to the poor who have fears. From a strategic perspective, putting key leaders in risky situations may appear to be questionable; in practice, this is the way the movements have been built. These are the qualities of the new leaders. The new leaders are not overpowering figures who conceive of themselves as indispensable, nor are they convinced by the legalist forms of an electoral system; nor are they privy to a false populism that curries social favor through effusive state give-aways. They gain their authority and respect by living the life of the move-ment, both in work and politics—a simplicity that is deceptive if one fails to perceive their astute analysis and understanding of the complexities of the struggles for popular power. Although they respect the rule of law, they are realists in the sense that they recognize that the bourgeoisie has placed prop-erty rights above human life and majority rule. They condition their support for the existing laws according to the rule of survival, self-defense, and the right to a decent life. The new leaders are very much in solidarity with active producers and those willing to occupy land, resist repression, and produce. They have little affinity with slackers, lumpen, and ne'er-do-wells.

The new leaders are indeed instrumental in forging the new movements, but it would be a mistake not to see them also as a product of the social movement—its ethics as well as its socioeconomic interests. That is because a fundamental fact leading to the deep and pervasive popular disenchantment with the electoral Center-Left has been the endemic corruption that has fil-tered down from the multinational corporations and traditional leaders. The mystique of the insurgent politicians of the 1980s is gone and the resurgence of the new peasant and urban movements of the 1990s can best be under-stood by taking account of the personal integrity of their leaders. If they were to lose that, their movements would dissolve or become fragmented into electoral clientele for the electoral vultures of the Center-Left.

The Violent Rupture with the Past

Many of the top leaders and theoreticians of the 1960s and 1970s have bro-ken violently with the past, in a literal as well as a figurative fashion. To take some recent cases, the Movement of the Revolutionary Left (MIR) of Bo-livia (a 1960s guerrilla group) closed the mines and eradicated coca, re-sponding to the commands of the U.S. government—and they jailed hundreds, wounded or killed scores, and displaced thousands.[74] In Chile, the Socialist ministers and administrators send the police carabineros to repress student demonstrators, fire militant coal miners, and administer one of the most lopsided income distribution systems in Latin America. The Socialist ministers expressed approval of the Pinochet-led military, describing them as solid professionals and defenders of constitutionism.[75] And these were the same military officers who murdered former Socialist president Salvador Allende and overthrew his democratically elected government.

In Brazil, President Cardoso, the former Marxist sociologist, has joined the most retrograde landlord classes in the countryside, represented in the PFL. Allied with local and international business, he sells off lucrative public enterprises to private monopolies. In pursuit of his agenda, he has dispatched the military police to break the chemical and petroleum workers' strike, militarized the *favelas* (slums) of Rio, blocked the agrarian reform, and failed to prosecute military and civilian officials (including the governor from his own party) responsible for the massacre of over forty landless peasants.[76]

In Argentina, ex-Montonero guerrillas advise and collaborate with the Menem regime, which has privatized the economy and doubled the unemployment rate in five years to a record 18 percent, while tripling the poverty level in greater Buenos Aires and in the interior.[77]

In Venezuela, the former leftist Teodoro Petkoff, of the Movement to Socialism, or MAS, Party sits in the Cabinet, presiding over a savage "adjustment" program enforced by the militarization of Caracas, a precipitous decline in income, and privatization of oil.[78]

In Nicaragua, the FSLN competes with the Right in seeking U.S. and European capital to create a Southeast Asian–style industrial export platform exploiting cheap labor.[79] Many of the self-styled "commandantes" are now private businessmen running lucrative businesses. Their political pact with Barrios de Chamorro led to the former head of the army, Humberto Ortega, repressing strikes and student protests and to the massacre of protesting ex-combatants in Esteli.

Cuba's turn to foreign investors and multinational corporations, especially in tourism, has served as the basis for a new discourse proclaiming the "Socialist" virtue of globalization and the inevitability of capitalist dependency.[80] Cuba's transition toward the one-party liberal Mexican model represents a challenge to socialism. The "burning out" of the 1960s generation has had significant influence on the "second wave" of leftists—fusing in some cases and in others simply pushing the Center-Left toward a more accommodationist position concerning neoliberalism and electoral politics. What is striking however, is the *minimal influence* that the ex leftists of the 1960s have on the third wave revolutionaries of the 1990s. The "halo" effect of the past no longer creates any credibility. Today's revolutionaries perceive them for what they are: middle-aged reactionaries defending regressive policies through repressive means. The eruption of peasant land occupations, the politics of direct action, creates tension between the legalist, electoralist politics of the second wave and their pragmatic Center-Left coalitions. The new revolutionaries call on the Center-Left to support their struggles, to pass progressive legislation, to resign from repressive regimes, even as they develop the strategy of building autonomous centers of popular power in communities, cooperatives, and provincial municipalities. It appears to be only a question of time until the rightward-moving electoral coalitions and the leftward-moving new social-political movements part ways.

A Revival of the Trade Union Struggle?

In 1996 in Brazil (June) and Argentina (August), the trade unions' confederations organized successful general strikes that paralyzed the economies. In Argentina, the strike totally stopped industry and almost all of commerce.[81] In Brazil, 12 million strikers closed industry and most of provincial commerce.

The massive participation and the meager political impact reveal the dual realities surrounding the action. The deepening unemployment crises—in Argentina, over 17 percent of the labor force and one-fourth of the working class and in Brazil, close to 15 percent of the labor force in the greater São Paulo region—are historic highs for the last half of the century. At the same time, that mass discontent is increasingly directed not only at the Cardoso or the Menem regimes. There is growing disenchantment with the official trade union leadership, especially the national leaders in São Paulo and Buenos Aires.[82] The convocation of the general strikes by the CGT and CUT leaders was essentially an escape valve to deflect anger, a ritualistic action lacking a strategic perspective and largely confined to registering a protest. The political leaders understood it as such and made little or no effort to meet any of the demands, let along modifying their neoliberal agenda. Nevertheless, though the substantive results were meager, the symbolic meaning of the general strike evokes the specter of a possible urban-rural alliance: the growing bonds between the provinces and the big city proletariat in Argentina, the landless rural workers movement, and the São Paulo industrial belts.

As the bureaucratic institutional blockage weakens and regional and alternative trade union organizations emerge, fissures appear within the existing trade union structure. The regime's continuing attacks on social programs and wages are now directed at the "core workers"—those in the metalworking and export sectors—and affect essential issues, like family allowances and severance pay, as well as job security and subcontracting. The result is the further isolation and discrediting of the compliant "pactist" trade union leadership.

Two processes are unfolding: the further decay of the formal organization of the trade unions and the resurgence of militant autonomous actions based in the factories of the central city as well as among independent provincial trade unions.

Although the public sector workers, particularly in the provinces, have been far and away the cutting edge of the new trade union militancy (understandable given the budget cuts in education and health and the massive firings of public employees to meet World Bank and IMF budget goals), the new round of cuts is directed at lowering the labor costs of private sector capitalists and facilitating "no-cost" firings, in order to increase the profits of exporters (competitiveness) and attract new investors. The result is an emerging "confluence" of common interest between downwardly mobile public employees and private wageworkers who are incorporated in the export model but are threatened with redundancy and loss of social benefits (family allowances, bonus payments, vacations, and so forth).[83] The general strikes are thus the *first* indications of this new and potentially destabilizing confluence, which in its full expression and sustained over time could topple the neoliberal regimes. The question is how durable is the reemergence of the trade union struggle and industrial working-class combativity?

The principle feature of the trade union insurgency is a *defense* of existing social legislation and previous wage gains against the new wave of budget cuts and downward pressures on wages. The militancy is thus based on *conserving residual* elements from the *previous* populist and Social Democratic era: The trade unions have yet to define a new social regime to sustain, let alone expand, the socioeconomic position of labor. Thus, though the strikes and increasing militancy reflect a growing rejection of neoliberalism, they have not been accompanied by an alternative strategic conception that converts the periodic paralysis of capitalism into a transition to new forms of socialized production and distribution.

The upsurge of peasant movements, particularly in Brazil, Bolivia, Mexico, and Paraguay, has provided examples that have made a significant impact on urban labor, stimulating a new militancy that in turn opens channels for the creation of a "new trade unionism"—independent of the old-guard "pactism" and collaborationist leadership. As the political parties of the Center-Left abandon the social movements, the direct action movements of the countryside turn to land occupations, the provincial civic associations and the trade unions revert to general strikes, and armed groups create "liberated territories."

Organizational fragmentation increasingly poses a serious challenge to the paradox of sectoral struggles and radical ideology. The fragmented nature of the struggles (sectoral and territorial) is the single major obstacle to a serious challenge for power. This is most evident in Mexico, where hundreds of local militant peasant, debtor, Indian, and community groups are active, each in limited spaces and working against the centralized power of the dictatorial one-party state.[84]

In this circumstance, the revival of peasant militancy in the countryside requires a political instrument rooted at least in part in the cities and ultimately requires a national political-social organization.

It is important to understand that these are not simply "new social movements." They retain and develop Marxism in new circumstances, adapting it to new class actors engaged in novel types of class or national struggles with a clear perspective of changing the national, if not the international, structure of political and economic power. The constituents of these new revolutionary movements are, for example, ex-miners converted into coca cultivators; Indian communities linked to urban intellectuals reconverted into guerrilla leaders (the EZLN); rural landless workers building urban or rural antiliberal power blocs; and Guarani-speaking peasants challenging the hegemony of drug and contraband "capitalists" in Paraguay. Marxism can be a creative tool for these new protagonists of Socialist revolution, depending on how its ideology is understood.

The United States: The New Colonialism

The attempt by the U.S. government to make its legislation (the Helms-Burton Act) the supreme law of the planet (referred to in legal terms as "extraterritoriality") reflects the growing centrality of imperial interests in defining U.S. foreign policy. This imposition is embedded in the context of de facto U.S. penetration of the higher echelons of the executive, military, and intelligence apparatuses of the Latin American states. Although most commentators have criticized the financial controls exercised by U.S. banks, particularly through the debt crisis, and others have questioned the pervasive influence exercised by the U.S. through its shared power in the World Bank and IMF, few have combined these powerful economic levers with the direct political and military control exercised by U.S. officials. Under the guise of fighting drug traffickers, Washington has organized Latin American military forces under U.S. command, a goal set in the 1960s and 1970s and unattainable until now. In Mexico, Bolivia, and Colombia, the U.S. ambassadors and State Department routinely dictate which military officials and cabinet ministers are acceptable and which are to be dismissed. And as a matter of routine, Latin American executive officials comply.[85]

The strengthening of U.S. control over Latin internal security affairs is paralleled by Washington's policy of pressuring the Latin American governments to reduce the size of their military, increase their dependence on the United States, while strengthening their *internal* police and military repressive apparatuses.

Even at the tactical level, FBI and DEA officials direct investigations and call in their Latin officials to provide intelligence and to oversee operations.[86] In Chaparé, Bolivia, and in the Upper Huallaga Valley of Peru, U.S. DEA officials make no effort to disguise who is in charge of directing operations. And most generals and presidents are very self-conscious of the fact that U.S. labeling ("drug trafficker") can cost them their position. The formidable influence at the presidential level is evident in the eagerness of President Menem to anticipate U.S. foreign policy positions and in the actions of Mexico's president, who makes debt payments *in advance,* despite the deepening impoverishment of millions of his fellow citizens.

The drug issue is confined to increasing U.S. power in Latin America. The use of drug money in financing U.S. trade imbalances through U.S. bank laundering never emerges in the drug eradication programs. The *Latin American Purchase* at the end of the twentieth century is in full force, parallel to the continental purchase extending U.S. boundaries in the nineteenth century. On the one hand, all of the major lucrative public petroleum companies are on the selling block (Brazil, Mexico, Venezuela, Argentina, Bolivia, and so on). On the other hand, the *maquiladora,* or sweatshop free-trade zones, are becoming emblematic of the new foreign-directed industrial export strategies. U.S. corporations now control greater shares of the fast food industry and cultural and media sales.[87] U.S. corporations are active in real estate as well as in retail outlets and shopping malls. U.S.-sponsored militarization is directed at safeguarding the "Purchase." The "new imperialism" is not "neocolonial"; it is direct executive control exercised through a routine command structure via Latin American executive officials evaluated on U.S. criteria of responsibility and effectiveness.

The new imperialism attempts to strengthen its declining global position through the more intensified exploitation of the Latin economies. In the process, it has established two new vehicles for containing unrest: an ideology and an organizational network. The ideology is "globalization"; nonprofit NGOs compose the organizational network. The first is to mystify intellectuals into submission before the Inevitable Wave of the Future; the second, to provide intellectuals with the means to dismantle the national welfare state.[88]

Nonetheless, the scope and depth of imperial penetration continues to undermine an ever-widening circle of social classes: the bankruptcy of medium and small firms, the downwardly mobile public employees, the displaced peasants, the temporary or low-paid factory workers. Even minority sectors of the intellectuals have begun to tentatively revive the notion of imperialism as a central concept for analysis and politics. But this latter move is very tentative and confined to very limited circles.

Conclusion

From opposite ends of the political and economic spectrum, two dynamic forces are in an increasingly confrontational mode: peasants versus the U.S.

empire. The dynamic behind the U.S. empire is built around internal economic imperatives and external political-military opportunities. The dynamic expansion of the new peasant movements is centered on the economic, cultural, and social transformations that have transformed isolated peasants into a cohesive, class-conscious, and revolutionary force.

The pattern of empire building is built around rentier extraction of interest payments, pillage of natural resources, and large-scale transfer of public property to multinationals. Together these forces have put tremendous pressure on the Latin American social system to heighten the extractions of value, income, and labor from workers and peasants. In this process of extraction and appropriation, the "provinces" and the rural areas have been especially hard-hit—since the "local power structure" is located in the central cities. The intensification of exploitation is accompanied by the penetration of cultural commodities that facilitate the fragmentation and alienation, particularly of uprooted urban groups. The dynamics of exploitation and fragmentation accompany the imperial-sponsored circulation of "market ideologies" through NGO and intellectual think tanks that drive a wedge between middle-class professionals, intellectuals, and labor. The imperial hegemonic bloc is strengthened by the "overdetermined" nature of U.S. influence in the military and police institutions, largely through the antinarcotic campaigns.

The underlying drive of U.S. empire building is determined by the decisive dependence of the largest U.S. multinationals on overseas profits and by the reliance of the U.S. economy on favorable accounts with Latin America to compensate for deficits in Asia and Germany.[89]

The logic of the expansion of the new peasant movements is intimately related to the internal transformations of the peasantry (politically, culturally, and economically) as well as to a dialectical resistance to the deepening encroachment of imperial demands. The "peasantry" today is both "market-oriented" and "worker-oriented." Small producers' access to credit, markets, and technical aid is linked to their increasing class conditions as wageworkers. The displacement of educated (self-taught or formally educated) peasants linked to modern urban centers creates a new peasantry with modern organizational and media skills that link agricultural activities to urban styles of class combat.

It would be a serious mistake to dismiss contemporary peasant movements as the last gasp of rebellion before they disappear from the map. The persistence and rootedness of the peasantry and the increasing displacement of urban workers, high-crime cities, and the decline of social services has narrowed the gap between countryside and city. As movements realize land takeovers and build communities, there could be a stabilization, if not a reversal, of the rural to urban migration. There is no inherent historical logic that compels the demographic change. In large part, it is a political question. The core regions are affected by imperial penetration in the countryside via the subordination of the state to imperial obligations: interest payments, the repression of coca farmers, the subsidy of agro-export conglomerates—all of these are *state directed.*

The fundamental dynamics of resistance are the "end product" of this imperial state exploitative chain. And it is at that end point that the reverse process of resistance and transformation is occurring.

The process of empire building is not a result of conjunctural events or particular policies but rather reflects deep structural processes built into the production and profit balances of major economic institutions at the pinnacle of the U.S. economic system.

To date, the U.S. empire has flourished as never before: Conditions for mineral appropriation, access to markets, low labor costs, and influence over governments and the military have never been better in this century. The space of "reforms" are almost nonexistent within the imperial formula of free markets, electoral regimes, and military oversight.[90] The dialectical opposite pole, however, is the decay of urban middle-sector mediating forces and the rapid accumulation of downwardly mobile workers and public employees moving toward the poles of direct social action. It is in this ambience of imperial excesses, unprecedented accumulation, and massive degradation of labor that new poles of social action in the countryside are gaining national political influence and prominence.

The fundamental turn from agrarian issues toward social transformation is built around the renewal of a Socialist praxis that links cultural autonomy and small-scale production with control over the strategic heights of the economy. That can only become a reality when socialism becomes integrated into the endogenous forms of cultural and social practices and if the basic producers are infused with the new values of gender equality and environmental compatibility. The empire has struck and torn asunder the economic, cultural, and political fabric of Latin American societies. It has assimilated a few and exploited the many.

But now the Left has struck back: From the villages of Paraguay and Bolivia, from the rural squatter settlements of Brazil to the jungles of Mexico, a new movement is taking hold that is writing its own history and practicing its own theory.

Notes

1. Basic history of the MST is found in João Pedro Stedile e Frei Sergio, *A Luta pela Terra No Brazil* (São Paulo: Scritta, 1993); *Documento Basico do MST* (São Paulo: MST, 1994). See *Jornal do Brasil,* June 23, 1996, p. 17.

2. Alex Contreras Baspineiro, *La Marcha Historica* (Cochabamba: CEDIB, 1994); interview with Evo Morales in Carlos D. Mesa Gisbert, *De Cerca* (La Paz: BBA, 1994).

3. *Informativo Campesino* (Asunción), no. 91 (April 1996).

4. *La Jornada,* August 10, 1996, p. 3; *Chiapas* (Mexico City), no. 2.

5. Eric Hobsbawm, *The Age of Extremes: A History of the World* (New York: Pantheon, 1994), pp. 8, 289.

6. Interview with Evo Morales, June 10, 1996. Many of the names of the peasant unions are taken from mining centers of Oruro.

7. Ibid.

8. Interview with regional leaders of the Landless Rural Workers Movement of Brazil at I Curso Latinoamericano de Formacion, March 19–29, 1995, Instituto Cajamar, São Paulo.

9. Interviews with Brazilian rural women workers of the MST at the Conference on Peasant Women in Rural Struggles, June 22, 1996, Cajamar, São Paulo.

10. There are regional organizations in Latin America, among them, CLOC (Congreso Latinoamericano de Organizaciones del Campo) and, internationally, Via Campesina, where rural worker leaders share experiences and debate such issues as the globalization of production (imperialism) and its impact on rural producers and strategies for combating neoliberation.

11. *Como Organizar a la Masa,* Direccion Nacional MST, São Paulo, September 1991; *Documento Basico do MST,* São Paulo, July 1994.

12. Interviews with MST leaders João Pedro Stedile, Ademar Bobo Egidio Brunetto, March 19–29, 1995. See also *Documento Basico do MST,* pp. 24–30.

13. In discussion with CUT leaders in Rio de Janeiro, Fortaleza São Paulo, Florianopolis, it was clear that the MST was at the cutting edge of the struggle. Most urban trade union leaders readily admitted that the MST was far more cohesive and organized for confrontation than the industrial unions in the cities. It was clear from the posters plastered on the walls of downtown Rio condemning the massacre at Pará that the rural struggle had became a "cause" for the militant sectors of the CUT. Interview with Iña Meireles, president of CUT Rio de Janeiro, May 17, 1996; Vito Giannotti, educational director, Aeronautical Workers, Rio de Janeiro, May 16, 1996.

14. In June 1996, during a seminar I conducted in Bolivia at the training school attended mostly by coca-growing peasants in La Paz, the relation of class and nation was the central topic of debate. In Paraguay, the issue is less clearly defined, though in everyday conversations with peasant leaders it was clear that the Guarani cultural-linguistic universe was central. As one peasant leader (Alberto Areco) said to me on July 6, 1996, at Asunción, "I think in Guarani and then have to translate it to Spanish when we are discussing; that's why I speak slower."

15. At a seminar in Cajamar (São Paulo) on May 21, 1996, there were over eighty peasant women leaders from all regions of Brazil discussing issues of gender equality in cooperatives, greater leadership roles, greater acceptance of married women attending cadre schools, and so on. In a seminar that I conducted, the class-gender framework was generally accepted, and the debate flowed within the parameters of a rejection of bourgeois (classless) feminism and class-reductionist economism. At the second meeting of the CLOC, almost 40 percent of the peasant delegates were women, up from 10 percent three years earlier.

16. This thesis is developed in James Petras, Henry Veltmeyer, and Steve Vieux, *Neoliberalism and Class Conflict in Latin America* (London: Macmillan, 1997), in particular, in chap. 2, "The Global and Local Dynamics of Latin American Develop-

ment." The fact that neoliberalism is a capitalist development strategy should not obscure the fact that it has had a devastating effect on local small and medium-size manufacturers and farmers. In Argentina and Mexico, bankruptcies are occurring at a historically record rate, and a similar problem is occurring among Brazilian farmers in the South and manufacturers in the Southeast.

17. Interview with João Pedro Stedile of the MST, May 13, 1996.

18. This was the case at least in part in some industries and factories in Argentina. The Montoneros and Peoples Revolutionary Army did have influence in specific unions, particularly in Cordoba and Rosario. This was generally not the case in the major metallurgical industries in the greater Buenos Aires area.

19. Chile was the classic case during the late 1960s and early 1970s. See my *Politics and Social Forces in Chilean Development* (Berkeley: University of California Press, 1968).

20. A typical list of declarations from the FORO appears in *America Libre* (Buenos Aires), no. 7 (July 1995), pp. 115–118.

21. This section as well as other discussions in this chapter are based on a series of interviews, informal discussions, and seminars that have taken place between 1993 and 1996. Between May and August 1996, I was invited to lead seminars by the MST and CUT of Brazil, the Miners' Union and coca peasant growers in Bolivia, the Peasant Federation in Paraguay, and the EZLN in Mexico. Much of the discussion in this essay reflects a "participant observer" perspective.

22. *A Luta pela Terra No Brazil,* pp. 23–39.

23. Interview with João Pedro Stedile, May 13, 1996. The new tactics are directed at building strategic alliances in the cities with trade unions and urban movements, both to prevent repression and to create the basis for a new national political movement.

24. An example of the redistributive *and* productionist approach of the MST—and a favorable response from the mass media—is found in "De Sem-Terra a Productor Rural," *A Noticia,* May 31, 1996, p. 1. On the data, see *Brazil Report: Latin American Regional Report,* September 19, 1996, pp. 6–7.

25. *Jornal dos Trabalhadores Rurais Sem-Terra* (São Paulo), August 1995.

26. Ibid., July 1996, p. 8.

27. Interviews with regional leaders of MST Santa Catarina.

28. "Sem-Terra Não Aceitan a Trégua Dos Ruralistas," *Jornal do Brasil,* June 4, 1996, p. 1B.

29. Interview, June 22, 1996.

30. *Los Tiempos* (Cochabamba), May 12, 1996, p. A9.

31. Gabriel Tabera Soliz, "Mineria Boliviana en Manos de Comsur e Inti Raymi," *La Razon* (La Paz), January 21, 1996, pp. D8, 9.

32. See H.C.F. Mansilla and Maria Teresa Zegada, *Politica, Cultura, y Etnicidad en Bolivia* (La Paz: CEBEM and CESU-UMSS, 1996).

33. Interview with Evo Morales (Cochabamba), June 12, 1996.

34. Ibid. See also Alex Contreras Baspineiro, *La Marcha Historica* (Cochabamba: CEDIB, 1994); Maria Lohman et al., *"Guerra a las Drogas": Un Vision Desde las Andes* (Cochabamba: CEDIB, 1994).

35. Discussion with coca farmers in leadership training school, La Paz, June 6, 1996.

36. The debates and controversies with the Bolivian trade union congress are summarized in Washington Estellano, "El Congreso Interrumpedo," *Punto Final* (Santiago), July 15, 1996.

37. Ibid. Estellano comments that the strong presence of the peasants led to a second secretary general being nominated by the peasant confederation.

38. Interview with Evo Morales in Mesa Gisbert, *De Cerca*.

39. *Los Tiempos* (Cochabamba), June 13, 1996, pp. A1, A9.

40. Ibid.

41. Daniel Campos Ruiz and Dienisio Borda, *Las Organizaciones Campesinas en la Decada de los 80* (CIPAE: Asunción, n.d.); *Guia de Organizaciones Campesinas, 1992–1993* (Asunción: CDE, 1994); *Censo de Organizaciones Campesinas, 1992–1993* (Asunción: CDE, 1994); Myriam Cristina Davalos and Jose Carlos Rodiguez, *Organizaciones Campesinas de Mugeres, 1992–1993* (Asunción: CDE, 1994).

42. In 1990, there were 49 land occupations and 51 evictions (at times the same land is occupied more than once); in 1991, 17 occupations and 23 evictions; in 1992, 16 and 16; in 1993, 14 and 17. In the same period, 1600 peasants were arrested. The same pattern persists in 1996: In April there were 11 occupied farms and 4 evictions. Monthly data are found in *Informativo Campesino* (Asunción: CDE, December 1993 and April 1996).

43. Interview with Alberto Areco, member of the executive committee of the National Peasant Federation (FNC), July 7, 1996.

44. See Campos and Borda, *Las Organizaciones Campesinas*.

45. Interviews with Eladio Flecha and Alfonso Cohere, July 1, 1996, members of the executive committee of the FNC.

46. See *Noticias* (Asunción) May 8, 1996; June 19, 1996; May 9, 1996. On May 8, 1996, peasant leaders walked out of negotiations, protesting the jailing of 160 peasants.

47. Interview with Alfonso Cohere, vice president of the FNC, July 1, 1996.

48. The peasant settlement Santa Carmen was in the department (county) of Caguazu, 250 kilometers from Asunción. The landowner was the ex-general Roberto Knopfelmacher.

49. Interview with Alberto Areco, FNC president.

50. To reach the villages where we held meetings, the FNC either borrowed a car from the CUT or else we needed good soles on our shoes to help the car brake.

51. *Clarin* (Buenos Aires), June 30, 1996. See also *Resistencia* (the organ of the FARC), May 15, 1996.

52. Ibid.

53. Interview with FARC spokesperson in Buenos Aires, June 15, 1996, and with comunicados of the FARC, February—April 1996.

54. *New York Times*, August 22, 1996.

55. The Communist Party increased its representation in the executive committee of the CUT by 44 percent, the Christian Democrats declined by 33 percent, and the Socialists lost 6 percent. The present executive committee includes 16 Communists (up from 10 previously), 15 Socialists (down from 16), 11 Christian Democrats (down from 17), and 6 others from other groups *El Siglo* (Santiago), April 19–25,

1996. See also "Como Avanzan los Comunistas," *El Mercurio,* May 26, 1996, pp. D1, D22, D23.

56. See James Petras, Fernando Leiva, and Henry Veltmeyer, *Democracy and Poverty in Chile* (Boulder: Westview Press, 1994), especially chap. 5, pp. 85–89, on institutional continuities.

57. Ibid. On the intellectuals, see chap. 4, "From Critics to Celebrants," pp. 46–75.

58. Interview with Gladys Marin, March 29, 1996. See also *El Mercurio,* May 26, 1996, pp. D1, D22, D23.

59. One of the best sources on popular struggles is the monthly published by the Madres de Plaza de Mayo, which carries the same name. See also "El Fuego de Santiago," *America Libre,* no. 5 (June 1994), pp. 92–100.

60. Interview with Hebe Bonafini, June 20, 1996.

61. Nestor Lopez and Alberto Minujin, "Nueva Pobreza y Exclusion: El Caso Argentino," *Nueva Sociedad,* no. 131 (May–June 1994), pp. 88–105. By the end of September 1996, the Menem regime's popularity had plummeted to its lowest level since Menem was elected—under 25 percent. And in the mayoral election in Buenos Aires, which has almost one-third of the electorate, his hand-picked candidate came in third, with almost one-fifth of the votes.

62. There has been a flood tide of books written on the EZLN. One of the best ongoing analytical sources is found in *Chiapas,* edited by Ana Esther Ceceña (Mexico City: UNAM, 1996).

63. Regis Debray, "Talking to the Zapatista," *New Left Review,* no. 218 (July-August), pp. 128–137.

64. Interview and discussion with Marcos of the EZLN, July 29, 1996, during the Encounter Against Neo-liberalism and for Humanity in *La Realidad* (Chiapras), July 27–August 3, 1996.

65. Leticia Hernandez Montoya, "Rechazamos el Dialogo; Derrocar al Estado, Nuestro Objetivo: EPR," *Excelsior,* August 10, 1996, pp. 1, 8, 17, 25; *Mexico City Times,* August 10, 1996, p. 1.

66. John Saxe-Fernandez interview, August 7, 1996, Mexico City. His forthcoming study on U.S.-Mexican relations draws heavily on nineteenth-century Porfirismo and U.S. annexation policies to explain NAFTA and the U.S. buyout of Mexican resources.

67. Interview-discussion with Marcos, July 29, 1996.

68. Since the initial Zapatista uprising, the Mexican government has invested tens of millions in building roads that lead to the jungles of Chiapas—strictly for counterinsurgency purposes. Passing over these roads leading to the Zapatista communities, I had the sensation that a military blitz could be launched within a matter of minutes, exterminating a substantial part of the social base of the movement.

69. The road leading toward the EZLN communities is covered by military camps and military checkpoints. During the encounter, helicopters hovered over the meetings, in a clear display of power. It is within this security context that the ruminations on democracy of critics like Debray and Gilly have to be understood.

70. Alan Touraine, who was at the encounter, made this comparison, thus reconciling his support for the EZLN with his earlier opposition to the French workers'

strikes against Chirac's social cuts in December 1995. Both Chirac and Marcos could be seen, in this version, as republican citizens.

71. Interview-discussion, July 29, 1996.

72. Ibid.

73. This section draws on observations based on discussions and political collaboration with sociopolitical movements in Paraguay, Brazil, Bolivia, Argentina, and Chile. It also draws on interviews with movement leaders and activists in Mexico, Colombia, and El Salvador. The time span varies from decades in Chile and Argentina to the past five years in Brazil to shorter periods in Paraguay and Bolivia.

74. See Mesa Gisbert, *De Cerca,* interview with Evo Morales.

75. *Punto Final* (Santiago), June 1996, p. 3; *El Siglo,* May 31–June 6, 1996, pp. 4–7.

76. Communiqué MST "Informaes Sobre o Massacre de Eldorado dos Carajas," July 30, 1996. See also "Balanco do Governo Comprova Não Cumprimento das Metas Estabelecidas para a Reforma Agraria (MST, July 17, 1996) for a devastating critique of Cardoso's falsification of data regarding land settlements for 1996. There have been four peasant massacres under Cardoso's regime, in Candelaria, Carandiru, Corumbiara, and Eldorado dos Carajas, as of September 1996.

77. In August 1966, the unemployment rate in Buenos Aires was 20.4 percent, while the national rate was 17.1, according to *Latin American Research Report: Southern Core Report,* August 8, 1996, p. 1.

78. Teodoro Petkoff "has left no doubt that privatization is a fundamental element of the government's economic policies" (*LARR Andean Group Report,* August 1, 1996, p. 6). Petkoff is chief economic architect of neoliberal policies that led to the closing of all major hospitals in June 1996 and to an 80 percent poverty rate in Venezuela.

79. The Sandinista leaders welcomed the pope, stating that they shared basic principles, extended support to neoliberal President Zedillo of Mexico, and had shed the last thread of reformist-welfare policies.

80. Carlos Lage Davila, "La Recuperacion de la Economia Cubana," *Punto Final,* September 1996.

81. Correio Sindical (Rio de Janeiro), June 1996, p. 3; *Jornal do Brasil,* June 22, 1996, pp. 1, 12.

82. Interview with Ina Meireles, president CUT Rio de Janeiro, June 4, 1996; seminar meeting with dissident trade unionists, São Paulo, May 23, 1996. Interviews with dissident trade union leaders of the CTA in Rosario, Cordoba, Neutuen, and Resistencia.

83. This confluence is clearly seen in Argentina in recent weeks. After over seven years of collaboration between the CGT and the Menem regime, the launching of two successful general strikes in a matter of days suggests that the revival of class struggle in the metalworking sectors could spell deep trouble for the regime and a possible end to neoliberal economic policy.

84. The striking fact about Mexico is the tremendous number of activists at the local level (municipality, village, barrio) and the absence of a national sociopolitical organization to articulate and project "local power." Mexico at the moment is the only country where there is no mass-based peasant organization. I am excluding the PRI-run peasant confederation. The arguments about Mexican "localism" are less con-

vincing than the long arm of the party-state in repressing or co-opting potential national leaders.

85. In all of these countries, U.S. hit lists result in potential appointees being withdrawn, officers being retired, and a quickening of the pace of implementation of U.S. policies, whether those for drug eradication, repression of coca-producing peasants, or expeditious payments of debt service.

86. A visit to Chaparé disabuses any observer of the sovereignty of the Bolivian state. Even everyday operational activities are overseen by the dozen or so DEA officials stationed there.

87. Between 1983 and 1993, U.S. media services exports increased by 138 percent compared to total service exports, which grew only 90 percent. U.S. media goods exports increased 2,143 percent, while total goods exports increased only 110 percent. U.S. Bureau of the Census, *Statistical Abstract of the United States, 1995,* 115th ed. (Washington, D.C.: Government Printing Office); *Bureau of Economic Analysis* (September 1995); *Survey of Current Business,* pp. 85, 93, 104.

88. See my *Intellectuals: A Marxist Critique of Post-Marxism* (forthcoming in *America Libre*).

89. James Petras and Todd Cavaluzzi, "Lucratives Bases Arrière pour l'Economie Américaine," *Le Monde Diplomatique,* February 1995, pp. 6–7. U.S. transfers (rent, interest, profits, and favorable trade balances) have covered 40 percent of the negative trade balance with Japan over the last decade.

90. For a critique of the "reformist" perspective, see ours, in James Petras and Steve Vieux, "Pragmatism Unmasked: History and Strategy in Castañedas' *Utopia Unarmed,*" in *Science and Society,* vol. 60, no. 2 (Summer 1996), pp. 207–219.

3

Intellectuals: A Marxist Critique of Post-Marxists

With the triumph of neoliberalism and the retreat of the working class, post-Marxism has become a fashionable intellectual posture. The space vacated by the reformist Left has in part been occupied by capitalist politicians and ideologues, technocrats and the traditional and fundamentalist churches (the Vatican and the Pentecostals). In the past, this space was occupied by Socialist, nationalist, and populist politicians and church activists associated with the "theology of liberation." The Center-Left was very influential within the political regimes (at the top) and among the less politicized popular classes (at the bottom). The vacant space of the radical Left refers to the political intellectuals and politicized sectors of the trade unions and urban and rural social movements. It is among these classes that the conflict between Marxism and post-Marxism is most intense today.

Nurtured and, in many cases, subsidized by the principal financial institutions and governmental agencies promoting neoliberalism, a massive number of "social" organizations have emerged whose ideology, linkages, and practices are in direct competition and conflict with Marxist theory and practice. These organizations, in most cases describing themselves as "nongovernmental" or as "independent research centers," have been active in propounding ideologies and political practices that are compatible with and complement the neoliberal agenda of their financial patrons. This chapter will proceed by describing and criticizing the components of their ideology and will then turn to describe their activities and nonactivities, contrasting these with those of the class-based movements and approaches. This will be followed by a discussion of the origins of post-Marxism and its evolution and future, in relation to the decline and possible return of Marxism.

Components of Post-Marxism

The intellectual proponents of post-Marxism in most instances are ex-Marxists, whose point of departure is a "critique" of Marxism and the elaboration of counterpoints to each basic proposition as the basis for attempting to provide an alternative theory or at least a plausible line of analysis. It is possible to more or less synthesize ten basic arguments that are usually found in the post-Marxist discourse.

1. Socialism was a failure and all "general theories" of societies are condemned to repeat this process. Ideologies are false (except post-Marxism!) because they reflect a world of thought dominated by a single gender- or race-culture system.
2. The Marxist emphasis on social class is "reductionist" because classes are dissolving; the principal political points of departure are cultural and are rooted in diverse identities (race, gender, ethnicity, sexual preference).
3. The state is the enemy of democracy and freedom and is a corrupt and inefficient deliverer of social welfare. In its place, "civil society" is the protagonist of democracy and social improvement.
4. Central planning leads to and is a product of bureaucracy, and it hinders the exchange of goods between producers. Markets and market exchanges, perhaps with limited regulations, allow for greater consumption and more efficient distribution.
5. The traditional Left's struggle for state power is corrupting and leads to authoritarian regimes that then subordinate civil society to its control. Local struggles over local issues by local organizations are the only democratic means of change, along with petition or pressuring national and international authorities.
6. Revolutions always end badly or are impossible: Social transformations threaten to provoke authoritarian reactions. The alternative is to struggle for and consolidate democratic transitions to safeguard electoral processes.
7. Class solidarity is part of past ideologies, reflecting earlier politics and realities. Classes no longer exist. There are fragmented "locales" where specific groups (identities) and localities engage in self-help and reciprocal relation for "survival," based on cooperation with external supporters. Solidarity is a cross-class phenomenon, a humanitarian gesture.
8. Class struggle and confrontation does not produce tangible results; it provokes defeats and fails to solve immediate problems. Government and international cooperation around specific projects does result in increases in production and development.

9. Anti-imperialism is another expression of the past that has outlived time. In today's globalized economy, there is no possibility of confronting the economic centers. The world is increasingly interdependent, and in this world, there is a need for greater international cooperation in transferring capital, technology, and know-how from the "rich" to the "poor" countries.

10. Leaders of popular organizations should not be exclusively oriented toward organizing the poor and sharing their conditions. Internal mobilization should be based on external funding. Professionals should design programs and secure external financing to organize local groups. Without outside aid, local groups and professional careers would collapse.

Critique of Post-Marxist Ideology

The post-Marxists thus have an analysis, a critique, and a strategy of development—in a word, the very general ideology that they supposedly condemn when discussing Marxism. Moreover, it is an ideology that fails to identify the crises of capitalism (prolonged stagnation, periodic financial panics, and so on) and the social contradictions (inequalities and social polarization) at the national and international level that impinge on the specific local social problems they focus on. For example, the origins of neoliberalism (the sociopolitical and economic milieux in which the post-Marxists function) is a product of class conflict. Specific sectors of capital allied with the state and the empire defeated the popular classes and imposed the model. A non-class perspective cannot explain the origins of the social world in which the post-Marxists operate. Moreover, the same problem surfaces in discussion of the origins of the post-Marxists—their own biography reflects the abrupt and radical shift in power at the national and international levels and in the economic and cultural spheres, limiting the space and resources in which Marxism operated while increasing the opportunities and funds for post-Marxists. The sociological origins of post-Marxism are embedded in the shift in political power away from the working class and toward export capital.

Let us shift now from a sociology of knowledge critique of post-Marxist ideology and its generally inconsistent view of general theorizing to discuss its specific propositions. Let us start with its notion of the "failure of socialism" and the "end of ideologies." What is meant by the "failure of socialism"? The collapse of the USSR, of Eastern European Communist regimes? First, that is only a single concept of socialism. Second, even here it is not clear what failed: The political system? The socioeconomic system? Recent election returns in Russia, Poland, Hungary, and many of the ex-Soviet Republics suggest that a majority of voters prefer a return of aspects of past social welfare policies and economic practices. If popular opinion in the ex-Communist countries is an indicator of "failure," the results are not definitive. If by the "failure of socialism" the post-Marxists mean the decline in power of the Left, we must insist on a distinction between "failure" due to internal inadequacies of Socialist practices and political-military defeats by external aggressors. No one would say that Hitler's destruction of Western European democracies was a "failure of democracy." Terrorist capitalist regimes or U.S. intervention in Chile, Argentina, Bolivia, Uruguay, the Dominican Republic, Guatemala, Nicaragua, El Salvador, Angola, Mozambique, and Afghanistan played a major role in the "decline" of the revolutionary Left. Military defeats are not failures of the economic system and do not reflect on the effectiveness of Socialist experiences. Moreover, when we analyze the internal performances during the period of relatively stable Socialist or popular governance, the results are far more favorable by many social indicators than that which came afterwards: Popular participation, health, education, and equitable growth under Allende compared very favorably to what came afterward with Pinochet. The same indicators under the Sandinistas compared favorably to Chamorro's regime in Nicaragua. The Arbenz government's agrarian reform and human rights policies compared favorably to the CIA-installed government's policy of land concentration and 150,000 assassinations.

Today, although it is true that neoliberals govern and Marxists are out of power, there is hardly a country in the Western Hemisphere where Marxist- or Socialist-influenced mass movements are not leading major demonstrations and challenging neoliberal policies and regimes. Successful general strikes in Paraguay, Uruguay, and Bolivia; major peasant movements and Indian guerrillas in Mexico; the landless workers' movements in Brazil—all reflect Marxist influence.

Socialism outside of the Communist bloc was an essentially democratic, popular force that secured major support because it represented popular interests freely decided. The post-Marxists confuse Soviet communism with grassroots revolutionary democratic Socialist movements in Latin America. They confuse military defeats with leftists' political failures, accepting the neoliberal amalgamation of the two opposing concepts. Finally, even in the case of Eastern communism, they fail to see the changing and dynamic nature of communism. The growing popularity of a new Socialist synthesis of social ownership, welfare programs, agrarian reform, and council democracy is based on the new sociopolitical movements.

In this sense, the post-Marxist view of the "end of ideologies" is not only inconsistent with its own ideological pronouncements but with the continuing ideological debate between past and present Marxists and present debates and confrontations with neoliberalism and its post-Marxist offspring.

The Dissolution of Classes and the Rise of Identities

The post-Marxists attack the Marxist notion of class analysis from various perspectives. To begin with, they claim that it obscures the equal or more significant importance of cultural identities (gender, ethnicity). They accuse class analysts of being "economic reductionists" and of failing to explain gender and ethnic differences within classes. They then proceed further to argue that these "differences" define the nature of contemporary politics. The second line of attack on class analysis stems from a view that class is merely an intellectual construction—essentially a subjective phenomenon that is culture determined. Hence, there are no "objective class interests" that divide society since "interests" are purely subjective and each culture defines individual preferences. The third line of attack argues that there have been vast transformations in the economy and society that have obliterated the old class distinctions. In postindustrial society, some post-Marxists argue, the source of power is in the new information systems and the new technologies and those who manage and control them. Society, according to this view, is evolving toward a new society in which industrial workers are disappearing in two directions: upward into the "new middle class" of high technology and downward into the marginal "underclass."

Marxists have never denied the importance of racial, gender, and ethnic divisions within classes. What they have emphasized, however, is the wider social system that generates these differences and the need to join class forces to eliminate these inequalities at every point: work, neighborhood, family. What most Marxists object to is the idea that gender and race inequalities can and should be analyzed and solved outside of the class framework: that landowner women with servants and wealth have an essential "identity" with the peasant women who are employed at starvation wages, that Indian bureaucrats of neoliberal governments have a common "identity" with peasant Indians who are displaced from their land by free market economic policies. For example, Bolivia had an Indian vice president who presided over the mass arrest of cocoa-growing Indian farmers. Identity politics in the sense of consciousness of a particular form of oppression by an immediate group can be an appropriate point of departure. This understanding, however, will become an "identity" (race or gender) prison, isolated from other exploited social groups unless it transcends the immediate points of oppression and confronts the social system in which it is embedded. And that requires a broader class analysis of the structure of social power that presides over and defines the conditions of general and specific inequalities.

The essentialism of identity politics isolates people into competing groups unable to transcend the political-economic universe that defines and confines the poor, workers, peasants, and employees. Class politics is the terrain within which to confront identity politics and to transform the institutions that sustain class and other inequalities.

Classes do not come into being by subjective fiat: They are organized by the capitalist class to appropriate value. Hence, the notion that class is a subjective notion dependent on time, place, and perception confuses class and class-consciousness. Whereas the former has objective status, the latter is conditioned by social and cultural factors. Class-consciousness is a social construct that, however, does not make it less "real" and less important in history. Although the social forms and expressions of class-consciousness vary, it is a recurring phenomenon throughout history and most of the world, even as it is overshadowed by other forms of "consciousness" (i.e., race, gender, national) at different moments or is combined with them (nationalism and class-consciousness).

It is obvious that there are major changes in the class structure, but not in the direction that the post-Marxists point to. The major changes have reinforced class differences and class exploitation, even as the nature and conditions of the exploited and exploiters' classes have changed. There are more temporary wageworkers today than in the past. There are many more workers employed in unregulated labor markets (the so-called informal sector, today) than in the past. The issue of unregulated exploitation does not describe a system that "transcends" past capitalism: It is the return to nineteenth-century forms of labor exploitation. What requires new analysis is capitalism after the welfare populist state has been demolished. This means that the complex roles of states and parties that mediated between capital and labor have been replaced by state institutions more clearly and directly linked to the dominant capitalist class. Neoliberalism is unmediated ruling-class state power. Whatever the "multiple determinants" of state and regime behavior in the recent past, today the neoliberal model of accumulation depends most directly on centralized state control horizontally linked to the international banks to implement debt payments and to export sectors to earn foreign exchange. Its vertical tie is to the citizen as subject, and the primary link is through a repressive state apparatus and the parastatal NGOs that defuse social explosions.

The dismantling of the welfare state means that the social structure is more polarized: On the one hand, there are unemployed public employees in health, education, social security, and on the other hand, there are the well-paid professionals linked to multinational corporations, NGOs, and other externally financed institutions linked to the world market and centers of political power. The struggle today is not only between classes in factories; it is also between the state and its uprooted classes in the streets and the markets that have been displaced from fixed employment and forced to produce and sell and bear the costs of social reproduction. Integration into the world market by elite exporters and medium and small compradors (importers of electronic goods; tourist functionaries of multinational hotels and resorts) has its counterpart in the disintegration of the economy of the interior: local industry and small farms, with the concomitant displacement of producers to the city and overseas.

The import of luxury goods for the upper middle class is based on the earnings remitted by "exported" labor of the poor. The nexus of exploitation begins in the impoverishment of the interior, the uprooting of the peasants and their immigration to the cities and overseas. The income remitted by exported labor provides hard currency to finance imports and neoliberal infrastructure projects to promote the foreign and domestic export and tourist business. The chain of exploitation is more circuitous, but it is still located ultimately in the capital-labor relation. In the age of neoliberalism, the struggle to recreate the "nation," the national market, and national production and exchange is once again a basic historic demand, just as the growth of deregulated employment (informality) requires a powerful public investment and regulatory center to generate formal employment with livable social conditions. In a word, class analysis needs to be adapted to the rule of unmediated capital in an unregulated labor market with international linkages in which the reformist redistributive politics of the past have been replaced by neoliberal policies reconcentrating income and power at the top. The homogenization and downward mobility of vast sectors of workers and peasants formerly in the regulated labor market creates a great objective potential for unified revolutionary action. In short, there is a common class identity that forms the terrain for organizing the struggles of the poor. In summary, contrary to what the post-Marxists argue, the transformations of capitalism have made class analysis more relevant than ever.

The growth of technology has exacerbated class differences, not abolished them. The workers in microchip industries and those industries in which the new chips have been incorporated have not eliminated the working class. Rather, the sites of activity and the mode of producing within the continuing process of exploitation have been shifted. The new class structure, insofar as it is visible, combines the new technologies with more controlling forms of exploitation. Automation of some sectors increases the tempo of work down the line; TV cameras increase worker surveillance while decreasing administrative staff; "quality work circles," in which workers pressure other workers, increase self-exploitation without giving increases in pay or power. The "technological revolution" is ultimately shaped by the class structure of the neoliberal counterrevolution. Computers allow for agribusiness to control the costs and volume of pesticides, but it is the low-paid temporary workers who do the spraying and are poisoned. Information networks are linked to putting out work to the sweatshop or household (the informal economy) for production of textiles, shoes, and so forth.

The key to understanding this process of combined and uneven development of technology and labor is class analysis and, within that, gender and race.

State and Civil Society

The post-Marxists have painted a one-sided picture of the state. The state is described as a huge inefficient bureaucracy that plundered the public treasury and left the people poor and the economy bankrupt. In the political sphere, the state was the source of authoritarian rule and arbitrary rulings, hindering the exercise of citizenship (democracy) and the free exchange of commodities (the market). The post-Marxists argue that, by contrast, "civil society" was the source of freedom, social movements, and citizenship. Out of an active civil society would come an equitable and dynamic economy. What is strange about this ideology is its peculiar capacity to overlook fifty years of history. The public sector was of necessity instrumental in stimulating industrialization in the absence of private investment and because of economic crisis (the world crisis of the 1930s, war in the 1940s, and so on). Further, the growth of literacy and basic public health was largely a state initiative.

In the century and a half of free enterprise, roughly from the eighteenth century to the 1930s, Latin America suffered the seven scourges of the Bible, while the invisible hand of the market looked on: Those scourges were genocide, famine, disease, tyranny, dependency, uprootedness, and exploitation.

The public sector grew in response to these problems and deviated from its public functions to the degree that it was privately appropriated by business and political elites. The "inefficiency of the state" is a result of its being directed toward private gain—either by subsidizing business interests (through low costs of energy) or by providing employment to political followers. The inefficiency of the state is directly related to its subordination to private interests. The state's comprehensive health and educational programs have never been adequately replaced by the private economy, the church, or the NGOs. Both the private sector and the church fund private clinics and education to cater to a wealthy minority. The NGOs, at best, provide short-term care and education for limited groups in local circumstances but are dependent on the whims and interests of foreign donors.

As a systematic comparison indicates, the post-Marxists have read the historical record wrong: They have let their antistatist rhetoric blind them to the positive comparative accomplishments of the public over the private.

The argument that "the state" is the source of authoritarianism both is and is not true. Dictatorial states have existed, and will exist in the future, but most have little or nothing to do with public ownership, especially if it means expropriating foreign business. Most dictatorships have been antistatist and pro free market—today, in the past, and probably in the future.

Moreover, the state has been an important supporter of citizenship, promoting the incorporation of exploited sectors of the population into the polity, recognizing legitimate rights of workers, blacks, women, and others. States have provided the basis for social justice by redistributing land, income, and budgets to favor the poor.

In a word, we need to go beyond the statist-antistatist rhetoric to define the class nature of the state and its basis of political representation and legitimacy. The generalized ahistorical and asocial attacks on the state are unwarranted and only serve as a polemical instrument to disarm citizens of the free market from forging an effective and rational alternative that is anchored in the creative potentialities of public action.

The counterposition of "civil society" to the state is also a false dichotomy. Moreover, much of the discussion of civil society overlooks the basic social contradictions that divide "civil society." To be more accurate, it is the leading classes of civil society, not "civil society," that while attacking the "statism" of the poor have always made a major point of strengthening their ties to the treasury and military to promote and protect their dominant position in "civil society." Likewise, the popular classes in civil society when aroused have sought to break the ruling classes' monopoly of the state. The poor have always looked to state resources to strengthen their socioeconomic position in relation to the rich. The issue is and always has been the relation of different classes to the state.

The post-Marxist ideologues who are marginalized from the state by the neoliberals have made a virtue of their impotence. Uncritically imbuing the stateless rhetoric from above, they transmit it below. The post-Marxists try to justify their organizational vehicles (the NGOs) for upward mobility by arguing that they operate outside of the state and in "civil society," when in fact they are funded by foreign governments to work with domestic governments.

"Civil society" is an abstraction from the deep social cleavages engendered by capitalist society, social divisions that have deepened under neoliberalism. There is as much conflict within civil society between classes as there is between civil society and the state. Only in exceptionally rare moments do we find it otherwise. For example, under fascist or totalitarian states that torture, abuse, and pillage the totality of social classes, we find instances of a dichotomy between the state and civil society.

To speak or write of "civil society" is to attempt to convert a legalistic distinction into major political categories to organize politics. In doing so, the differences between classes are obscured and ruling class domination is not challenged.

To counterpose the "citizen" against the "state" is to overlook the profound links of certain citizens (the export elites, the upper middle class) to the state and the alienation and exclusion of the majority of citizens (workers, un-employed, and peasants) from effective exercise of their elementary social rights. Elite citizens, using the state, empty citizenship of any practical mean-ing for the majority, converting citizens into subjects. Discussion of civil soci-ety needs to specify the social contours of social classes and the boundaries im-posed by the privileged class, and discussion of the state needs this as well. The way the post-Marxists use the term as an uncritical, undifferentiated concept serves to obscure more than reveal the dynamics of societal change.

Planning, Bureaucracy, and the Market

There is no question that central planning in the former Communist countries was "bureaucratic"—authoritarian in conception and centralized in execution. From this empirical observation, the post-Marxists argue that "planning" (central or not) is by its nature antithetical to the needs of a modern complex economy with its multiple demands, millions of consumers, and massive flows of information. Only the market can do the trick. Democracy and the market go together—another point of convergence between the "post-Marxists" and the neoliberals. The problem with this notion is that most of the major institu-tions in a capitalist economy engage in central planning.

General Motors, Wal-Mart, Microsoft—all centrally program and plan di-rect investments and expenditures toward further production and market-ing. Few, if any, post-Marxists focus their critical attention on these enter-prises. The post-Marxists do not call into question the efficiency of central planning by the multinational corporations or their compatibility with the competitive electoral systems characteristic of capitalist democracies.

The theoretical problem is the post-Marxists' confusion of central plan-ning with one particular historic political variant of it. If we accept that plan-ning systems can be embedded in a variety of political systems (authoritarian or democratic), then it is logical that the accountability and responsiveness of the planning system will vary.

Today in capitalist societies, the military budget is part of state planning and expenditures based on "commands" to the producers (and owners of capital), who have responded in their own inefficient way, producing and profiting for over fifty years. Although this is no "model" of planning, the point that needs to be made is that central state planning is not a phenome-non confined to Communist systems. The defects are generalized and are also found in capitalist economies. The problem in both instances (the Pen-tagon and communism) is the lack of democratic accountability: the mili-tary-industrial complex elite fix production, costs, demand, and supply.

The central allocation of state resources is essential in most countries be-cause of regional inequalities in resource endowment, immigration, produc-tivity, and demand for products or for a wealth of historical reasons. Only a decision made at the center can redistribute resources to compensate less-developed regions, classes, gender, and racial groups adversely affected by the above factors. Otherwise, the "market" tends to favor those with historic advantages and favorable endowments, creating polar patterns of development or even fostering interregional or class exploitation and ethnic conflicts.

First, the fundamental problem of planning is the political structure that informs the planning process. Planning officials elected and subject to organized communities and social groups (producers, consumers, youth, women, and racial minorities) will allocate resources among production, consumption, and reinvestment that are different from those who are beholden to elites embedded in industrial-military complexes.

Second, planning does not mean detailed specification. The size of social budgets can be decided nationally by elected representatives and can be allocated according to public assemblies where citizens can vote on their local priorities. This practice has been successful in Porto Alegre in Brazil for the past several years under a municipal government led by the Workers Party. The relation between general and local planning is not written in stone, nor are the levels of specification of expenditures and investments to be determined at the "higher levels." General allocations to promote strategic targets that benefit the whole country (infrastructure, high technology, education, and so forth) are complemented by local decisions on subsidizing schools, clinics, and cultural centers.

Planning is a key instrument in today's capitalist economy. To dismiss Socialist planning is to disarm an important tool in organizing social change. To reverse the vast inequalities, concentration of property, and unjust budget allocations requires an overall plan with a democratic authority empowered to implement it. Together with public enterprises and self-management councils of producers and consumers, central planning is the third pillar in a democratic transformation.

Finally, central planning is not incompatible with locally owned productive and service activities (restaurants, cafés, repair shops, family farms, and so on). Clearly, public authorities will have their hands full managing the macrostructures of society.

The complex decisions and information flows are much easier to manage today with the mega-information processing computers. The formula "democratic representation plus computers plus central planning" equals efficient and socially equitable production and distribution.

"State Power Corrupts"

One of the principal critiques of Marxism among the post-Marxists is the notion that state power corrupts and that the struggle for it is the original sin. They argue that this is so because the state is so distant from the citizens that the authorities become autonomous and arbitrary, forgetting the original goals and pursuing their self-interest. There is no doubt that throughout history, people seizing power have become tyrants. But it is also the case that the rise to power of individuals leading social movements has had an emancipating effect. The abolition of slavery and the overthrow of absolutist monarchies are two examples. Thus, "power" in the state has a double meaning, depending on the historic context. Likewise, local movements have had successes in mobilizing communities and improving immediate conditions, in some cases significantly. But it is also the case that macropolitical economic decisions have undermined local efforts. Today, structural adjustment policies at the national and international level have generated poverty and unemployment, depleting local resources and forcing local people to migrate or to engage in crime. The dialectics between state and local power operate to undermine or reinforce local initiatives and changes, depending on the class power manifested at both levels. There are numerous cases of progressive municipal governments that have been undermined because reactionary national regimes cut off their funding. Nonetheless, progressive municipal governments have been a very positive force in helping neighborhood and local organizations, as has been the case with the Socialist mayor of Montevideo in Uruguay or the leftist mayor in Puerto Alegre in Brazil.

The post-Marxists who counterpose "local" against "state" power are not basing their discussion on historical experience, at least not that of Latin America. The antinomy is a result of the attempt to justify the role of NGOs as mediators between local organizations and neoliberal foreign donors (the World Bank, Europe, or the United States) and the local free market regimes. In order to "legitimate" their role, the post-Marxist NGO professionals, as "agents of the democratic grassroots," have to disparage the Left at the level of state power. In the process, they complement the activity of the neoliberals by severing the link between local struggles and organization and national or international political movements. The emphasis on "local activity" serves the neoliberal regimes just right, as it allows its foreign and domestic backers to dominate macrosocioeconomic policy and to channel most of the state's resources on behalf of export capitalists and financial interests.

The post-Marxists as managers of NGOs have become skilled in designing projects and transmitting the new "identity" and "globalist" jargon into the popular movements. Their talk and writing about international cooperation, self-help, and microenterprises creates ideological bonds with the neoliberals while forging dependency on external donors and their neoliberal socioeconomic agenda. It is no surprise that after a decade of NGO activity, the post-Marxist professionals have "depoliticized" and deradicalized whole areas of social life: those that relate to women and to neighborhood and youth organizations. The case of Peru and Chile is classic: Where the NGOs have become firmly established, the radical social movements have retreated.

Local struggles over immediate issues are the food and substance that nurture emerging movements. The crucial question is over their direction and dynamic: whether they raise the larger issues of the social system and link up with other local forces to confront the state and its imperial backers or whether they turn inward, looking to foreign donors and fragmenting into a series of competing supplicants for external subsidies. The ideology of post-Marxism promotes the latter; the Marxists promote the former.

Revolutions Always End Badly:
The Possibilism of Post-Marxism

There is a pessimistic variant to post-Marxism that speaks less of the failures of revolution than of the impossibility of socialism. These post-Marxists cite the decline of the revolutionary Left, the triumph of capitalism in the East, the "crisis of Marxism," the loss of alternatives, the strength of the United States, the coups and repression by the military. All these arguments are mobilized to urge the Left to support "possibilism": the need to work within the niches of the free market imposed by the World Bank and structural adjustment agenda and to confine politics to the electoral parameters imposed by the military. This is called "pragmatism," or incrementalism. Post-Marxists have played a major ideological role in promoting and defending the so-called electoral transition from military rule in which social changes were subordinated to the reintroduction of an electoral system.

Most of the arguments of the post-Marxists are based on static and selective observations of contemporary reality and are tied to predetermined conclusions. Having decided that revolutions are out of date, they focus on neoliberal electoral victories and not on the postelectoral mass protests and general strikes that mobilize large numbers of people in extraparliamentary activity. They look at the demise of communism in the late 1980s and not to its revival in the mid-1990s. They describe the constraints of the military on electoral politicians without looking at the challenges to the military by the Zapatista guerrillas, the urban rebellions in Caracas, the general strikes in Bolivia. In a word, the possibilists overlook the dynamics of struggles that begin at the sectoral or local level within the electoral parameters of the military and then are propelled upward and beyond those limits by the failures and impotence of the electoral possibilists to satisfy the elementary demands and needs of the people. The possibilists have failed to end the impunity of the military. They have been impotent to force the neoliberal regimes to pay the back salaries of public employees (in the provinces of Argentina). They have failed to end crop destruction of the coca farmers (in Bolivia).

The post-Marxist possibilists become part of the problem instead of part of the solution. It has been a decade and a half since the negotiated transitions began, and in each instance, the post-Marxists have adapted to neoliberalism and deepened its free market policies. The possibilists are unable to effectively oppose the negative social effects of the free market on the people but are pressured by the neoliberals to impose new and more austere measures in order to continue to hold office. The post-Marxists have gradually moved from being pragmatic critics of neoliberals to promoting themselves as efficient and honest managers of neoliberalism, capable of securing investor confidence and pacifying social unrest.

In the meantime, the pragmatism of the post-Marxists is matched by the extremism of the neoliberals: The decade of the 1990s has witnessed a radicalization of neoliberal policies, designed to forestall crisis by handing over even more lucrative investment and speculative opportunities to overseas banks and multinationals.

This has meant exploiting petroleum production in Brazil, Argentina, Mexico, Venezuela and lower wages and fewer social security payments, greater tax exemption, and fewer constraints from past labor legislation everywhere else. The neoliberals are creating a polarized class structure, much closer to the Marxist paradigm of society than the post-Marxist vision. Contemporary Latin American class structure is more rigid, more deterministic, and more linked to class politics and the state than in the past. In these circumstances, revolutionary politics are far more relevant than the pragmatic proposals of the post-Marxists.

Class Solidarity and the "Solidarity" of Foreign Donors

The word "solidarity" has been abused to the point that in many contexts it has lost meaning. The term "solidarity" for the post-Marxists includes foreign aid channeled to any designated "impoverished" group. Mere "research" or "popular education" of the poor by professionals is designated as "solidarity." In many ways, the hierarchical structures and the forms of transmission of "aid" and "training" resemble nineteenth-century charity, and the promoters are not very different from Christian missionaries.

The post-Marxists emphasize "self-help" in attacking the "paternalism and dependence" on the state. In this competition among NGOs to capture the victims of neoliberals, the post-Marxists receive important subsidies from their counterparts in Europe and the United States. The self-help ideology emphasizes the replacement of public employees for volunteers and upwardly mobile professionals contracted on a temporary basis. The basic philosophy of the post-Marxist view is to transform "solidarity" into collaboration and subordination to the macroeconomy of neoliberalism by focusing attention *away from* state resources of the wealthy classes toward *self-exploitation of the poor.* The poor do not need to be made virtuous by the post-Marxists for what the state obligates them to do.

In contrast, the Marxist concept of solidarity emphasizes class solidarity and, *within* the class, solidarity of oppressed groups (women and people of color) *against* their foreign and domestic exploiters. The major focus is *not* on the donations that divide classes and pacify small groups for a limited time period. The focus of the Marxist concept of solidarity is on the *common action* of the *same members* of the class *sharing* their *common economic predicament* and struggling for *collective* improvement.

It involves intellectuals who write and speak *for* the social movements in struggle, committed to sharing the same political consequences. The concept of solidarity is linked to "organic" intellectuals who are basically *part* of the movement—the resource people providing analysis and education for class struggle. In contrast, the post-Marxists are embedded in the world of institutions, academic seminars, foreign foundations, international conferences, and bureaucratic reports. They write in esoteric postmodern jargon understood only by those "initiated" into the subjectivist cult of essentialist identities. For the Marxists, solidarity means sharing the risks of the movements, not being outside commentators who question everything and defend nothing. For the post-Marxists, the main object is "getting" the foreign funding for the "project." The main issue for the Marxists is the *process* of political struggle and education in securing social improvement. Movement is crucial in raising consciousness for societal change: It leads to the construction of political power to transform the general condition of the great majority. "Solidarity" for the post-Marxists is divorced from the general object of liberation; it is merely a way of bringing people together to attend a job-retraining seminar, to build a latrine. For the Marxists, the solidarity of a collective struggle contains the seeds of the future democratic collectivist society. The larger vision or its absence is what gives the different conceptions of solidarity their distinct meaning.

Class Struggle and Cooperation

The post-Marxists frequently write of "cooperation"—of everyone, near and far—without delving too profoundly into the price and conditions for securing the cooperation of neoliberal regimes and overseas funding agencies. Class struggle is viewed as an atavism in a past that no longer exists. Today, we are told "the poor" are intent on building a new life. They are fed up with traditional politics, ideologies, and politicians. So far, so good. The problem is that the post-Marxists are not so forthcoming in describing their role as mediators and brokers, hustling funds overseas and matching the funds to projects acceptable to donors and local recipients. The foundation entrepreneurs are engaged in *a new type of politics* similar to the "labor contractors" *(enganchadores)* of the not-too-distant past: herding together women to be "trained," setting up microfirms subcontracted to larger producers or exporters. The new politics of the post-Marxists is essentially the politics of the compradors: They produce no national products but rather link foreign funders with local labor (self-help microenterprises) to facilitate the continuation of the neoliberal regime. In that sense, the post-Marxists in their role as managers of NGOs are *fundamentally political actors,* whose projects, training, and workshops do not make any significant *economic impact* either on the gross national product (GNP) or in terms of lessening poverty. But their activities do make an impact in diverting people from the class struggle into *harmless and ineffective* forms of collaboration with their oppressors. The Marxist perspective of class struggle and confrontation is built upon the real *social divisions* of society: between those who extract profits, interest, rent, and regressive taxes and those who struggle to maximize wages, social expenditures, and productive investments. The results of post-Marxist perspectives are today evident everywhere: The concentration of income and the growth of inequalities are greater than ever, after a decade of preaching cooperation and microenterprises and self-help. Today, banks such as the Inter-American Development Bank (IDB) fund the export agribusinesses that exploit and poison millions of farm laborers while providing funds to finance small microprojects. The role of the post-Marxists in the microprojects is to neutralize political opposition at the bottom while neoliberalism is promoted at the top. The ideology of cooperation links the poor *through the post-Marxists* to the neoliberals at the top. The post-Marxists are the intellectual policemen who define *acceptable research,* distribute research funds, and filter out topics and perspectives that project a class analysis and struggle perspective. Marxists are excluded from the conferences and stigmatized as "ideologists" while post-Marxists present themselves as "social scientists." The control of intellectual fashion, publications, conferences, and research funds provide the post-Marxists with an important power base—but one that is ultimately dependent on avoiding conflict with their external funding patrons.

The critical Marxist intellectuals have their strength in the fact that their ideas resonate with the evolving social realities. The polarization of classes and the violent confrontations are growing, as their theories would predict. It is in this sense that the Marxists are tactically weak and strategically strong vis-à-vis the post-Marxists.

Is Anti-imperialism Dead?

In recent years, anti-imperialism has disappeared from the political lexicon of the post-Marxists. The ex-guerrillas of Central America turned electoral politicians and the professionals who run the NGOs speak of international cooperation and interdependence. Yet debt payments continue to transfer huge sums from the poor in Latin America to the European, U.S., and Japanese Banks. Public properties, banks, and, above all, natural resources are being taken over at very cheap prices by U.S. and European multination-als. There are more Latin American billionaires with the bulk of their funds in U.S. and European banks than ever before. Meanwhile, entire provinces have become industrial cemeteries and the countryside is depopulated. The United States has more military advisers, drug officials, and federal police di-recting Latin American "policing" than ever before in history. Yet we are told by some former Sandinistas and ex-Farabundistas that anti-imperial-ism/imperialism disappeared with the end of the Cold War. The problem, we are told, is not foreign investments or foreign aid but their absence, and these people ask for more imperial aid. The political and economic myopia that accompanies this perspective involves the failure to understand that the political conditions for the loans and investment are the cheapening of labor, the elimination of social legislation, and the transformation of Latin America into one big plantation, one big mining camp, one big free trade zone stripped of rights, sovereignty, and wealth.

The Marxist emphasis on the deepening of imperial exploitation is rooted in the social relations of production and state relations between imperial and dependent capitalism. The collapse of the USSR has intensified imperial ex-ploitation. The post-Marxists (ex-Marxists) who believe that the unipolar world will result in greater "cooperation" have misread U.S. intervention in Panama, Iraq, Somalia, and elsewhere. More fundamentally, the dynamic of imperialism is imbedded in the *internal* dynamic of capital, *not* in *external* competition with the Soviet Union. The decline of the domestic market and the growth of the external sector of Latin America is a return to a "prena-tional" phase: The Latin economies begin to resemble their "colonial" past.

The struggle against imperialism today involves the *reconstruction* of the nation, the domestic market, and the productive economy and a working class that is linked to social production and consumption.

Two Perspectives on Social Transformation:
Class Organizations and NGOs

Advancing the struggle against imperialism and its domestic neocomprador collaborators means passing through an ideological and cultural debate with the post-Marxists inside and on the periphery of the popular movements. Neoliberalism operates today on two fronts, the economic and the cultural-political; and it operates at two levels, the regime and the popular classes. At the top, neoliberal policies are formulated and implemented by the usual characters—the World Bank, the IMF working with Washington, Bonn, and

Tokyo—and in association with neoliberal regimes and domestic exporters, big business conglomerates, and bankers.

By the early 1980s, the more perceptive sectors of the neoliberal ruling classes realized that their policies were polarizing the society and provoking large-scale social discontent. Neoliberal politicians began to finance and promote a *parallel* strategy "from below," in support of "grassroots" organizations with an "antistatist" ideology to intervene among potentially conflictual classes, to create a "social cushion." These organizations were financially dependent on neoliberal sources and were directly involved in competing with sociopolitical movements for the allegiance of local leaders and activist communities. By the 1990s, these organizations, described as "nongovernmental," numbered in the thousands and were receiving close to $4 billion worldwide.

The confusion concerning the political character of the NGOs stems from their earlier history in the 1970s during the days of the dictatorships. In this period, they were active in providing humanitarian support to the victims of the military dictatorships and in denouncing human rights violations. The NGOs supported "soup kitchens" that allowed victimized families to survive the first wave of shock treatments administered by the neoliberal dictatorships. This period created a favorable image of NGOs even among the Left. They were considered part of the "progressive camp." Even then, however, the limits of the NGOs were evident. Although they attacked the human rights violations of local dictatorships, they rarely denounced their U.S. and European patrons who financed and advised them. Nor was there a serious effort to link the neoliberal economic policies and human rights violations to the new turn in the imperialist system. Obviously, the external sources of funding limited the sphere of criticism and human rights action.

As opposition to neoliberalism grew in the early 1980s, the U.S. and European governments and the World Bank increased the funding of NGOs. There is a direct relation between the growth of social movements challenging the neoliberal model and the effort to subvert them by creating alternative forms of social action through the NGOs. The basic point of convergence between the NGOs and the World Bank was their common opposition to "statism." On the surface, the NGOs criticized the state from a "Left" perspective defending civil society, while the right did so in the name of the market. In reality, however, the World Bank, the neoliberal regimes, and Western foundations co-opted and encouraged the NGOs to undermine the national welfare state by providing social services to compensate the victims of the multinational corporations (MNCs). In other words, as the neoliberal regimes at the top devastated communities by inundating the country with cheap imports, increasing external debt payments, and abolishing labor legislation, thereby creating a growing mass of low-paid and unemployed workers, the NGOs were funded to provide "self-help" projects, "popular education," job training, and so on to absorb temporarily small groups of poor, to co-opt local leaders, and to undermine antisystem struggles.

The NGOs became the "community face" of neoliberalism, intimately related to those at the top and complementing their destructive work with local projects. In effect, the neoliberals organized a "pincer" operation, or dual strategy. Unfortunately, many on the Left focused only on "neoliberalism" from above and the outside (the IMF and the World Bank) and not on neoliberalism from below (NGOs and microenterprises). A major reason for this oversight was the conversion of many ex-Marxists to the NGO formula and practice. *Post-Marxism was the ideological transit ticket* from class politics to "community development," from Marxism to the NGOs.

While the neoliberals were transferring lucrative state properties to the private rich, the NGOs were *not* part of the trade union resistance. On the contrary, they were active in *local private projects*, promoting the private enterprise discourse (self-help) in the local communities by focusing on microenterprises. The NGOs built ideological bridges between the small-scale capitalists and the monopolies benefiting from privatization—all in the name of "antistatism" and building civil societies. While the rich accumulated vast financial empires from the privatization, the NGO middle-class professionals got small sums of funds to finance offices, transportation, and small-scale economic activity. The important political point is that the NGOs *depoliticized* sectors of the population, undermined their commitment to public employees, and co-opted potential leaders in small projects. NGOs abstain from public schoolteacher struggles, as the neoliberal regimes attack public education and public educators. Rarely, if ever, do NGOs support the strikes and protests against low wages and budget cuts. Since their educational funding comes from the neoliberal governments, they avoid solidarity with public educators in struggle. In practice, "nongovernmental" translates into antipublic spending activities, freeing the bulk of funds for neoliberals to subsidize export capitalists while small sums trickle from the government to NGOs.

In reality, nongovernmental organizations are *not* nongovernmental. They receive funds from overseas governments or work as the private subcontractors of local governments. Frequently, they openly collaborate with governmental agencies at home or overseas. This "subcontracting" undermines professionals with fixed contracts, replacing them with contingent professionals. The NGOs cannot provide the long-term comprehensive programs that the welfare state can furnish. Instead, they provide limited services to narrow groups of communities. More important, their programs are not accountable to the local people but rather to overseas donors. In that sense, NGOs undermine democracy by *taking social programs out of the hands of the local people* and their elected officials and creating dependence on non-elected, overseas officials and their locally anointed officials.

NGOs shift people's attention and struggles away from the national budget toward self-exploitation to secure local social services. This allows the neoliberals to cut social budgets and transfer state funds to subsidize bad debts of private banks, loans to exporters, and so forth. Self-exploitation (self-help) means that in addition to paying taxes to the state and not getting anything in return, working people have to work extra hours with marginal resources, expending scarce energies to obtain services that the bourgeoisie receives from the state. More fundamentally, NGO ideology of "private voluntaristic activity" undermines the sense of the "public": the idea that the government has an *obligation* to look after its citizens and provide them with life, liberty, and the pursuit of happiness; that political responsibility of the state is essential for the well-being of citizens. Against this notion of public responsibility, the NGOs foster the neoliberal idea of private responsibility for social problems and the importance of private resources to solve these problems. In effect, they impose a double burden on the poor: paying taxes to finance the neoliberal state to serve the rich; private self-exploitation to take care of their own needs.

NGOs and Sociopolitical Movements

NGOs emphasize projects, not movements; they "mobilize" people to produce at the margins, not to struggle to control the basic means of production and wealth; they focus on technical financial assistance of projects, not on structural conditions that shape the everyday lives of people. The NGOs co-opt the language of the Left: "popular power," "empowerment," "gender equality," "sustainable development," "bottom-up leadership," and so on. The problem is that this language is linked to a framework of collaboration with donors and government agencies that subordinate practical activity to nonconfrontational politics. The local nature of NGO activity means "empowerment" never goes beyond influencing small areas of social life with limited resources within the conditions permitted by the neoliberal state and macroeconomy.

The NGOs and their post-Marxist professional staff directly compete with the sociopolitical movements for influence among the poor, women, the racially excluded, and the like. Their ideology and practice diverts attention from the sources and solutions of poverty (looking downward and inward instead of upward and outward). To speak of *microenterprises* as the solution, instead of admitting to the problem of exploitation by the overseas banks, is based on the notion that the problem is one of individual initiative rather than the transference of income overseas. The NGOs' aid affects small sectors of the population, setting up competition between communities for scarce resources, generating insidious distinctions and inter- and intracommunity rivalries, thus undermining class solidarity. The same is true among the professionals: Each sets up *his or her* NGO to solicit overseas funding. They compete by presenting proposals closer to the liking of the overseas donors for lower prices, while claiming to speak for more followers. The net effect is a proliferation of NGOs that fragments poor communities into sectoral and subsectoral groupings unable to see the larger social picture that afflicts them and even less able to unite in struggle against the system. Recent experience also demonstrates that foreign donors finance projects during "crises"—political and social challenges to the status quo. Once the movements have ebbed, they shift funding to NGO-regime "collaboration," fitting the NGO projects into the neoliberal agenda. Economic development compatible with the "free market" rather than social organization for social change becomes the dominant item on the funding agenda. The structure and nature of NGOs, with their "apolitical" posture and their focus on self-help, depoliticizes and demobilizes the poor. NGOs reinforce the electoral processes encouraged by the neoliberal parties and mass media. Political education about the nature of imperialism, the class basis of neoliberalism, and the class struggle between exporters and temporary workers are avoided. Instead, the NGOs discuss "the excluded," the "powerless," "extreme poverty," and "gender or racial discrimination" without moving beyond the superficial symptom, without engaging the social system that produces these conditions. Incorporating the poor into the neoliberal economy through purely "private voluntary action," the NGOs create a political world where the *appearance* of solidarity and social action cloaks a conservative conformity with the international and national structure of power.

It is no coincidence that as NGOs have become dominant in certain regions, independent class political action has declined and neoliberalism goes uncontested. The bottom line is that the growth of NGOs coincides with increased funding from neoliberalism and the deepening of poverty everywhere. Despite its claims of many local successes, the overall power of neoliberalism stands unchallenged, and the NGOs increasingly search for niches in the interstices of power. The problem of formulating alternatives has been hindered in another way. Many of the former leaders of guerrilla and social movements, trade union, and popular women's organizations have been co-opted by the NGOs. The offer is tempting: higher pay (occasionally in hard currency), prestige, and recognition by overseas donors; overseas conferences and networks; office staff; and relative security from repression. In contrast, the sociopolitical movements offer few material benefits but greater respect and independence and, more important, the freedom to challenge the political and economic system. The NGOs and their overseas banking supporters (the Inter-American Bank, the World Bank) publish newsletters featuring success stories of microenterprises and other self-help projects—without mentioning the high rates of failure as popular consumption declines, low-priced imports flood the market, and interest rates spiral—as is the case in Mexico today.

Even the "successes" affect only a small fraction of the total poor and succeed only to the degree that others cannot enter into the same market. The propaganda value of individual microenterprise success, however, is important in fostering the illusion that neoliberalism is a popular phenomenon. The frequent violent mass outbursts that take place in regions of microenterprise promotion suggest that the ideology is not hegemonic and the NGOs have not yet displaced independent class movements.

Finally, NGOs foster a new type of cultural and economic colonialism and dependency. Projects are designed or at least approved in the "guidelines" of priorities of the imperial centers or in their institutions. They are administered and "sold" to communities. Evaluations are done by and for the imperial institutions. Shifts in priorities funding or bad evaluations result in the dumping of groups, communities, farms, and co-operatives. Everything and everybody is increasingly disciplined to comply with the donors' demands and their project evaluators. The new viceroys supervise and ensure conformity with the goals, values, and ideologies of the donor as well as the proper use of funds. Where "successes" occur, they are heavily dependent on continued outside support, otherwise they could collapse.

Although most NGOs are increasingly instruments of neoliberalism, there is a small minority that attempt to develop an alternative strategy that is supportive of class and anti-imperialist politics. None of them receive funds from the World Bank or from European and U.S. governmental agencies. They support efforts to link local power to struggles for state power. They link local projects to national sociopolitical movements, occupying large landed estates, defending public property and national ownership against multinationals. They provide political solidarity to social movements involved in struggles to expropriate land. They support women's struggles linked to class perspectives. They recognize the importance of politics in command, in defining local and immediate struggles. They believe that local organizations should fight at the national level and that national leaders must be accountable to local activists. In a word, they are not post-Marxists.

4

Pragmatism Unarmed

WITH STEVE VIEUX

Jorge Castañeda's book *Utopia Unarmed* has spawned a cottage industry of favorable reviews and comments in both mass circulation and liberal newspapers and in left-wing journals. Beyond the literary world, his writing reflects an influential current of thought in Latin America and to a much lesser degree in Europe and the United States. His book provides a more or less coherent doctrinal point of reference for a growing number of intellectuals and politicians who are critical of the liberal Right, reject the Left policies of the 1960s and 1970s, and look toward fashioning reformist coalitions that bring together bankers, businesspeople, workers, peasants, and the urban poor in a grand alliance that transcends past divisions and moves Latin America forward to a progressive future.

Whatever the intellectual merits of the book, *Utopia Unarmed* requires a close reading and a thorough critique. It is a political statement that resonates with an increasingly influential sector of the Latin American Center-Left and provides many of the arguments that sustain it. Its importance lies less in its originality—since many of its arguments and critiques have been voiced or written in numerous Social Democratic and liberal texts—than in its ability to bring these partial and fragmentary comments together in a single manuscript.

Castañeda's appeal and influence stems from several sources. In the first place, his virulent critique of leftist politics in the 1960s and 1970s echoes the critical posture of many renovated Socialists engaged in electoral-parliamentary politics and their intellectual brain trusts in the NGOs. Second, his method of analysis, which focuses on a set of dichotomous political elites (guerrillas and the military) and doctrines (neoliberal and Social Democratic), is a congenial way of simplifying otherwise complex, inconveniently challenging realities. Third, his entertaining anecdotal approach (on gun-running, political ransoms, and so on) to political history provides his narra-tive with a semblance of "insider knowledge," compensating the reader for the lack of in depth analysis of the links among social interests, movements, and political choices.

We will proceed through a brief exposition of Castañeda's approach and his method of arguing for a Social Democratic agenda. We will then turn to outlining the political context for the emergence of Castañeda's "new prag-matism," focusing on the growth of Center-Left political coalitions. We will follow with a systematic critique of his method, analytical framework, and the major substantive historical and contemporary issues that engage writers attempting to fashion a theoretical perspective for Latin America's Left.

Castañeda's Argument

Utopia Unarmed combines a lengthy narrative of the history of the Left in Latin America with several thematic chapters on important questions facing the Left today. The historical treatment of the Left begins with the author's analysis of the Communist parties and populist movements and govern-ments in the region, especially emphasizing their contributions to demo-cratic traditions and the expansion of welfare expenditure. The author com-bines his discussion of the rise and defeat of the first wave of urban and rural guerrilla activity in the 1960s with an analysis of the influence of the Cuban government on these struggles. He particularly stresses the role of Cuban in-telligence in aiding these struggles. This emphasis is carried over into his dis-cussion of the second wave of guerrilla struggles in Nicaragua and El Sal-vador, in which he emphasizes the role of the Cubans in arming these movements and the role of the Sandinistas in militarizing the revolutionary government when it was finally established. Castañeda's historical narrative concludes with a discussion of present-day political currents in the region that are either Social Democratic—the post-Pinochet governing coalition in Chile, the Venezuelan Movimiento al Socialismo, the Brazilian Social Demo-cratic Party—or are on the road to social democracy, such as the Brazilian Workers Party. With the increasing marginalization of populism, the collapse of the Communist parties in the wake of the passing of the Soviet Union and the electoral defeat of the Sandinistas—symbolizing the defeat of the second wave of guerrilla struggles—social democracy is well placed to assume lead-ership of the Left in Latin America, as he sees it.

More than half of *Utopia Unarmed* is devoted to discussion of a series of themes. Castañeda discusses the traditional role of intellectuals in Latin America and their rightward movement and the increasing weight of grass-roots movements such as women's groups, ecological groups, and Christian-based communities. The author devotes two chapters to analyzing the nature of nationalism in Latin America and the ways in which it ought to be reformulated in the post–Cold War period. He devotes two chapters to democracy in Latin America, focusing in particular on the failings of the Left in this area, the defects of the current electoral regimes in the region, and the principal reforms he thinks are essential to strengthening electoral rule. Castañeda concludes the work by arguing that the left must reconcile itself to capitalism but must struggle to devise a capitalism that uses extensive state intervention to right the wrongs of the market and to protect local economies from the hazards of the world economy.

Traumatic Politics and the Emergence of the New Pragmatists

One of the major weaknesses of Castañeda's account is the absence of any serious discussion of the long-term, large-scale traumatic effects on the Left caused by state terrorism, economic shock treatment, and the new U.S.-centered world order. There is no effort to analyze the harsh political conditions that have eliminated leftist political discourses or weakened their social bases and facilitated the ascendance of the new pragmatists. The ascendance of the new pragmatists over the revolutionary Left is a product of the success of the authoritarian regimes in eliminating the revolutionary Left and tolerating the new pragmatists.

Castañeda's discussion of state repression is impressionistic. Without supporting documentation, he places the upper limit of state repression in a single country in Latin America during the 1970s and 1980s at 30,000, the number killed in the repression in Colombia (Castañeda 1993, 116). This grossly underestimates the extent of the mass murder carried out in the region during these years, especially in the cases of El Salvador and Guatemala. Castañeda himself describes the slaughter in Guatemala during the Rios Montt years as "virtual genocide" (Castañeda 1993, 94; on Guatemala, see Schirmer 1991; on El Salvador, see Instituto de Derechos Humanos 1986). The point is that repression has been such a crucial formative force for the contemporary Left in Latin America that a history of the Left must seriously reckon with it, as Castañeda does not.

For almost two decades, Latin America has endured the hardships and inequalities associated with the free market: Inequalities have deepened, poverty has increased, natural resources have been plundered, and public enterprises have been privatized at outrageous prices. The overseas dollar accounts of the wealthy have fattened; the number of billionaires has tripled; the United States, Europe, and Japan have recovered their original loans several times over.

Yet despite the severity of the exploitation, the political response had been relatively weak: sporadic riots and protests, political-social movements struggling to defend the remains of the social and labor legislation of previous eras. The principal social forces of the Left experienced a series of traumatic shocks that have seriously impaired their capacity to react. In the first instance, the violent eruption of military dictatorships and the associated authoritarian political regimes destroyed labor unions, neighborhood organizations, and civic groups. Immediately afterward, the draconian economic shock tactics—the application of the free market policies—virtually dismantled a half century of social legislation and labor rights. Finally, the collapse of the Communist regimes and the accompanying disappearance of an ideological and political reference point further divided and disoriented the Left. As a consequence of the "shocks," the discontent and malaise among the populace engendered by the application of neoliberal policies was disconnected from political movements.

After almost two decades of free market policies, there are signs everywhere that the end of the neoliberal cycle is approaching. Electoral movements call into question the supposedly benign effects of free market policies and demand changes in social programs and state policy.

Latin America is entering a period of transition from free markets to postliberalism. The protagonists of the new politics can be divided into two sectors. One sector, occupied by pragmatists like Castañeda, proposes to manage the liberal economy with greater attention to the social costs. The other, the consequential Left, calls for systemic changes, structural transformations that affect power, property, and production.

Two types of political actors are struggling to define the politics of postliberalism. The first type, protagonists of the pragmatist vision, are electoral personalities and parties that seek to negotiate better salaries, increase taxes to finance poverty programs, and renegotiate the foreign debt in order to free funds to stimulate local industry and increase employment. In a word, Castañeda and his supporters hope to convince the free market establishment to share wealth and power with the popular classes, without touching the changes wrought by neoliberal policies (Castañeda 1993, 451–471). The second group of actors includes the sociopolitical movements composed basically of the urban and rural poor, who want to transform property relations (land and enterprises) and to create new forms of political representation and redistribute income.

Below the surface unity between the electoral politicians and the sociopolitical movements, real tensions exist, not only over the methods of struggle and the nature of the changes but also over the character of the social actors. Throughout Latin America, the social movements are pressuring the organized electoral parties. In Mexico, the pragmatic programs of the leaders of the Revolutionary Democratic Party compete with the revolutionary demands of the Zapatista movement. In Brazil, the pragmatists involved in electoral politics are pressured by the Landless Workers Movement and the urban movements.

In overlooking the historical bases of political power and the compromises that spawned the new pragmatists, Castañeda ignores the real interests of the antagonists of reform and the links between the neoliberal economic agenda and the class interests and state institutions that defend them. In effect, Castañeda fails to integrate political and social history into his contemporary prescription for reforming the neoliberal economies.

Distorting the Past in the Service of Pragmatism

The upsurge of the Center-Left has its own ideologues, and its defenders include a significant contingent of intellectuals who, like Jorge Castañeda, have elaborated a vision of a social democracy built on the foundation of a liberal economy.

The regrouping of an array of social movements and political intellectuals like Castañeda in an antiliberal coalition is a positive development, particularly as they articulate a critique of the worst social abuses incurred in the process of implementing the so-called structural adjustment policies. However, the theoretical, historical, and empirical analysis developed by the pragmatic politicians and ideologues is deeply flawed.

In the first place, the attempt to locate the "new pragmatism" in recent history is totally inadequate. Castañeda distorts the experiences of the 1960s and 1970s—reducing a rich mosaic of experiences into a simplistic dichotomy between utopian or apocalyptic guerrillas and reactionary military forces. In his discussion, the revolutionary Left and revolutionary mass movements are reduced simply to the "military Left." He says that "an entire wing of the left has been nothing but militaristic for at least thirty years." He speaks of the "largely dominant chapter of the military left during the last three decades" (Castañeda 1993, 271).

The successful experiments in direct democracy in the rural cooperative settlements, the self-managed factories, the assembly-style democracy in the work sites, the experimental schools and mental institutions are not taken into account. One possible reason is because they highlight successful popular experiences that go far beyond the pragmatic doctrines and programs of the ideologues of the Center-Left.

The problem of understanding the positive experiences of revolutionary change through popular organizations is evaded. Instead of analyzing the workers' councils in Chile, the experimental schools and democratic patient-doctor committees in the mental institutions of Argentina, the new forms of political representation found in the popular assemblies in the neighborhoods and trade unions in Uruguay and Bolivia, Castañeda chooses to focus on the military confrontations and failures of the guerrilla movements. The experiences of popular representation did not fail; they were defeated by force and violence. They were not utopian yearnings dissociated from everyday experiences. For the pragmatists to recognize this other reality of the 1960s and 1970s would certainly raise important alternatives to their current preoccupation with channeling politics among electoral leaders and enlightened elites. The pragmatists, by posing the false dichotomy of the guerrillas and army of the 1960s and 1970s, can dismiss the relevance of popular democratic forms of governance to the 1990s. By denying the past, the pragmatists can present the contemporary choices as between military authoritarianism or electoral politics. The pragmatists have rewritten the past in the service of their current doctrinal preferences.

The second serious flaw in Castañeda's pragmatic approach is his idealized vision of the trajectory of European social democracy. Basically, he envisions a version of Northern European social democracy, vintage 1960s–1970s— which has little or no relation to current practices and certainly is distinct from the policies adopted by Southern European social democracy (Castañeda 1993, 433–447). Castañeda extrapolates the politics of the democratic social welfare state from the expansive phase of European capitalism at a time when the Communist parties and countries and the extraparliamentary Left served as formidable competitors. By decontextualizing the politics of European social democracy from its world-historic setting, Castañeda fails to confront the decisive shift of social democracy toward liberal politics in the 1980s and 1990s. The policies of high unemployment, of privatization and reduction of social expenditures, which have been pursued in various degrees by all Social Democratic regimes, cloud the "vision" presented by Castañeda. More to the point, the Social Democratic parties operating in countries most proximate in structure and experience to those of Latin America (Spain and Portugal) have gone the furthest in undermining the welfare state and labor rights and have proceeded the furthest in introducing the neoliberal political agenda that the Latin American pragmatists purport to criticize. The Spanish and Italian versions of pragmatic Social Democratic politics are deeply immersed in judicial processes for massive corruption scandals and supporting policies that erode the historic gains of the working class and small farmers (Petras and Kurth 1993).

Third, Castañeda fails to come to grips with the failures of contemporary pragmatists in Latin America. The lessons of recent history are fairly well known. In Peru, the American Popular Revolutionary Alliance (APRA) regime, headed by Alan Garcia, attempted to harness social reforms to a liberal economic regime and ended in failure. In Venezuela, former vice president of the Socialist International Carlos Andres Perez was forced to resign after two major urban uprisings (brutally repressed) and one military revolt, and he was charged and convicted of fraud and misuse of state funds. The "pragmatic" Social Democratic regime of Jaime Paz Zamora (of the Movement of the Revolutionary Left) in Bolivia likewise ended up implementing neoliberal policies and repressing peasant and worker protest; Zamora left office under a cloud of accusations of corruption, contraband smuggling, and drug trafficking. The guerrillas in Colombia's MR-19 pragmatically joined a coalition with the liberal regime of President Gavira and saw their vote decline from 20 percent to barely 4 percent, displaced to the margin of electoral politics. And in the most recent case, a Center-Left coalition supported the candidacy of the Social Christian Rafael Caldera and subsequently participated in the violent repression of student demonstrations and labor protests against the privatization and wage cuts pragmatically determined by the Social Christian regime.

The lack of "historicity" in the political proposals put forth by pragmatists like Castañeda puts their ideals on the same level as the "utopians" they purport to criticize. What is even more serious, the absence of a critical analysis of the rise and decline of European social democracy and its conversion to neoliberalism condemns the pragmatists to repeat these errors and experiences.

Both in Southern Europe and in Latin America, the "pragmatists" in government exceeded the norms of corruption to such an extent as to subject their maximum leaders to judicial processes. In other words, the liberal–social democratic compromises and the elite agreements among reformers, generals, and bankers have neither strengthened democracy nor provided an opening for the advance of social welfare legislation.

Attempts were made to harness social welfare policies to capitalism in a context where capital mobility undermined the efforts of reform. The Center-Left coalitions today no longer have the instruments to discipline capital: to force capital to share profits, power, and growth with the popular classes as was possible twenty years ago. Over the past decade, capital has constructed international circuits and greatly enhanced its independence from national controls. State institutions and international banks reinforce and facilitate movements of capital in and out of the region. More basically, the conditions for investment today are premised on long-term, large-scale conditions favoring lower wages and social costs and weak social legislation and trade unions. Efforts to strengthen labor or correct the asymmetry of power have resulted in disinvestment, and threats of financial reprisals.

Current Center-Left coalitions face the same intransigence and resistance: deeply entrenched capital linked to the neoliberal model as the only form to advance their interests. Center-Left regimes discard major sections of their social programs and conform to the neoliberal model, trying to cushion the social costs with "poverty programs" that change little in the way of power, income inequalities, or quality of life. They do not advance toward deep structural changes that take the investment initiatives out of the hands of the dominant liberal coalition. As the Center-Left advances to power, it confronts a crisis in "confidence": the threat or reality of capital flight or disinvestment.

Historical Method

The bulk of Castañeda's history of the Left focuses on organizations and organizational elites at the expense of social history. His lengthy synopsis of the history of the Left since the 1920s, which occupies some two hundred pages of the book, fails to link these organizations with the history of popular social forces and their efforts to defend their perceived interests against the local ruling classes, the state, and foreign interests. The result is old-fashioned political history with the masses left out.

The author provides many lively stories of gunrunning, guerrilla kidnappings, bank robberies, and political reprisals. But one of the most peculiar aspects of *Utopia Unarmed* (one that has escaped most of the celebrants of the book) is that there is not a single, sustained analysis of any independent mass mobilization in the entire book.[1] Strikes, insurrections, land seizures, mutinies, factory occupations: One will search his book in vain for thorough analyses of such high points of mass struggle in the history of the Latin American Left in this century. This is the history of the Left without the Bolivian miners, the Cordobazo, the wave of factory occupations under Allende, land seizures in Peru, and the revolt of the *pobladores* (squatter settlers) against Pinochet. The Bolivian Revolution of 1952 does not merit even a full sentence. Castañeda's fascination with the operational details of bank robberies and gunrunning is the stuff of Hollywood film scripts—a Latin version of *Bonnie and Clyde.*

Of course, even organizational history is badly served by such an approach. It is impossible to understand the "elite" behavior of the guerrillas in Peru in the mid-1960s without an analysis of the vast peasant land-occupation movement that swept the sierra in the 1950s and early 1960s. The emergence of the Tupamaros in the late 1960s and early 1970s is directly linked to Raul Sendic's activities among the sugar workers a decade earlier. The movement of the revolutionary Left in Chile is directly related to the urban squatter movement and the *campamentos* that were established in the late 1960s.

Castañeda's neglect of the conflict of social forces seriously mars his discussion of the history of constitutionalism and democratic procedure in Latin America. He claims that the parliamentary reformism of the Communist parties of Latin America was the greatest contribution of the Left to the rise of electoral regimes (Castañeda 1993, 39, 42). In fact, mass movements and struggles, variously mediated by Left leadership, have driven democratization rather than organizational elites. The long period of Chilean constitutionalism at midcentury—a crucial episode in the history of Latin American parliamentary rule—resulted from the popular upheavals of the 1920s and early 1930s. Strike waves, mutinies, and urban revolts—together with the Great Depression and the economic blunders of the Ibañez dictatorship—foreclosed a return to oligarchical rule, military dictatorship, or the continuation of Ibañismo under another name. It was not patient reformism that made Chilean constitutionalism a realistic option but rather mass upsurge and the fissuring of the military (Rueschmeyer, Stephens, and Stephens 1993; on Chile, see Vieux 1994).

The recent wave of constitutionalism in Latin America confirms this pattern. This wave follows the Sandinista breakthrough in Nicaragua and is shadowed by the growing strength of the revolutionary movement in El Salvador. The Sandinista victory was itself one of a number of worldwide upheavals, beginning with Ethiopia and the Iranian Revolution, which demonstrated the vulnerability of long-standing, even quite well-armed, dictatorships to popular revolt. This global trend was seconded locally in Chile, for example, where the steadily radicalizing street protests of the *pobladores* began to shake the dictatorship as the bottom fell out of the Chilean economic miracle in the early 1980s. It was against this backdrop that regional elites and Washington began to envision a transition from the dictatorships. Castañeda neglects this real history of the origins of parliamentary rule in Latin America because he fails to integrate the social and organizational history of the Left (Robinson 1992).

Inevitably, Castañeda's neglect of conflicting social interests weakens his discussion of the foes of the Left as well, the local ruling elites and their international allies, principally the U.S. government. Beyond a few pages on Brazil, the author does not provide a clear picture of the Latin American bourgeoisie or the landed upper classes. He does provide a blistering overview of the economic failures of neoliberal policy and the benefits that these classes have derived from it (Castañeda 1993, 255–264). But this economic analysis is not integrated into a discussion of the local elites as political actors with definite social interests embodied in strategies and defended by means of political parties and state action. He accepts in a general way that the interests of the bourgeoisie may be threatened by an impoverished mass electorate (Castañeda 1993, 338–339). However, he does not pursue this insight to reveal the mainsprings of the strategy of the Right in key episodes of confrontation with the mass movements of the Left, such as the bloody repression in the Southern Cone during the 1970s or the imposition of neoliberal policies in a whole series of countries in the 1980s.

Castañeda ignores the history of the largely nonmilitarist left-wing mass movements—only the "utopian," "armed" groups are defined as the Left. The result is a false picture of what happened to "the Left." It was not "utopians" (guerrillas) who were disarmed but grassroots leaders who were killed. What was dismantled was not "utopia" but civic, neighborhood, peas ant, and trade union organizations and their program of structural transfor-mations leading to a new Socialist society. What Castaneda has produced is "history" that lacks history of major actions embodying concrete social in-terests and engaged at decisive moments of time in contested sociopolitical spaces. Presented without a clear discussion of the interests and strategies of the Right, the significance of the repression of the 1970s and the imposition of neoliberalism in the 1980s for the development of the Left and its future strategies remains unclear.

The Missing Link: U.S. Interests and Latin America

Castañeda's discussion of U.S. interests and intervention in the region is also very weak. The author devotes many more pages to the discussion of the ac-tivities of Cuban intelligence in Latin America than he does to those of the U.S. government. He provides no overview of the extent of U.S. confronta-tion with movements and governments of the Latin American Left. In Cas-tañeda's view, U.S. actions during the Cold War were motivated primarily by geopolitical considerations—the desire to deny the region to Soviet influ-ence—than by the defense of markets, access to raw materials and labor, in-vestment opportunities, debt repayment, and so on (Castañeda 1993, 295). Such an explanation ignores the extent of U.S. intervention before the Cold War (the extensive interventions in the Caribbean before 1917), during peri-ods of détente with the Soviets, the actions taken against the Allende gov-ernment, and after that, in Panama and Haiti. A geopolitical explanation based on the dynamics of the Cold War cannot account for these historical episodes.

The most consequential effort to introduce an advanced welfare program in Latin America occurred in Chile during the Allende period. This process was blocked by the United States and was subsequently derailed in large part through concerted action by the U.S. government and its Chilean clients. Elected Social Democratic governments in Guatemala (Arbenz in 1954), the Dominican Republic (Bosch in 1963; Camaño in 1965), Guyana (Jagan in 1953–1954), and Grenada (Bishop in 1984) provide strong evidence that persistent U.S. intervention is not a conjunctural occurrence but rather a strong structural-ideological antagonism. Castañeda's failure to provide suf-ficient analysis of the strict controls imposed by U.S. imperial policy on So-cial Democratic regimes leaves his current prescriptions in a historical-struc-tural vacuum.

In keeping with the author's stress on the political-strategic determinants of U.S. behavior in the region, he has little to say about the role of the World Bank and International Monetary Fund in the imposition of neoliberal policies throughout the 1980s in Latin America. This oversight is especially damaging since the history of the Left in Latin America is closely bound up with the origins and spread of structural adjustment. These techniques—tariff cutting, deep devaluations, budget reductions, privatization, and other measures—were pioneered in the Southern Cone dictatorships after the destruction of the Left made them possible. These policies were enthusiastically welcomed by the IMF and the World Bank, then generalized and replicated on a global scale, not least in Latin America. Between 1982 and 1989, Latin American and Caribbean governments signed eighteen stand-by arrangements, ten extended fund facilities and two structural adjustment facilities with the IMF. Over the same period, fifteen structural adjustment loans were signed with the World Bank (World Bank 1990, 12). The spread of adjustment drastically altered the political terrain of the Left as general strikes, uprisings, and riots spread in the wake of the implementation of these policies. Again, Castañeda avoids discussing the actions of the central political actors in the region in defense of their perceived social interests, preferring to limit his analysis to the ideological preoccupations and interactions of party political elites and state elites.

From Defective History to Flawed Strategy

Castañeda's neglect of conflicting social interests follows a clear political logic. A frank discussion of the role played by regional and U.S. elites in the destruction of the Left and the imposition of neoliberal governments and the benefits they have gained from this course of action would render highly implausible his favored strategic recommendations for the Left. He urges the Left to reconcile itself to capitalism in hopes of constructing a Social Democratic order along European lines (Castañeda 1993, 451–471). The desired regime would raise taxes, spur social spending, enhance regulation of the market, defend state industries, protect local industries from foreign competition, and so on. Such a program is only plausible as long as one conceives of the chief political actors in Latin America as organizational elites fundamentally dissociated from antagonistic social classes and projects. Such free-floating elites are capable of endless compromise. Castañeda's book is a monumental effort to establish an historical pedigree for his current strategic outlook by demonstrating that antagonistic social interests need not block the road to reconciliation and accommodation between Left and Right on the basis of capitalist social relations. Such conflicts were not decisive to the history of the Left; they need not decisively shape its future.

The difficulty is this: Increased taxation, social spending, regulation of industries, the nurturing of state enterprises, and protection of markets all involve the rejection of the neoliberal model and the fruits of structural adjustment. Why should the regional and U.S. elites reconcile themselves to the rejection of this model? They cannot be expected to lightly abandon it after all the economic disruption, the social unrest, and the political risks they ran to impose it so recently. They have benefited handsomely from it. Over $200 billion flowed to the United States in debt repayment and profit remittances during the neoliberal decade of the 1980s. A new class of billionaires sprouted in Latin America in this decade, many of them nourished by heavily subsidized privatizations. Throughout the decade, the distribution of income shifted decisively in favor of the wealthy, as Castañeda himself shows. None of this would have been possible without the defeat of the Left in the 1970s and 1980s. Why should regional and U.S. elites abandon the field of battle to a defeated enemy and permit encroachments on the privileges their victory brought them? Only a wild utopian could expect such an outcome.

Throughout *Utopia Unarmed,* Castañeda continually criticizes the Left for its indifference or contempt or instrumental attitude toward the procedures of democratic rule. The irony is that the author's enthusiasm for a reconciliation between the Left and capitalism exceeds his enthusiasm for reconstructing parliamentary rule in Latin America. Thus, the author regards the Aylwin regime in Chile—with the subordinate participation of the Socialist Party—as the "archetype" of permissible reform experiments in Latin America. He frankly admits that this regime is "conserving the economic accomplishments of the Pinochet regime," a curious admission, since elsewhere in the book he describes in detail the dubious character of these accomplishments: incomes "below the cost of a basic food basket" for 70 percent of the population, per capita consumption below the Allende years until 1989, gross and widening income inequality, and dependence on primary exports (Castañeda 1993, 166–167, 255–261). Moreover, Castañeda makes only a few passing remarks about the limitations of democracy in Chile under Aylwin: the parliamentary strength of the Right guaranteed by parliamentarians appointed by the military, guaranteed military budgets, electoral rules designed to marginalize small parties, impunity for crimes committed under the dictatorship, and the lifetime tenure of Senator Pinochet. Later in the book, in a chapter entitled "Democratizing Democracy," Castañeda discusses a large number of changes he would like to see in the current crop of Latin American electoral regimes. Many of these suggestions are unobjectionable: strengthening civil society, decentralization and municipal democracy, combating electoral fraud, insuring the right to vote, increasing proportional representation, cleaning up campaign financing and media access, and insuring freedom from intimidation (Castañeda 1993, 378–373). But again, the most striking issue is the one that Castañeda ignores: digging up the remnants of the dictatorships. He avoids discussing the antidemocratic heritage of the dictatorships, such as parliaments rigged to strengthen the Right, military hierarchies unencumbered by civilian control, intelligence networks free of democratic oversight, continuing impunity for those who committed crimes under the dictatorships, and the inflation of executive power through decree rule. These issues are crucial to the future vitality of the electoral regimes in Latin America, but they are anathema to Castañeda because raising them will break the spell of accommodation and reconciliation with the ruling elites and their military backers that the author seeks to conjure up. Castañeda seems to have subordinated his concern for democracy to his broader political agenda of Left accommodation to the ruling elites and the military. Is this not precisely the kind of subordination of democracy to other, grander social goals that he found so objectionable in the theory and practice of the Left over the past several decades?

Conclusion

Castañeda's weak treatment of the social forces in conflict during the travail of the Latin American Left in this century makes it less than satisfying as history or thematic political analysis. His potted histories of communism, populism, and the revolutionary Left are too thin descriptively to nourish alternative interpretations or debate. As has been argued here, the missing dimension of social struggle results in a history of the Left that inflates the role of elites and organizations. Castañeda's assessment of nationalist and democratic impulses in the region slights the driving forces behind them: the realities of U.S. intervention and the mass pressure for popular rule. These failings are condensed in the strategic sketch that Castañeda offers the Left at the conclusion of his book. This sketch requires reconciliation between the elites of Left and Right, domestic and foreign, on the terms of the neoliberal Right, with the hope that in the medium term, higher taxes, greater regulation, more social spending, and tighter constraints on foreign capital can be imposed. This sketch fails to reckon with mass antipathy toward the "logic of the market" and the failings of electoral rule as currently practiced in Latin America, as exemplified in the numerous riots, general strikes, and armed uprisings launched against neoliberalism during the 1980s and 1990s. At the same time, the sketch fails to take into account the antipathy of the Right toward meddling with neoliberal policy formulas. Castañeda's strategic recommendations are as lacking in social analysis as his history of the Latin American Left.

In the end, *Utopia Unarmed* is less important as an intellectual investigation of the past and prospects of the Left than as a reflection of a particularly prominent current within the contemporary Latin American Left. Castañeda's work reflects the strategy and policies of such organizations as Mexico's Revolutionary Democratic Party, the Columbian MR-19, the Sandinistas, reformist trends inside the Brazilian Workers Party, and the renovationist Chilean socialism. Castañeda has gathered many fragmentary analyses from these sources, outfitted postures with arguments, captured a mood of disillusion and anti-utopianism and systematized this whole assemblage into something like a Social Democratic doctrine for the 1990s. His is a polished, forceful, and sober presentation of this doctrine. But it lacks historical depth and strategic realism.

Notes

1. Castañeda does discuss social movements that are under the control of guerrilla leaderships, an approach that is congruent with his reductionist guerrilla-military dichotomy.

References

Castañeda, Jorge. 1993. *Utopia Unarmed*. New York: Knopf.

Instituto de Derechos Humanos. 1986. *Los Derechos Humanos en El Salvador Durante el Año 1985*. San Salvador: Universidad Centroamericano Jose Simeon Canas.

Petras, James, and James Kurth. 1993. *Mediterranean Paradoxes: Politics and Social Structure in Southern Europe*. New York: Berg.

Robinson, William I. 1992. *A Faustian Bargain*. Boulder: Westview Press.

Rueschmeyer, Dietrich, Evelyn Huber Stephens, and John Stephens. 1992. *Capitalist Development and Democracy*. Chicago: University of Chicago Press.

Schirmer, Jennifer. 1991. "The Guatemalan Military Project: An Interview with General Hector Gramajo." *Harvard International Review* (Spring):10–13.

Vieux, Steve. 1994. *Democratization by Revolt: The Foundations of Mid-Century Chilean Democracy, 1920–1932*. Ph.D. diss., State University of New York at Binghamton.

World Bank. 1990. *Adjustment Lending Policies for Sustainable Growth*. Washington, D.C.: World Bank.

5

Perspectives for Liberation: The Ambiguous Legacy

In the face of the pessimistic assessment of the recent history of the Left by critical intellectuals and the triumphalist rhetoric of the neoliberal ideologues, it is necessary to reassess the historical trajectory of the radical movement over the last quarter century. It is important to do so for several reasons. First, a good deal of the negative appraisals from the Left are largely products of their current predicament—which is read backwards into history. In effect, there is a failure of historical memory. Second, many leftists have succumbed to the criticism emanating from neoliberal and ex-leftist sources who today command the main cultural outlets, foundations, and research centers. Third, the emergence of NGOs has eclipsed many of the historical transformative organizations of the past, and in their haste to justify their existence, the NGOs have contributed to the negative assessment of past social struggles, analysis, and more important political organizations.

However, the neoliberals have an obvious interest in painting a harsh portrait of the "failures" of the past Left sociopolitical movements in order to avoid confronting them in the near future, hence the effort to minimize the important social gains, the massive social mobilizations, and the real alternative to capitalism that the Left posed. Among the techniques used to discredit the leftist past is *reducing* the Left to an adjunct of the ex-USSR (or Cuba or China) and to amalgamate its decline to that of the "failed Communist" system. In other cases, the physical *repression* of the Left by the Right is transformed into the "failure" of the Left. In other words, the current weakness of the Left is described as self-induced, a result of its supposed internal inadequacies rather than the result of superior force. The neoliberal Right has gained hegemony over important sectors of the Left in the sense that it has induced the Left to deny its past successes and the relevance of past struggles to the present. This leads some sectors of the Left to "self-destruct." This takes the form of some intellectuals' "renovating" basic concepts and principles in line with the free market practices established by the Right. The "renovation of the Left" in this context denies the success of the Left in the past and its ability to shape policy and transform institutions and even to question the capitalist system.

This chapter will argue that in both the past and the present, the perspectives for liberation were and are *ambiguous*—neither inevitable victories nor defeats. This will be followed by a discussion of three *possible* moments of change leading up to the present: (1) the 1960s and early 1970s and the potential for transformation in the crises of the national-populist period; (2) the 1980s and the crises of the transition from military rule; and (3) the contemporary period and the crises of neoliberalism. The last half of the chapter will focus on analyzing and discussing the "ambiguities" in the contemporary period: the deepening crises of neoliberalism *and* the more radical application of neoliberal measures; the increasing "subjective" rejection of neoliberalism and the forms of adaptation. The chapter will conclude by examining the theoretical and practical basis for liberation in Latin America today.

Why Ambiguity?

In discussing the perspectives for liberation, it is essential to focus on the ambiguity of the past and the present. In both the past and the present, the Left has had *opportunities* to change the course of history but has lost them because of an unfavorable correlation of power or because of strategic failures. Thus, recent history is one of promise and possibility as well as disenchantment and frustration.

The Left today faces another opportunity to change the course of history and defeat the neoliberal power structure and create a new power configuration based on the working poor. As in the past, the present situation presents ambiguities, in a double sense. First, the *objective decay of neoliberalism* (the decline of infrastructure, the massive unused capacity of labor, the emptying of the provinces, the disarticulation of the domestic market, the lack of endogenous technological capacity) is accompanied by the continued weakness of the subjective opposition to neoliberalism, in short, economic polarization without a decisive sociopolitical polarization.

Second, contemporary "expressions of subjectivity"—political and social responses to neoliberalism—are both negative and positive, in the sense that there is a *turning away* from collective action and a *turning toward* individual and local activities and mass struggle.

In summary, to define the perspectives for liberation requires us to accept the dual realities of the past and present: The Left has created a positive legacy and has lost strategic struggles; and we have positive and negative subjective conditions in the present. There is no "automatic" postliberal period on the horizon. Nor, of course, is there an "end of history," as some neoliberal ideologues argue. There is no certainty of victory or defeat. There is no "end of history" or "beginning of a new epoch." Everything is *contingent* on the political, cultural, and ideological (and perhaps in some circumstances, military) intervention. The Left must learn to live in an ambiguous world in which there are firm principles and shifting realities, commitments, and leaders. There are no permanent alliances. There are only permanent interests. Yesterday's revolutionary leaders and critical intellectuals are today's parliamentary neoliberals and NGO functionaries. And vice versa: Yesterday's apolitical schoolteachers and unemployed young people are today building barricades.

Contemporary History: Moments of Change

It is important to review the past and present "moments of change" or *possible* rupture to highlight the principle of *historic ambiguity:* of struggle and advance as well as retreat and defeat. This allows us to locate the current process of struggle against neoliberalism in a similar framework that emphasizes the *centrality of voluntarism,* of action, in creating or losing opportunities resulting from the contradiction of neoliberalism.

Today, the major theoretical-analytical challenge of the Left is overcoming "objectivism" and economic determinism, learning to reject history as determined by "globalism," "technology," and "interdependence." The Left must refuse to see human subjects as shaped by impersonal, abstract, "global" forces—and reject choices that are fixed and actions limited to liberal alternatives. The "objectivist" approach is both "deductive" and linear: Power is identified from the top down and linked to institutional position.

The appropriate approach is "inductive-historical": Power is embedded in basic relations of production, consumption, and habitation, and it works in both directions, depending on the subjective forces of the contesting classes.

To say that subjective action is central in deciding the future of neoliberalism, however, requires that in discussing contemporary sociopolitical responses, we combine harsh realism with transformative possibilities. When we refer to "harsh realism," it means recognizing that there are among those victimized by neoliberalism a whole range of attitudes that are *not in opposition to neoliberalism.* Whether they are "survival strategies" or "reciprocal" forms of petty exchanges or "antisocial forms" of behavior, they are still *adaptations, not confrontations,* with neoliberalism, even as they are rooted in the harsh consequences of neoliberal policies. In the end, their adaptive responses are negative forms of subjectivity because they deny the possibilities of liberation.

Nonetheless, the "positive subjectivity" is a process that grows out from and parallels these negative responses. In many cases, oppressed and exploited people combined both negative and positive subjective responses, depending on circumstances: the availability of organized channels of revolt, the levels of "social desperation," and so forth. In some cases, the very type of social action (crime) can have an ambiguous content—both positive and negative, defined in context.

By taking the perspective of subjectivity and sociopolitical action, we reject the intellectual trend toward conceptual novelties that focuses on "globalization" and "world market imperatives." I take it for granted that we are historically minded enough to know that the market, including the global market, is an economic construct of social classes; that economic systems are historical phenomena; that there never has been and never will be an "end of history," with the ascendancy of any specific economic system. All systems pass through cycles: They rise, consolidate, and decay. This is observable today with neoliberalism, though not in any linear and universal fashion, nor is the outcome predetermined.

If "globalism" has been present for centuries and the degree of participation in national or international markets varies from time to time, depending on class policies, it is clear that the *struggle between classes* is a determinant of market relation, not vice versa. It is the imperative of class interests that shapes whether to produce locally or "globally." Thus, our discussion is neither about "models of accumulations" nor about an economic reading of neoliberalism. What is proposed is a *political reading* of the current socioeconomic conjuncture and the revolutionary and nonrevolutionary responses to the *decay and deepening* of neoliberalism.

Three Periods of Change

There are three identifiable periods in which the Left had an opportunity, and in many cases played a major or minor role, in attempting to transform the capitalist system. These include: (1) the crises of the "national-popular" or "welfare state" regime, (2) the crises of the transition from authoritarian military regimes, (3) the crises of neoliberal regimes.

In each one of these periods, the Left had an *opportunity* to pose an *alternative* to capitalism. The fact that the Left alternative was not usually successful should not obscure the fact of the historical relevance of the left.

During the 1960s and early 1970s, both in Latin America as well as in Europe (to a much lesser degree), the national-popular and welfare state regimes were under severe pressure from both the leftist and the rightist ends of the spectrum.

In Latin America during the early 1960s, massive peasant and urban movements took hold in Brazil, which increasingly pressured the Goulart regime to radicalize its program—to implement a comprehensive agrarian reform, nationalize foreign enterprises, and redistribute income. In Bolivia from the late 1960s to 1970, a popular assembly was elected in which workers and peasants predominated and legislated a series of laws challenging the capitalist system. In Chile, the Allende government, pressured by the factory councils and peasant movements, moved toward socialism. Implicit in the crises of the national-popular welfare regime was a revolutionary Socialist and neoliberal counterrevolutionary alternative. To a lesser degree, similar challenges to capitalism took place in Europe, particularly in France in 1968 and Italy in 1969. Even in the United States, the radicalization of the massive anti–Vietnam War movement and the black movement contributed to the defeat of imperialism and the enactment of comprehensive social legislation. The "radical break" proposed by the Left raised basic issues that threatened the capitalist system. Not only did the Left call into question the capitalist system, but it implemented substantial institutional and policy changes that strengthened the political power, social organization, and legislation benefiting the working poor.

Throughout Latin America, this "breakdown" of the national popular state resulted in a major confrontation with what is today the neoliberal Right. The implantation of neoliberalism was the result of the military defeat and destruction of the Left by right-wing political-military power. Neoliberalism did not succeed because of the "failure" of the Left as much as because it was a result of superior force. In historical perspective, the Left experience during the national popular crises reveals a dual legacy of opportunity and defeat, advances and regression, Left insurgency and neoliberal victory. This is the first important component of the ambiguous legacy.

The second historic opportunity for the Left occurred during the crises of the authoritarian regimes and the so-called transition period. By the beginning of the 1980s (earlier in the case of the Dominican Republic and Peru), the authoritarian regimes implementing neoliberal policies had gone into crises. In Peru, successful general strikes and a constituent assembly with strong left-wing influence threatened to bring about a systemic change. In Chile and Bolivia, major mobilizations and even armed struggle called into question not only military rulership but also the capitalist system. Earlier in 1965, in the Dominican Republic, a major urban insurrection of the urban and rural poor called into question the oligarchical-imperial alliance. In Brazil, major social mobilizations and general strikes calling for an end of the military dictatorship took place beginning in 1979.

In Southern Europe (Spain, Portugal, and Greece) major antidictatorial movements led by Communist and radical Left popular leaders took hold in the mid-1970s. In the early 1980s in South Korea and in South Africa, the struggle for social transformation accompanied the struggle for democracy. The "transitions" took on radical expression in Nicaragua and earlier in Cuba. But in practically every other country in Latin America as well as in Southern Europe and Asia (South Korea and the Philippines), the Left strategy was to subordinate the socioeconomic struggle to legal political changes, ensuring bourgeois hegemony. The opportunity for a radical rupture was instead channeled into "democratic transition," which ensured the continuity of the neoliberal socioeconomic model. The imperial formula of an intact military, free market economic policies, and an electoral regime was consolidated. Although the Left played a role in undermining the military and forcing political change in the direction of greater individual and personal freedoms, the neoliberal power configuration was the main beneficiary of the transition. The transition from authoritarian rule reflects the ambiguous legacy of the Left: an opportunity to displace the military and a political defeat in the consolidation of the neoliberal electoral regime.

The third historical moment is the contemporary crisis of neoliberalism. The neoliberal policy follows the distinct path of reconcentrating income to the top, transferring public property to major private owners, shifting state subsidies from domestic consumers to private exporters. The neoliberal policy cycle begins by forced reconcentration of income, property, and power; it then consolidates its rule via foreign flows of capital and the electoral process. The process of decay begins as capital outflows and inflows become increasingly speculative, privatized firms are exhausted, free-flowing imports undermine local production, and the regional concentration of income disarticulates the internal market. Neoliberal society becomes increasingly polarized as many, from factory workers to petty commodity producers and local industrialists, become indebted or impoverished or go bankrupt. One financial crises precedes another, and the costs of "recovery" add a further burden toward accelerating the next crisis: The debt payments, the decline of the productive forces, and the growing unused capacity of labor accompany the weakening role of the state as an employer of last resort or as an instrument to stimulate demand. Public employees in health, education, and productive activities go unpaid; provincial industries go bankrupt, and local governments lack funds for essential services. Everybody not involved in parliaments and externally funded NGOs suffers.

As the cycle enters decay, the neoliberal politicians and their international advisers impose harsher measures, deepening the immersion in class austerity, debt, free markets, and privatization. At the same time that the social support for the regime declines, economic resources to respond to the crises diminish and the reliance on short-term speculative capital increases.

Neoliberal Crises: Subjectivity and Ambiguity

The decay and deepening of neoliberalism has evoked both positive and negative responses. There is no clear unambiguous revolutionary movement, nor is there any longer any illusion of future improvement, at least for the great majority of working people.

First, on the negative side, the deepening of neoliberalism has been accompanied by political disorientation, disinterest, depoliticization, and disorder. This "disorder," however, has an ambiguous character, in that it holds forth responses that are both adaptive and threatening to neoliberalism. On the positive side, there is the growth of widespread forms of extraparliamentary activity that involve new forms of struggle and a wide range of groups and cover new geographical regions.

Second, the resistance to neoliberalism is spreading beyond the boundaries of Latin America to some of the advanced capitalist countries. The basic problem for the Left is the gap between the prolonged decline in *living standards* and the *lack of massive resistance*. This can be explained in part by examining the political impact of the abrupt and radical shift in orientation of prestigious Left leaders and movements. This change has had the effect of totally disorienting popular supporters and shifting their attention away from radical politics toward sectoral, local, and private activities.

Political Disorientation

The ambiguity of popular responses to the deepening of neoliberalism is in part rooted in widespread political disorientation. First, the political leaders and organizations identified with the alternatives to neoliberalism have gone over to the other side, thus creating political confusion. Second, recognized leaders of the Left tend to use a double discourse, criticizing "neoliberalism" while implementing "structural adjustment" policies and allying with neoliberal politicians. The result is a growing "distrust" of the leaders and loss of belief in alternatives.

The most damaging example of this process was the behavior of the Sandinista regime and party. Because of their success in overthrowing Anastasio Somoza, their tenacious struggle against the CIA-funded mercenary armies (the Contras), and initial social reforms, the Sandinistas were a basic reference point for the Left throughout Latin America and beyond (to Europe and the United States). The turnaround and embrace of neoliberalism had a devastating effect not only on the popular movement in Nicaragua but on the worldwide solidarity movements in the United States and Nicaragua. Policies and institutions that had been described as adversarial were converted overnight into people-friendly.

The examples are numerous. In the late 1980s, after years of defending the welfare state and attacking the IMF and structural adjustment policies, the Sandinistas embraced an IMF-style austerity plan that severely reduced living standards. The FSLN, or Sandinistas, correctly defined the Chamorro-Lacayo-led political coalition as class enemies and proimperialist during the electoral campaign of 1989. Subsequently, they allied themselves with the Chamorro regime. The Sandinista army was for many years a prime defender of the revolution against U.S. counterrevolutionary aggression. With the election of Chamorro, the "popular army" was directed by Humberto Ortega to repress popular demonstrations, which culminated in the massacre of scores of Sandinista activists in Esteli. For over two decades, the FSLN denounced U.S. intervention and exploitation as imperialist. After the Sandinistas lost the election, they announced the "end of anti-imperialism" and turned to seeking to collaborate with U.S. aid programs. Throughout the revolutionary struggle, the FSLN practiced internationalism—and received a great deal of international solidarity. In the late 1980s, the FSLN's historic leader Tomas Borge supported the Mexican PRI and Carlos Salinas and, in 1994, Ernesto Zedillo—both notorious U.S. clients, and neoliberals. In 1996, the same Borge welcomed the pope to Nicaragua, stating that they shared the same basic ideas. During the revolutionary struggle, the FSLN called on the population to sacrifice. Upon leaving office, the Sandinistas seized luxury houses and lucrative businesses. The case of the Sandinista switch from social reform to neoliberalism was duplicated by many other movements and leaders throughout Latin America.

In Mexico, Cardenas, the candidate of the Left, presented himself as the champion of nationalism and popular interests. Yet during the presidential campaign of 1994, he wrote an article in the *Wall Street Journal* supporting NAFTA—after years of opposing it in front of vast audiences. In El Salvador, the FMLN declared that the peace accords were a "historic victory" of the people. Subsequently, two components of the coalition, the People's Revolutionary Army (ERP) and National Renovation (RN), joined the neoliberal National Republican Alliance (ARENA) government. In the years that followed, the army has remained intact and ARENA remains fully in control of government. Neoliberal socioeconomic measures are being applied as harshly as ever; land reform is forgotten. El Salvador's popular movements protesting declining living standards are repressed by the "democratic" regime. The export economy is the centerpiece of government policy, and El Salvador is still dependent on foreign aid and remittances from overseas Salvadoreans. And as socioeconomic conditions decline and human rights abuses continue, more and more people have turned away from politics and toward private activity and crime.

In Chile, the "Socialists" and many former members of the Movement of the Revolutionary Left have embraced a governmental alliance with the Christian Democrats (the Concertación), which practices one of the most unadulterated forms of neoliberalism. The government shares power with the military, led by General Pinochet, responsible for the mass slaughter of thousands of Chilean popular leaders from 1973–1988.

In Bolivia, the Left Revolutionary Movement had been a major focus of popular resistance in the 1970s. In the 1980s, it joined in an alliance with former right-wing dictator Hugo Banzer, narco-traffickers, and notorious free marketeer Jeffrey Sachs to impose harsh neoliberal policies, lowering living standards, firing thousands of miners, and harassing tens of thousands of coca-growing peasants.

In Guatemala, a former leader of the human rights group called the Guatemalan Mothers Group (GAM), newly elected by the leftist front to Congress, recently declared that it was important to become "pragmatic" and forget about punishing the genocidal military officials accused of human rights violations. She added that it was also utopian to even publicly name the institutions and criminals—in order to achieve "reconciliation," "peace," and democracy. Meanwhile, as the "peace talks" progress and "democracy" flourishes (of the sort that the GAM leader participates in), numerous political murders take place in Guatemala.

Militants and activists in the rank-and-file peasant movements ask themselves and their former revolutionary leaders what happened to the struggle for agrarian reform and the redistribution of land and credit, for which they fought and died by the thousands. And more likely than not, the "renovated" leaders answer (if they answer at all) that "we" must first "consolidate" democracy; "we" must "modernize the economy"; we must attract "foreign investment." In a word, the ex-revolutionary leaders are looking upward and outward. And when some of these leaders do turn toward the populace, it is as professional functionaries of well-financed NGOs who no longer fight for structural changes but for "local projects" of self-help and microenterprises, many of which go bankrupt very quickly and do very little for the mass of the people.

Human rights activists ask their ex-revolutionary leaders about bringing to justice those officials responsible for torture, disappearances, and mass killings. And their leaders say that it is not opportune and they should stop wasting their time counting the dead. They argue for reconciliation and political amnesia. People asked what happened to the virtuous leaders-turned-parliamentary-statesman who engage in empty debates and restrain mass mobilization in favor of political pacts and conflict management; and what about popular leaders-turned-NGO-bureaucrats who move to affluent neighborhoods, send their children to private school, and attack public social programs as "statism"?

As debt payments mount and profits of multinationals soar from exploiting cheap labor and raw materials, people ask these renovated leaders who now embrace "modernization" and "new thinking": What happened to imperialism?

The fundamental source of disorientation is the reorientation of the leaders from nationalism, popular power, and socialism to neoliberalism. Disoriented people suffer the consequences of neoliberalism but have lost their political reference. The former leaders have been co-opted into the neoliberal electoral system (as deputies, cabinet ministers, or even presidents), the government, and foreign-funded NGO international "survival" networks. They have converted political influence into lucrative professional or business careers. By solving some of the problems of the leaders, neoliberalism has deepened the process of "privatization" and ruling-class enrichment.

Disinterest

The second negative subjective factor affecting popular consciousness is the growing disinterest in parties, radical ideologies, and even politics itself. This is true not only for Latin America but for Europe and the United States. As a result of the dramatic transformation in political-social programs and leadership—the abandonment of welfare legislation—there is a sharp decline in public activity and less interest in general strikes, demonstrations, and protests. As people note the real behavior of leaders, they are increasingly alienated by the "double discourse." There is a sense that, after all the struggles, the leaders benefit and the people are forgotten. The disinterest of the ex-Left in essential issues of the poor has its counterpart in the disinterest of the people in "politics."

The withdrawal from movements is accompanied by an increasing focus on family, individual, and locality. Survival strategies organized around household economies and the pursuit of individual mobility over class tends to become the norm.

Cynicism is accompanied by increasingly turning inward toward private life. There is a decline of solidarity, and the view that ideologies are a "deception" is reinforced by the growing social distance between leaders and followers.

At best, activists turn to local struggles for concrete demands and to organizing activities that have an immediate payoff and benefit local people. Many people turn to the unofficial economy (contraband, drugs, and the rest). The "economy" in the local immediate sense takes precedence over politics. People increasingly turn to and look for political favors rather than ideological visions.

Depoliticization

The decline of interest in party politics is accompanied by a deeper rejection of politics—growing electoral abstention, the increase of religious fundamentalism, and the importance of family networks. As the ex-Leftists concentrate on their new pursuits of looking abroad for aid, the people look increasingly toward the mini-economy. Poverty in the absence of political alternatives encourages "familism," pooling resources among family members. As neoliberal governments and the World Bank dismantle the welfare state, people are forced to relay on the mini-economy.

To discourage popular protests, the World Bank and European and U.S. foundations and government agencies have been pouring close to $5 billion into funding NGOs. The great majority of NGOs do not engage in political activity that involves class or anti-imperialist struggles. Instead, they replace the comprehensive national state welfare programs with local projects directed to limited groups under overseas control. They encourage self-exploitation and avoid solidarity with trade unions, peasant land occupations, and general strikes.

The NGOs co-opt popular leaders and convert them into professional careerists answerable to overseas donors. They are no longer responsible to the members of the popular movements, nor do they share their lifestyle. In effect, the "technical," nonconfrontational, local, private activity fragments social movements, setting off competition among groups for external funding and depoliticizing their members.

Disorder

"Disorder" here refers to the increase in individual violence, growth of criminal gangs, and personal greed. Yet "disorder" has two faces: a negative side that undermines social solidarity in pursuit of personal enrichment and a positive side that involves attempts to seize private wealth for social consumption. As the renovated leftists turn to political pacts with the neoliberal political class, as socialist ideology is emptied of content and practice, as NGOs fragment the social movement and foment depoliticization and individual careerism, the popular classes turn away from collective action and class struggle toward individual violence and personal gain. Crime replaces rebellion. There is a massive increase in crime throughout Central America with the decline of revolutionary politics and the ascendancy of ineffective electoral politics and impotent leftist electoral machines. In El Salvador, during the last eight years of the conflict (1982–1990), the number of average deaths per year was 4,500. In 1994, homicides totaled 9,135—almost double the deaths during the war. The "peace agreements" have ended the political war in the mountains and have brought the criminal war to the city streets. It is, of course, not "peace" itself, but rather the political failure to secure reforms for the poor and to provide meaningful social movements and mobilization to the former activists, the young, and the unemployed. According to Salvadoran professor Ricardo Ribera the growth of the narco trade and inequalities accompanies the deepening of neoliberalism. Crime has increased exponentially in Mexico, Venezuela, Brazil, Colombia, Chile, and Argentina, as well as in Central America. Gangs replace defunct movements among the unemployed youth. Gang bosses replace political leaders—providing wages, influence, and status for the poor, abandoned by the leftists who have gone to Congress and the NGO international conference in Europe and the United States to present reports on the poor, women, and the like. The demobilization of revolutionary fighters in Nicaragua and El Sal vador without land or future—provides trained disciplined and organized forces to engage in contraband and other illicit activities.

In the context of the ascendancy of neoliberalism, the "drug trade" replaces revolution as a means of social mobility and self-improvement, along with immigration to wealthy countries. As the renovated Left uses electoral politics as an escalator to a professional career, the poor create their own informal channels to pursue the same goals. Negative disorder is the popular *adaptation* to crises of neoliberalism *and a means to compete for its benefits*.

But "disorder" has a positive side. There are various types of *positive disorder* that lead to the creation of revolutionary subjectivity.

Spontaneous Uprisings in the Provinces. These movements result in attacks on government buildings because of lack of payment of salaries when the populace identifies the local representatives of neoliberalism. In Bolivia and Paraguay, the blocking of highways is another instance of seeking justice by paralyzing the networks of the system.

Sacking of Municipal Buildings, Supermarkets, and Trains. Mass intervention to redistribute food and consumer goods is a form of "social banditry"—taking from the state and the beneficiaries of neoliberalism and giving to the poor. Some examples include train assaults in Brazil's Northeast and in Argentina, the sacking of supermarkets in provincial areas.

Military-Popular Uprisings. In Venezuela, large-scale urban uprisings protesting structural adjustment policies were followed by nationalist populist military rebellions protesting the intervention of imperial powers, the dictating of policy by the IMF.

Political Kidnapping. In Columbia, guerrilla groups engage in kidnapping wealthy businesspeople who are benefiting from the neoliberal model in order to finance their peasant armies and their support for a social transformation. Self-financing is an element in sustaining movement autonomy.

Popular Justice. The failure of public authorities to bring to justice notorious torturers and public officials involved in mass killings has led to popular justice—popular judgments in the courts or the streets of Port au Prince in Haiti.

Positive disorder is the *first* step toward creating collective action for social transformation. *In itself,* it is limited by being "spontaneous," "local," and unsustained. But it breaks the constraints imposed by the renovated Left on mass mobilization and the limits of "institutionalized" groups (trade unions tied to electoral parties of the renovated Left, externally funded NGOs). Positive disorder focuses national attention and delegitimizes authority—but it can also fade from sight when the "disorder" ends. Nevertheless, this social side of disorder leads directly to the positive subjectivity emerging today primarily in the growth of the extraparliamentary movements. As the neoliberals win elections, the extraparliamentary forces increasingly control the politics of the streets and the parliaments of the plazas.

Positive Subjectivity: Extraparliamentary Activity

Resistance to neoliberalism over the last decade has been largely through extraparliamentary activity. Electoral processes have not been effective either as forms of resistance or as means of implementing alternatives. Today, elections are not where the action against neoliberalism is taking place.

A new alternative political culture is growing out of the mass struggles occurring outside of Congress—before and after elections. The major paradox today is that although neoliberals win elections, after the elections the same voters turn to mass mobilizations and general strikes attacking the neoliberal policies. What accounts for this paradoxical behavior? What is more representative of the popular will: elections or the postelectoral popular attacks on neoliberalism?

To understand why neoliberals win elections, it is important to examine the so-called transitions. In all cases, the authoritarian institutions of the past have remained intact (the state, the socioeconomic system, the repressive culture). These form the parameters of political debate prior to the electoral campaign. The Center-Left is obligated to accept these parameters to compete in the elections. Thus, electoral competition inhibits the Center-Left from engaging in social action, which polarizes the electorate and provides the popular classes with a distinct political identity. In the absence of class struggle and polarization prior to the electoral campaign, the neoliberals, with their superior financial resources, control over the mass media, and demagogic "populist" propaganda can gain the votes of the depoliticized masses. The Center-Left competes on the basis of being more honest and being better managers with greater social concerns—but this is inadequate to define basic differences with lower-class voters who are subject to the short-term economic payoffs of the neoliberals. *After the elections,* the neoliberals apply their concrete programs of austerity, privatization, and social cuts—programs that adversely affect the majority, thus provoking mass discontent and the growth of extraparliamentary movements.

For example, in the recent elections in Bolivia, the combined vote of the neoliberals was close to 90 percent. Yet after the vote count and the application of the structural adjustment policies, a general strike was called by the miners, coca growers, and others that was totally effective and was prolonged for over two weeks. Likewise, in the Dominican Republic, Balaguer

was elected on a neoliberal program and subsequently faced mass urban revolts that led to the death of several dozen protesters. Similar events took
place in Venezuela after the election of Carlos Andres Perez in 1989 and
subsequent to the election of Caldera in 1994: The electorate votes for the
neoliberals campaigning for popular program and then rebels against neoliberal "adjustments."

In Brazil shortly after Cardoso was elected, the Landless Workers Movement, or MST, began a large-scale program of land occupations, challenging
Cardoso's neoliberal policies. In Mexico after Salinas was elected through
fraudulent means, his electoral program was not forcefully challenged by the
electoral opposition of the PRD but by the Zapatistas of Chiapas. In Argentina
after Menem won a majority of votes in the provinces, there were major
provincial revolts in Salta, Rio Negro, Córdoba, Tierra del Fuego, Jujuy, San
Juan, and elsewhere. In Uruguay, although the traditional parties win the elections, the trade union confederations, the National Confederation of Labor
(PIT-CNT), convoke successful general strikes. Even in Europe, the right-
wing Chirac political forces won the elections, but effective public-sector general strikes block the implementation of the neoliberal agenda, while the opposition Socialist Party sits impotent on the margins of the conflict.

The revival of extraparliamentary activity and the role of a new kind of trade
union linked to the social movements struggling directly with the state have
marginalized the purely "identity" politics (feminist, ecology, and ethnic) that
are divorced from the class struggle. The new subjectivity grows out of the extraparliamentary mass action confronting the state, rejecting both the electoral
politics and the NGOs. Extraparliamentary action is moving away from defensive actions against the neoliberal policies (cuts in budgets for the provinces,
failure to pay public employees, closure of factories due to imports, bankruptcy of small farmers, unemployment of miners, and declining living standards of wageworkers) toward liberating territory (Chiapas), establishing
hegemony in the struggle for national independence against the DEA (coca
farmers of Chaparé), and forming a political pole of opposition to neoliberalism (the MST in Brazil). The positive side of the new subjectivity is engaged in
a two-front struggle: against neoliberalism from above and against negative
popular subjectivity from below. The young leaders of the new extraparliamentary movements are replacing the "renovated" ex-revolutionaries of the
1970s and 1980s. They are once again providing an orientation and creating
trust; they are challenging the NGOs to support the mass struggles or be rele-
gated to the camp of reaction or irrelevance.

Conclusion

Once again we return to the major theme of this chapter, the ambiguous
legacy of contemporary neoliberalism, the *deepening* of neoliberalism and its
decay. Today, politicians everywhere are taking new measures extending and

deepening social cuts and privatizations. Cardoso in Brazil and Zedillo in Mexico follow Caldera in offering up lucrative oil resources to foreign investors. Labor rights continue to be eliminated, and social legislation abolished. Each crisis requires deeper cuts as investment is secured through offers of higher interest rates and profits, leading to the decline of domestic investment and downward pressures on wages and salaries, which in turn leads to declining investment, production, and local demand. In order to "roll over" the debt, more social cuts are demanded, as are more tax concessions that impoverish the state's capacity to stimulate the economy. Short-term recoveries have built-in crises that continue in a downward spiral, resulting in a "permanent counterrevolution." The logic of neoliberalism has no limits in the rollback of social welfare; the process has no internal constraints. Only "outside" political intervention can constrain or reverse the logic. And "outside intervention," meaning social forces not benefiting from the model, can change the class relations and state within which neoliberalism functions. *Political intervention,* however, does not "necessarily" emerge because of downward mobility and loss of consumption or employment; it depends on the development of subjective factors, politically conscious organized sociopolitical movements. As noted here earlier, "subjectivity" today is an ambiguous phenomenon, reflecting various forms of adaptation or even "imitation" among the poor and exploited as well as forms of resistance. The recent growth of extraparliamentary action is one indicator of the reemergence of positive subjectivity—a force that is capable of breaking the constraints imposed by the Center-Left electoral opposition. This new subjectivity is rooted in the *decay* of neoliberalism that accompanies its deepening. The decay of neoliberalism is evident in its failure to innovate new products, technologies, and forms of social production. This is expressed more generally in the failure to develop the forces of production (particularly the growth of unused labor, the decline in professional training of labor, and so on). The reverse side of the decline of the productive forces is the boom of the stock market, based on windfall profits from privatization and lowering labor costs.

These economic factors have profound influences on the society, including the increasing disenchantment of social strata that once supported the neoliberal model. For example, in Mexico the middle-class farmers and industrialists heavily indebted to the state are organized in the million-member group called Barzon. Opposition is spreading from the working class to the middle-class public employees and professional and the self-employed. Opposition that is least manifested in elections is most powerfully expressed in the sphere of extraparliamentary action in the pre- or postelectoral periods.

Politically, the decline of social support has led neoliberal leaders to use authoritarian methods; Alberto Fujimori dissolves parliament, Menem concentrates executive and legislative power, Cardoso militarizes the oil workers' strike. The loss of legitimacy accompanies the increasing concentration of executive powers. The deepening of neoliberalism erodes the values and undermines the institutions that are the basis of its ideological appeal: the individual, the family, the community. As factories close, the community is riven by crime and violence; as capital moves from the provinces to the capital city and as export agriculture displaces family farms, peasants abandon the countryside and flee to the city slums. As the international banks draw interest and debt payments out of the country, families are abandoned as male heads of family seek to migrate overseas. As antilabor legislation decimates unions and minimum wages decline, the parallel economies grow and the young and desperate turn to drugs, contraband, and urban violence. The basic question is not the consolidation of a hegemonic neoliberalism, as the renovated leftists would have us believe, but the challenge of converting the negative subjectivity—particularly the hostility of youth—into the positive subjectivity of collective direct action.

Today, we have for the first time in this century the *objective* bases for international solidarity among workers in the advanced capitalist countries and the exploited in the Third World. Social imperialism has ended. The multinational corporations no longer share the profits of Third World exploitation with the trade unions of the North. On the contrary, the multinationals are exploiting and exporting their capital and profits overseas, eliminating the welfare state to provide state resources to subsidize overseas investment. Greater capitalist international integration is accompanied by increased domestic disintegration. As the empire grows, domestic society declines. The reactivization of the class struggle in the advanced capitalist countries, particularly the massive sustained strikes of French workers in December 1995, was the first major successful resistance to the neoliberal structural adjustment program. The best form of solidarity with Latin American people is the defeat by the working class of the neoliberal adjustments in the advanced capitalist countries. By undermining neoliberalism in the center of the capitalist system, it sets an example and provides potential allies for the popular movements opposing neoliberalism in Latin America. Solidarity in common struggle, North and South, and not NGOs funded by the World Bank, neoliberal regimes, and foundations is the road toward reinventing the state in the image of popular welfare and popular power.

PART TWO

Elections and Extraparliamentary Politics

Opposition to neoliberal regimes has utilized different tactics and strategies. Essentially, two approaches predominate: electoral politics and extraparliamentary politics. These differing methods usually coincide with differences in the composition of the sociopolitical coalitions and leaders and their respective programs. The electoralist opposition emphasizes, reforms, compromises with neoliberal elites and is predominantly made up of middle-class politicians and urban intellectuals. The extraparliamentary opposition is largely based on peasant movements, trade unions, and shantytown organizations. These groups engage in direct action, land occupations, general strikes, and so on. Their leaders tend to be drawn from among the peasantry, the working class or the lower middle class (schoolteachers, health workers, and the like). These diverse approaches compete for the loyalty of the majority of the populace that is adversely affected by neoliberal politics and coalesce in certain moments of crisis or in particular elections.

6

Alternatives to Neoliberalism

Two important issues that confront the Left in Latin America need to be discussed. First is the fact that neoliberal politicians have won relatively free elections, defeating prominent leftist and Center-Left political coalitions. Second, subsequent to the elections, large-scale social mobilizations against the newly elected regimes have occurred, involving significant sectors of the population and probably including many who voted for them (nonleftist voters).

For many years, most leftists associated the introduction of neoliberalism with the military regimes and the use of state terror. Historically, this made sense. The initial introduction of neoliberal policies and structural adjustments was made in the 1970s by military dictators, in the first instance by the Pinochet regime. A second line of reasoning, reinforcing the notion of neoliberalism with military repressive regimes, was the fact that the neoliberal policies adversely affected a majority of the population in a profound and continuing fashion. The point was that only military dictatorships could impose such draconian measures and contain popular discontent.

Recent history belies this contention. In recent presidential elections in Argentina, Brazil, Peru, Bolivia, and other countries, overtly neoliberal candidates have been elected (or reelected). This has led conservative commentators to argue that neoliberalism has become the hegemonic ideology or, in less elegant terms, that it has become the accepted political discourse of the masses. To a considerable extent, Center-Left politicians and intellectuals have been influenced by this line of reasoning, have adapted to the so-called new realities, and have moved toward accepting the main outlines of neoliberal political economy. Some Center-Left coalitions accept the neoliberal stabilization plan (Argentina); others accept at least part of the privatization agenda (Uruguay, Argentina, Brazil, Mexico). With this shift in the political spectrum, it would seem that neoliberalism has consolidated its position in Latin America.

However, both conservative celebrants and Center-Left pragmatists overlook the second basic fact of the contemporary period: the mass popular revolts, social mobilizations, general strikes, land occupations, and provincial revolts that follow almost immediately after the neoliberal electoral victories. These mass social movements reject in part or as a whole the neoliberal political agenda (privatizations, structural adjustments, wage constraints, increases in transport, and the rest). In some cases, these mobilizations include the vast majority of the labor force; some examples are the general strike in Bolivia in May 1995 and in Paraguay in 1994.

The point is that the large-scale social mobilizations explicitly rejecting part or all of the neoliberal agenda call into question the assumption of "consolidation." This opens up the perspective of the *decay* of neoliberalism and the opening toward the construction of a political alternative based on a different socioeconomic model.

What interpretation and what sense can we make of these dual and apparently contradictory events? What is more representative of the popular will: the elections or the mass movements and popular uprisings?

In the first place, it is important to recognize that the so-called transitions to democracy have been deeply marked by the authoritarian legacy of the previously military dictatorship. The military rulers and their civilian business and political collaborators played an essential role in defining and negotiating the conditions of the transition. As a result, most of the state institutions (military, police, judiciary, and so forth) from the authoritarian past remained intact. Second, the authoritarian socioeconomic system based on elite control of the mass media and the financial and productive system remained intact. The culture of fear and insecurity generated by the military authoritarian period continued and was in many cases cultivated by the neoliberal electoral politicians, who discouraged protests as a potential "provocation" that could cause the military to intervene. Finally, and most important, the civilian neoliberal politicians ruled in many ways by decree and used the military to enforce their policies of privatization and adjustment.

The point of this "continuity of authoritarianism" is that it limits citizen activity, undermines political debate, and forces politicians into the neoliberal framework. The continuities provide an institutional bias toward the neoliberal political candidates in the electoral process. The neoliberal candidates exploit the historical legacy, the repressive political culture, the concentration of mass media, and the major state institutions in order to force the political debate onto the terrain of the neoliberal agenda. Thus, the electoral politicians of the Center-Left are at a distinct disadvantage and, in the course of trying to compensate, attempt to compete by demonstrating their personal virtue (they are not corrupt), their managerial abilities (they manage the system more efficiently) and, at the margins, their greater social concern for the "costs" of neoliberalism (increased social expenditures). Thus, in effect, the Center-Left politicians reinforce the neoliberal argument that there are "no alternatives" to the basic model. The blurring of sociopolitical identities between Right and Left has had a negative impact on the electoral fortunes of the Center-Left. As most voters do not have strong political organizational identities, they become the objects of short-term electoral campaign propaganda in which the neoliberals, with their vast campaign funds and quasi-monopoly of the mass media, play a decisive role.

Thus, the elections represent the power of the legacy of the authoritarian past, the enormous capacity of the neoliberal politicians to concentrate organizational and financial resources in a limited time period (electoral campaigns) to secure favorable electoral outcomes.

In contrast, in the postelectoral period, the electoral propaganda and political machine is replaced by the concrete socioeconomic policies of the neoliberal regimes. These policies overwhelmingly reflect the interests of the economic elites. Privatization provides for a massive transfer of lucrative public resources to big business; price increases and wage reductions favor employers. *The social polarization absent* during the electoral *campaign comes sharply into focus when the newly elected president comes into office.* Using the so-called electoral mandate as a "legitimating cover," the neoliberal president then relies on the elitist authoritarian state institutions (military, courts, police) to impose their regressive socioeconomic policies on the protesting majority.

Under the neoauthoritarian electoral regimes, *force follows elections,* in contrast to the military regime, where force was applied before the implementation of neoliberal policies.

Clearly, there is a profound gap between the electoral processes and popular socioeconomic interests. This gap is the result of an electoral process embedded in an authoritarian elitist institutional matrix and is incapable of representing popular interests. However, the postelectoral period clearly focuses attention on the most significant socioeconomic issues of interest to the working majority: how to earn a livelihood, jobs, living standards, health, education, and so on. The *actions* of the neoliberal regime (much more than its campaign rhetoric) define the social nature of its policies. The popular reaction in the form of direct action rejecting those policies defines the populace's political preferences. Hence, the seeming political paradox of "people voting for the Right and acting with the Left" is easily resolved. The electoral process involves the legitimation of the neoliberal elite and its restricted political agenda, divorced from the interests and needs of the majority. The mass direct action movements provide an *open, grassroots* (base-oriented) *structure* in which *essential* day-to-day issues are linked to political expression.

The electoral processes capitalize on the structural weaknesses induced in the labor force by the repressive regime and the economic shock treatment:

The military disarticulated civic organizations, eliminated militant unionists, and domesticated politicians and intellectuals. The economic shock treatment weakened social legislation and labor unions and created a vast pool of unemployed and temporary workers. These structural conditions of atomization and fragmentation of the working class lessened class solidarity and made the "individualistic" appeals of neoliberal politicians more palatable.

All the same, the extreme socioeconomic measures of neoliberalism, the vast numbers affected, and the depth of the decline in living standards cut across classes, gender, races, class segments, and geographical regions, providing direct-action social movements with a broad array of forces that were concentrated and mobilizable. The sharp, steep decline in conditions compensated in part for the structural weakness. The loose "movement" structures and the call for "direct action" moved people who were otherwise passive and inactive into large-scale direct action.

Nonetheless, there is a sharp distinction between the outcomes of neoliberal electoral victories and leftist-led popular revolts. Through the electoral process, the neoliberals control the regime and state, and thus they have continuity and power even as their representativeness is questionable. The popular revolts reflect majoritarian interests but lack continuity and in most cases lack strong institutional bases to sustain them. In many cases, the mass movements ebb and flow in relation to specific neoliberal measures, thus revealing a lack of ideological capacity to sustain action.

In the following sections of this chapter, the problem of popular opposition to neoliberalism will be discussed in terms of the "geopolitics" of revolts, the limits of pragmatism, the contrasting strategies of neoliberal regimes and popular movements, the neoliberal political cycle and popular responses, and the issue of subjectivity and neoliberalism.

The Center-Left: The Dilemmas of Pragmatism

The period of the Center-Left electoral pragmatists was 1994–1995: There were presidential elections in Mexico, Venezuela, Argentina, Brazil, and Uruguay in which the pragmatists of the Left believed they could win. Although in most cases the Center Left increased its electoral presence in relation to past elections, it failed to defeat the neoliberal opponents. The striking phenomenon about these electoral campaigns was not the loss of the elections per se, or for that matter their increasing vote, but the gradual though perceptible abandonment of social democratic reform agendas. As the election campaigns advanced, the pragmatists moved almost uniformly toward a social liberal agenda. What is the difference between "Social Democrat" and "social liberal"? Essentially, the former is primarily concerned with redistributing income, reallocating public expenditures toward social welfare, elaborating a strong public sector and effective planning system, and shifting the costs of adjustments and stabilization policies onto the capital-ist class. Social liberals maintain the income-distribution pattern, increase social expenditures incrementally, and follow orthodox stabilization poli-cies within a basically privatized economy. As Social Democrats, the prag-matists discovered they could not win elections by demobilizing the masses and focusing exclusively on electoral politics. There were two alternatives: mobilize the populace or continue the demobilization strategy of the masses while moving increasingly toward competing with the neoliberals for the support of big business. In making the latter choice, the Social De-mocrats effectively shifted their programmatic commitments toward the Center-Right and became reconverted social liberals. As the pragmatists began to take seriously their capacity to become contenders for power, they began to *imitate* the existing holder of power, in the style and sub-stance of politics. Increasingly, the electoral campaign was shifted from the streets to the media. In the media, public appearance images of bourgeois respectability and political responsibility were projected. The pragmatists appealed to the middle class and to businesspeople's concerns about cor-ruption rather than heading up workers strikes, peasant land occupations, or shantytown demonstrations. Trips to the U.S., Western European, and Japanese embassies to assure the ambassadors of their fealty to private property became de rigueur. Overseas visits to Washington, Wall Street, and Brussels were undertaken to secure the approval of the respected elites. In effect, during the electoral campaigns, the pragmatists gained re-spectability while depoliticizing the voters. The Left voters were passive and, in most cases, were voting out of traditional allegiance or because of new clientelistic relations rather than participating with the energy needed to bring about a real social transformation. Televised electoral debates re-placed social confrontations, and the Center-Left lost its identity as a point of reference for the majority discontent with basic conditions. The prag-matist killed the élan, the hope, and vision that allows the Left to win the support of the very poorest, who are immersed in lethargy, dependency, and prejudices.

The pragmatists, who are long in image politics and short in historical memory, forgot the lessons of past successful electoral campaigns. In Latin America, the Social Democrats, or Left, won the presidency in Guatemala (1954), the Dominican Republic (1963), Guyana (1950s), Chile (1970), and Nicaragua (1984) when the elections were the *culmination* of mass mobilizations and struggles, land occupations, urban movements, and workers' factory assemblies. The social struggles politicized and activated the mass of the population while polarizing the society in a manner favor-able to an electoral victory by the Left. The politicized and active populace could reject the mass media propaganda of the Right because in each local committee there was an alternative political point of reference. The electoral outcome was one more victory, one more struggle in the effort to transform a polarized society.

At the international level, the attempt to regroup the Left in the post-Communist period in the Foro of São Paulo went through two phases. The first phase, essentially the "Social Democratic" phase, reflected the efforts by a broad array of Left forces to forge a common redistributive agenda based on a combination of mass struggle and electoral politics. In its search for inclusiveness, the Foro subsumed fundamental differences in style and content of politics toward the state, class structure, and economy. Working papers that promoted radical perspectives and resolutions that denounced neoliberalism were accompanied by political practices by many members of the Foro that gradually approached neoliberal policies and regimes. While the Foro initially served as a useful point of exchange of views on the politics of the late 1980s, by the mid-1990s it was losing its relevance. The assimilation of neoliberal doctrines, the deep commitments to purely electoral politics, the de facto political-social alliances with neoliberal regimes among leading pragmatists in the Foro undermined its practical and subversive nature. It became an increasingly ritualistic event, divorced from the radical social movements confronting the electoral regime and challenging the neoliberal regimes and their Foro partners.

Contrasting Strategies:
Neoliberal Regimes and Popular Movements

Neoliberal political regimes have had a strategic advantage in relation to their adversaries in the popular movements: They have a vision of coherent, global change involving reorganization of the state, the economy, the class structure, and personal values. The neoliberals have an image of the "New Person," not merely of economic changes to increase profits in a conjuncture. In sum, they have adopted a world-historical structural approach in the elaboration of their policies.

In the first instance, their position is take control over the state and shift state resources to the local propertied groups and multinational corporations, creating a class of super-rich billionaires. Their second goal is to increase exports to finance external debt payments, to lower wages to allow for the concentration of capital, and to destroy or control labor unions and undermine labor legislation to strengthen the power of capitalists in the workplace. Their social policy is to increase state expenditures (subsidies, loans, financing, and socializing financial losses) for the wealthy and lower their taxes, thus creating a polarized social structure. Their cultural policy toward the workers is to emphasize individual outlooks over collective; private problems over social; clientelistic relations over solidarity; mass spectacles over community organized cultural events. In summary, class cohesion at the top, fragmentation in the middle, atomization at the bottom.

The "global strategy" of the neoliberals has depended on two types of tactics. "Salami tactics" involve attacking workers sector by sector, or even industry by industry, for example, through sequential privatization, starting with the petroleum industry, then communications, transportation, and so on. In this way, all of state power and media propaganda is mobilized against a single sector isolated from other sectors of the population. Defeating one sector sets the stage (and provides an example) for moving on to other sectors, leading eventually to the global transformation.

The second line of attack is to combine repressive and even violent activity against an organized sector of the working class with appeals to lower-class unorganized sectors. For example, the Cardoso government attacks the petroleum workers as "privileged" and promises to provide low-cost consumer services and the income from privatization sectors to finance social services. In fact, the attack on one sector of the working class is accompanied by further attacks on others, thus perpetuating and deepening class inequalities, as newly privatized enterprises enrich a handful of private monopoly buyers.

In the recent past, when faced with the neoliberal attack, most popular movements have engaged in sector-by-sector resistance: prolonged strikes, mobilization, and confrontations between the affected sector and the neoliberal state. And practically every time, the popular movements lose in this uneven struggle.

Accompanying these popular struggles are appeals for solidarity that elicit limited support from militant sectors: one-day stoppages, financial contributions, symbolic declarations. But the "material bonds" that could change the correlation of forces in the struggle are absent. Each working-class sector has refused to risk pay or job loss to generalize the strike. Each sector has acted as if the state action is only directed against a particular group of workers and enterprises instead of the whole class and economy. They believe that they are dealing with traditional reactionaries instead of counterrevolutionary neoliberals.

Whereas the neoliberals rely on politicizing the state at every instance—drawing the army, the judiciary, and public administration into the battle to impose the neoliberal agenda—the popular movements look exclusively at "civil society." The neoliberal regime backed by the state and the ruling class is more than a match for the popular organizations, which rely only on organized civilians in civil society.

The Neoliberal Policy Cycle and Popular Responses

Neoliberalism, like previous political-economic regimes, is a historical phenomenon that contains contradictions. Neoliberalism goes through different phases: a beginning, a consolidation, and a decline. Obviously, "free market" capitalism is not the culmination of history, as some of its more enthusiastic apologists are prone to argue. At each stage, neoliberal policies have met popular resistance, though the highest levels of opposition tend to occur at the beginning, when the initial policies are imposed, and at the end, when the deep structural contradictions manifest themselves.

The origins of free market capitalism are written in the blood and gore of the military dictatorships of the 1970s. It was only after a massive attack on the working-class trade unions, urban civic associations, and peasant organizations that the neoliberal policies could be implemented. Popular resistance was not only against the dictatorships but against the socioeconomic policies that they pursued: in Uruguay, a prolonged general strike in the early 1970s; in Chile, resistance in the factories and shantytowns; in Argentina, the illegal strikes in factories and transport sectors; in Bolivia, the miners' general strikes—all were defeated by force and violence. The point is that neoliberalism did not establish its ascendancy because of the "failure" of the Left or because of the economic superiority of the market but because of the favorable correlation of military force.

In the subsequent period of implementation of the neoliberal agenda, there occurred a series of strikes in practically each sector affected by neoliberal policies; privatization of ports, telephones, airlines, mines, and factories frequently confronted strikes or popular resistance. As previously mentioned, these "sectoral actions" were defeated by the neoliberal regime because of their political and social isolation.

In the more recent period, a new and more powerful wave of opposition has arisen in the context of the decline of neoliberalism. This opposition has taken various forms, from electoral campaigns to guerrilla warfare. But what distinguishes this opposition is that it takes place when neoliberalism no longer has the economic resources, political reserves, and social support of the earlier periods. First, the prolonged process of privatization has deprived the neoliberal regimes of a potential source of income, of valuable assets to attract overseas loans. Second, the open economy has undermined the productive forces of the county, has increased trade imbalances, and has caused the regime to pursue speculative investments to balance external accounts.

In the social sphere, the unending series of adjustments—each implemented with the promise that this is the "final one" before takeoff into First World prosperity—has eroded popular and middle-class credibility. It is clear that the policies of adjustments simply provide short-term resources while depressing markets and weakening the capacity to produce, thus creating a new cycle of debt, balance-of-payments crises, and capital flight. The erosion of confidence in the middle and working classes is accompanied by downward social mobility for key supporters of the neoliberal model—not only the poor and public employees but also sectors of the professional and business classes who are badly hit by dollar-indexed debts and devalued earning. In its declining phase, pivotal sectors of the middle class, the trade union bureaucracy, and even sectors of the military and church hierarchy part ways with the neoliberal regime. In the political sphere, the neoliberal regimes increasingly rely on military force to impose their policies or retain power, thus calling into question the legitimacy of the regime.

Recent political history illustrates the growing heterogeneous opposition to neoliberalism. In the first instance, there was the prolonged general strikes of the workers and peasants in Bolivia in the mid-1980s. Then came the guerrilla movements in Chiapas in the mid-1990s and the massive mobilization of 400,000 workers and the middle class in Mexico City. The urban popular and military uprising in Caracas followed in the early 1990s in Venezuela. The industrial and public employee revolts hit the provinces of Argentina in the early 1990s. The growing peasant movements and general strike occurred in Paraguay in the mid-1990s. And in Brazil, the land occupations continued throughout the late 1990s.

After the defeat of the Center-Left electoral coalitions, popular opposition has increasingly assumed extraparliamentary methods of struggle; the limits of electoral policies in an authoritarian setting has ignited. Mass movements outside of the control of the pragmatic Left have occurred, appearing on the surface to be a defensive strategy against the deepening of the privatization strategy. But in a deeper sense, the new resistance is linked to new forms of production: The land occupations and peasant co-ops of Brazil and Paraguay and the coca farmers in Bolivia are linked to cooperative forms of production and allied with urban working-class organizations. The electoral losses of the Center-Left do not result in demobilization because the social movements are not disciplined or controlled by the pragmatic politicians. As evidenced in the recent strikes in Bolivia and elsewhere, there is a tendency to extend solidarity beyond particular sectors affected by neoliberal policies: to extend the resistance beyond sectoral protests into a "general struggle." The movement toward occupation of "state property" and the creation of the dual power of autonomous Indian communities evidenced in Chiapas and other regions in Mexico offers a glimpse into revolutionary processes that seek to accumulate forces and political spaces for sustained struggle. The efforts in Brazil by the Landless Workers Movement to unify diverse rural segments and concentrate on large-scale land occupation near urban centers is part of a new strategy to consolidate a multiclass popular alliance capable of opening divisions in civil society and the state.

As the neoliberals increasingly politicize the state, it is likely that a similar process can occur from the Left, causing fissures in the apparatus. Venezuela's nationalist-military revolt is one such indication. The resort to military violence, as in the case of Cardoso's use of the military to break the petroleum workers' strike, is an indication of the regimes' weakness in the popular sectors of civil society—the incapacity to mediate social forces. More important, the illusion of a peaceful transition to neoliberalism in Brazil is now open to question. The strategy of the Left must be to pose the question of a Socialist alternative to neoliberalism as the only "global alternative" available. The basic issue is how to move from massive, militant defensive struggles within capitalism to an antisystem transformation. The answer is in large part to be found in the problem of the *subjectivity* of the popular classes.

Subjectivity and Liberation

For too long, the left has defined revolution in economic terms: economic crises, poverty, exploitation. The problem is that these economic conditions have been abundantly present in the 1980s and 1990s and there has been no revolutionary change. However, the neoliberal Right has devoted extensive attention to capturing the minds of the people adversely affected by their policies.

The question of changing the subjective responses of the exploited majorities revolves around four areas of struggle: ideology, culture, consciousness, and ethics. The ideological level requires a clear definition of the social character of work and must consider unemployment and its contradictory relation to private ownership: the need for socialism or social ownership (in its self-managed form) as the socially necessary form for bring social needs into congruence with social production and distribution.

At the cultural level we must revive the critical view of contemporary conditions: the link between private discontents and social power; the macroeconomic world that infringes on personal intimacy; the music of the street instead of the touring millionaires performing spectacles at the price of a Third World worker's weekly or monthly salary; the theater and films that confront the contradictions of individualism and cultural imperialism, consumerism, and poverty—culture that begins at the personal, everyday levels of the universal themes of love, death, and personal desires and moves to the socially specific world we live in.

Consciousness can be learned, from experience, reading, and winning. It can only be sustained in the context of sustained everyday solidarity. Consciousness is about the individual in community, class, and family and about friendship, involving the way these social mediations define the conditions and ethics of everyday existence. Consciousness is about choices: to move up with the bosses or to link up with the workers. It is both "voluntary" and determined. It can never be imposed or forced. It is, in the final result, the product of "self-understanding": the realization that becoming class-conscious is a better way of living with oneself, with friends, lovers, family, and neighbors.

Socialism is not the unfolding of history: There are too many choices to make at every turn of history. Those choices are based on material interests, but those material interests involve more than commodities; they involve personal and social relations. How one pursues "material" or class interests is an ethical question: to pursue social advance through political corruption or through social solidarity.

The collective decisions of workers in Tierra del Fuego and Oruro, the decision of landless rural workers in Brazil and Paraguay to occupy factory, municipal building, or land—these are not only about material necessities but are also an affirmation of these workers' self-worth, dignity, and capacity to govern themselves, to become full human beings and share friendship and intimate relationships without the constant threat of abuse, hunger, and fear.

The subjective factor today is the great terrain of struggle: The economic and social conditions for the overthrow of neoliberalism are being re-created every day in each country, workplace, and neighborhood. What is necessary is the steady creation of a new social consciousness, culture, and ethics to convert those conditions into bases for transformation.

7

Neoliberal Political Cycles

WITH MORRIS MORLEY

Throughout Latin America there is a deepening popular disenchantment with neoliberal governments that have entrenched themselves across the continent over the past decade or more. Yet one of the paradoxes confounding analysts of the region's politics has been voter reluctance to repudiate these regimes at the ballot box: Devastating socioeconomic failures have been no obstacle to the election of successor regimes committed to the same kinds of policies.[1] Another paradox is just as striking: Political oppositions that have exploited voter hostility have waged successful election campaigns to oust incumbent neoliberal governments, but once in power, the new regimes have invariably and systematically repudiated their critical electoral posture in favor of deepening the neoliberal agenda of their predecessors.

This chapter explores the pattern of reproducing neoliberal regimes in Latin America and poses the question whether there can be a "resolution" to this debilitating political cycle. This political cycle is linked to, and interrelated with, upward and downward socioeconomic spirals that, in turn, are closely associated with a key part of the neoliberal repertoire—the so-called structural adjustment policies (SAPs). Based on an examination of the SAPs real socioeconomic impact, this chapter argues that too much attention has been paid to the SAPs as part of a purported *economic strategy* rather than comprehending them as primarily motivated by a *class-directed political strategy*.

First Wave Regimes

Neoliberal electoral regimes have followed a cycle of ascendancy, decay, and reproduction. Three broad "waves" of such regimes can be identified. For most countries, the first wave began during the 1980s, roughly coinciding with the negotiated transition from military dictatorship to civilian government that was taking place across the continent. The second wave followed toward the end of the decade through the first half of the 1990s. A third neoliberal wave has begun to take shape in the current period, the late 1990s.

Fernando Belaunde and Alan Garcia in Peru, Raul Alfonsín in Argentina, Miguel de la Madrid in Mexico, Julio Sanguinetti in Uruguay, and José Sarney in Brazil were prominent among those who headed the first wave of neoliberal electoral regimes that rode to power on the surge of euphoria accompanying the "redemocratization" process and the electorate's expectation that political change and economic opening would promote freedom and prosperity. Sooner or later, however, each of these "reformist" governments did an about-turn, jettisoning their populist campaign rhetoric in favor of extending the free market agenda originally proposed by the military dictatorships that they replaced. Exhibiting a newfound willingness to implement the "stabilization" and SAPs prescribed by the IMF and the World Bank, they began to dismantle social welfare programs, weaken labor legislation, take the first steps toward dismantling the state sector, permit large-scale foreign buyouts of public enterprises, and give priority to repaying the foreign debt at the expense of social and economic development at home.

But what was striking about this first wave of neoliberal regimes was their common failure to generate sustained, dynamic growth based on a more equitable distribution of wealth and income. As their terms reached conclusion, each confronted serious economic crises, in some cases compounded by major corruption scandals, producing widespread voter malaise and a burgeoning electoral and extraparliamentary opposition. The cases of Peru and Brazil are illustrative of these developments. In Peru, Belaunde's election to the presidency in 1980 was in large measure due to his ability to attract the votes of workers, peasants, and the urban poor with promises of jobs, improved living standards, and greater freedom to unionize. Once in office, though, he quickly signaled a new priority agenda: freeing the market, privatizing state enterprises, encouraging foreign investment, meeting international debt obligations, and imposing austerity-stability measures in return for new loans from the international financial institutions. By 1984, Belaunde's neoliberal policies had produced neither growth nor development. Instead, the economy was mired in a severe recession: Approximately 50 percent of export earnings were being siphoned off to maintain the foreign debt payments schedule, and agricultural and industrial production had plummeted downward. The social costs were equally devastating: growing unemployment, rising food prices, declining real wage levels, and a dramatic increase in reported cases of malnutrition and tuberculosis. The electoral support for the candidate of Belaunde's party in the 1985 presidential election collapsed to less than 10 percent.

The APRA Party's Alan Garcia won the 1985 contest on a platform that promised to reverse the process of economic decline and improve living standards by employing a strategy that combined lower foreign debt payments with increased government spending. During 1986–1987, Garcia presided over a limited but fragile economic recovery (lower inflation, rising employment, increased purchasing power of the masses), but it soon began to falter against a background of stagnant investment, capital flight, and balance-of-payments difficulties. Between 1988 and 1990, the regime dumped its populist pretensions and enacted three IMF-style structural adjustment programs in a failed effort to bring resurgent hyperinflation under control. The third and harshest of these economic packages included massive overnight price increases in basic food items and consumer goods, with the predictable devastating consequences for living standards. The austerity shock treatments impoverished a large segment of the population. This time, the neoliberal experiment triggered a major resurgence of political and class struggle: Hundreds of thousands of workers in the mining, textile, education, and state sectors participated in waves of strikes throughout the country.[2]

In Brazil, the sequence of events was much the same: from short-term, limited reforms to full-blown neoliberal policies and the collapse of the regime's political base. Through a combination of price freezes, currency reform, and other measures, the Sarney government (1985–1990) temporarily succeeded in bringing inflation under control and increasing real wage levels. By early 1987, however, most constraints on prices were lifted, signaling a major policy shift. By late 1988, the return of hyperinflation had devastated workers' purchasing power, the economy was in a state of crisis, and charges of government corruption were rife. Meanwhile, Sarney seemed more concerned with renegotiating payments on the country's massive $121 billion foreign debt, which involved new austerity measures in return for new loans from its international creditors. As inflation once again spiraled out of control, hundreds of thousands of organized workers took to the streets, engaging in strikes and other protests against the consequences of neoliberal policies. To reimpose law and order, the regime increasingly resorted to use of the army and police. In public opinion surveys conducted prior to the November 1988 municipal elections, in which the ruling Brazilian Democratic Movement Party suffered heavy losses, Sarney's approval rating hit a new low of 5 percent.[3]

The crises of first wave neoliberal regimes did not induce the preeminent international lending agencies—the IMF and the World Bank—to critically reassess the consequences of the initial "economic reforms" or "free market policies." On the contrary, they clung to their original diagnosis and found fault not with the prescriptions offered but with the failure of the first wave regimes to implement the neoliberal policies in a sufficiently forceful, consistent, and sustained fashion. This diagnosis, however, posed a major problem for the foreign financial aid donors, so influential in shaping the Latin American development agenda, and their local collaborators, insofar as the majority of the electorate felt that the "bitter medicine" prescribed for future prosperity was bitter enough, especially given that prosperity still seemed a distant prospect. The political issue facing the international actors and the emerging domestic electoral opposition who would form the second wave of neoliberal regimes revolved around pacifying the electorate sufficiently to get elected in order to implement a new and more radical neoliberal agenda.

Second Wave Regimes

The second wave of neoliberal electoral politicians—Carlos Andres Perez in Venezuela, Carlos Menem in Argentina, Fernando Collor in Brazil, Alberto Fujimori in Peru, Jaime Paz Zamora in Bolivia, Luis Lacalle in Uruguay, Carlos Salinas in Mexico—solved the dilemma of submitting to the electorate in order to serve their economic rulers by dividing the political process into distinct set of activities. The *electoral campaign* was characterized by sharp populist attacks on the *consequences* of *neoliberalism* (poverty, stagnation, capital flight) in order to defuse popular discontent with the first wave of neoliberal regimes and mobilize sufficient votes to gain office. The *postelectoral* period quickly witnessed a reaffirmation of support for the neoliberal agenda, combined with a powerful indication that these second-wave presidents were not simply part of a reshuffling process but were committed to a *radicalization* of the policies of their predecessors—whether it involved support for accelerated privatization formulas, harsher constraints on trade union activities, or more wage and job cuts to create a greater reserve army of cheap labor—that had savaged living standards across the region and made possible their political rulership.

After successfully campaigning for the Venezuelan presidency in late 1988 on a quasi-populist program, including support for a debtors' cartel to limit the social and economic costs of the country's repayments to its international creditors, Carlos Andres Perez began implementing a savage neoliberal program, almost from the moment he took over the reins of political power. In February 1989, he negotiated a $4.6 billion economic package with the IMF that reflected, in part, a decision to make foreign debt payments a high priority. Overnight, the government imposed massive increases in the cost of gasoline, transport, and basic foodstuffs, triggering explosive riots that left over 200 dead and more than 1,000 injured. Although the elimination of price controls and food subsidies and the freeing of interest charges halved the inflation rate during Perez's first eighteen months in office, these and other austerity measures (cutting tariff barriers, eliminating thousands of jobs in the state sector, and so on) significantly eroded the liv-

ing standards of both the lower and middle classes. Despite a 9 percent increase in gross domestic product (GDP) between mid-1991 and mid-1992,
Perez's public approval rate had plummeted to 6 percent, which was not surprising given that real wage levels had fallen to half of what they were in
1988 and around 60 percent of the population remained below the poverty
line.⁴ These consequences of the neoliberal reforms, together with increasingly pervasive graft and corruption within the regime, triggered nationwide
protests and work stoppages on an almost constant basis. In May 1993, the
Supreme Court ruled that sufficient evidence existed to prosecute Perez on
charges of embezzlement and misappropriation of public funds. Later that
year, he was impeached and subsequently incarcerated on charges of corrupt
behavior in office.

In Brazil, the Collor government (1990–1993) quickly dispatched its
populist electoral rhetoric and outlined an ambitious free market economic
plan based on deregulation, large-scale privatization, and letting the market
set wages and prices. Although efforts to sell off state-owned companies
barely got off the ground because of consistent popular opposition to privatizing most basic public services, the regime pushed ahead with its fiscal and
monetary policies leading to depressed demand, falling industrial activity, rising unemployment, hyperinflation, an unprecedented number of bankruptcies, and negative overall growth. By the end of 1991, Collor's popular support base had collapsed. As the neoliberal-induced recession entered its third
year, the president was confronted by another problem: In June 1992, a
congressional investigation found that he had knowingly used his public office for personal gain. In September, the Chamber of Deputies voted for im-
peachment; and three months later, he resigned from office, only to be subsequently convicted by the Senate of engaging in corrupt activities.

The Paz Zamora government in Bolivia (1989–1993) launched an aggressive neoliberal program to "stabilize" and "adjust" the economy. In close
consultation with the IMF and the World Bank, Paz Zamora, seeking to attract new loans and foreign investment, eliminated controls on goods and
services, cut tariffs supporting local industry, and instituted labor system
changes that gave employers more authority to reduce wages and increased
power over the hiring and firing of workers. However, the effort to launch
an ambitious privatization program in 1992 was also derailed for some, but
not all, of the same reasons that had frustrated Collor in Brazil: trade union
opposition, allegations of government corruption, and the military's discontent over losing some of its most lucrative sources of income.

In the case of the Menem government in Argentina (1989–1993), the division between the election campaign and postelection policies could not
have been sharper. To win the presidency, Menem promised an economic revival and a return to traditional Peronist prolabor policies. He promised to
increase workers' wages, which had declined substantially in real terms under

his predecessor, Raul Alfonsín; and he castigated Alfonsín for allowing debt payments to consume approximately 45 percent of the country's export earnings. He told voters his government would push for a five-year "grace period," in effect, a debt moratorium. At the same time, he also favored the sale of state-owned companies and supported new policies to increase foreign investment levels.

During his first hundred days in office, the order of priorities was comprehensively reversed. With the promise of new IMF assistance, he turned his back on the trade union movement that had played a major role in his electoral victory and proceeded to implement a set of neoliberal austerity measures, including support for massive rate increases by public utility, transport, communications, and energy enterprises. Simultaneously, he retreated from his advocacy of a debt moratorium, indicating a preparedness to negotiate a new schedule of repayment terms with the country's international creditors.

In 1991, Minister of Economics Domingo Cavallo launched a major program of neoliberal market reforms that was intended, among other objectives, to entice greater inflows of foreign capital. By mid-1993, the regime had privatized a large number of state enterprises and, more important in terms of maintaining popular support, had lowered the unemployment rate and pushed inflation down from a monthly growth rate of 200 percent in 1989 to an annual increase of only 12 percent.[5] But cracks in the neoliberal facade began to appear during late 1993 and early 1994 in the form of rising civil unrest, including popular uprisings in the northern province of Santiago del Estero over the failure of market reforms to improve the socioeconomic lot of traditionally marginalized sectors. Moreover, unemployment began an upward trend, reaching 18 percent in 1996, at a time when the government announced cuts in the national unemployment fund and in welfare and health benefits for workers. In December 1994, the state pension system suffered a similar fate; two months later, up to 500,000 civil servants were informed of salary cuts.[6] Nonetheless, Menem was reelected in May 1995 with nearly 50 percent of the vote. He had stabilized the economy, had presided over a GDP growth rate that averaged close to 8 percent annually during his first administration, and, above all, had effectively solved the inflation problem, thus the electorate appeared willing to return him to power, notwithstanding the austerity "adjustments" and growing poverty that accompanied the neoliberal experiment.

The victorious candidate in Peru's 1990 presidential election, Alberto Fujimori, campaigned against both his opponent, the rightist free marketeer Mario Vargas Llosa, and his neoliberal predecessors. He attacked the latter for failing to address the country's social problems and, in contrast to Vargas Llosa's call for harsh "shock treatment" measures, announced that he intended to reduce the country's hyperinflation on a gradual basis. The urban poor and rural peasantry swept him into office in a June runoff election.

Within weeks, Fujimori reversed course and announced a set of stringent austerity measures mandated by the IMF and World Bank in return for new loans. Dubbed "Fujishock," they were almost a mirror image of the Vargas Llosa campaign promises that the electorate had repudiated. The removal of subsidies on basic foodstuffs tripled prices overnight; soon after, hundreds of thousands of public sector workers were the victims of "downsizing." The immediate response to rising bread and milk costs and falling wages was mass demonstrations, riots, and confrontations between Lima's urban slum dwellers and the regime's security-military forces, as well as strikes by public sector unions whose members had suffered big job losses.

Fujimori's neoliberal commitment also extended to repayment of a $2 billion foreign debt in arrears owed to the IMF, the World Bank, and the Inter-American Development Bank. This headlong drive to regain favor within the international financial community translated into added burdens on the poor and the lower middle class. During the regime's first twelve months, debt servicing absorbed hundreds of millions of dollars, compared with an estimated $40 million spent on social welfare programs. Meanwhile, almost 90 percent of the workforce lacked stable, full-time employment, and the proportion of the population living below the poverty line more than doubled. However, even if the social costs of the neoliberal policies were catastrophic for many Peruvians, the Fujimori regime did halt runaway inflation and bring it under control for the duration of its first term in office.

By late 1994, Fujimori had successfully privatized a large part of the state sector, had established an enviable inflation-fighting record, and had produced growth and a stable economy, all of which contributed to his landslide reelection victory in April 1995—despite a worsening of social conditions, more people reduced to poverty status, and the passage of new laws "that virtually eliminated all forms of legal protection for salaried workers."[7]

The "adjustment" and "stabilization" measures promulgated by the second wave of neoliberal regimes effectively took on the character of annual rituals, each new round further shredding the remaining vestiges of the social net. Emblematic of deteriorating socioeconomic conditions in major capital cities such as Buenos Aires, São Paulo, Caracas, and Mexico City were the extraordinarily high levels of open and disguised unemployment. Although deflationary economic policies, international bank loans, and the influx of speculative capital stabilized these economies in the short term, all too often such recoveries were soon followed by new rounds of structurally induced crises.

As the "economic reforms" polarized these societies, the second-wave neoliberal presidents also began to increasingly centralize legislative and executive power. The prototype was the Fujimori *autogolpe* (self-induced coup) that was executed while maintaining the framework or facade of a bargaining electoral system. In April 1992, with the full backing of the military high command, the Peruvian president dismissed the Congress, closed down the judiciary, suspended all constitutional guarantees, and rewrote the constitution to permit his reelection to a second term.

This willingness to impose policies by executive fiat, overriding legislatures, and violating constitutional norms and individuals' civil rights was a defining feature of these second-wave neoliberal regimes. In the single-minded pursuit of an ideological doctrine, their leaders were often impervious to large-scale public protests or abysmally low public opinion ratings. Argentina's Carlos Menem, for instance, stated on more than one occasion that nothing—whether general strikes or collapsing popular support—would deter him from pursuing his free market agenda. Such rigidity and scorn toward any notion of a consultative regime was accompanied by the beginnings of a move to strengthen coercive institutions and remilitarize civil society. This shift, and its parallel creation of an increasing "bunker mentality" among neoliberal regimes, becomes more entrenched with the advent of the third-wave neoliberal presidents.

Two kinds of opposition emerged as the second-wave regimes declined: well-financed political parties that condemned the "harshness" of the austerity programs but once again were preparing a wave of neoliberal measures; and growing social movements desperately struggling to salvage the remnants of the social wage in order to avoid falling into deeper poverty. In the face of regime rigidity and the elimination of serious public interlocutors, even proregime conciliators among trade unions, civic associations, and neighborhood groups associated with clientelistic politics began to organize protest activities. Although a majority of the public increasingly favored a break with neoliberalism, the majority of the political opposition remained deeply embedded in that framework, unable to elaborate new initiatives outside of the "globalized" economies that they would ultimately administer. The option facing the third wave of new or reelected neoliberal presidents was, and remains, the *further deepening* of the free market exploitation and an increasing risk of *organized* social upheavals.

Third Wave Regimes

The third-wave neoliberal regimes that came to power between 1993 and 1995 range from those of Alberto Fujimori in Peru and Carlos Menem in Argentina, both reelected to second terms, to the administrations of Ernesto Zedillo in Mexico, Rafael Caldera in Venezuela, Gonzalo Sánchez de Lozada in Bolivia and Fernando Henrique Cardoso in Brazil. Like the second-wave neoliberals, they continue to demonstrate that the SAP is not a passing phenomenon; that social sacrifice is *not* a *temporary* condition on the way to long-term, large-scale prosperity; that what the lower middle and working classes are now experiencing is a *continuous spiral of declining living stan-*

dards, as temporary "stabilizations" are followed by new sets of "adjustment" measures that further erode living standards. Increasingly, intellectuals and professionals experiencing downward mobility realize that SAPs do not serve the development project. Rather, they facilitate an *upward spiral* of the very wealthy, creating polarized societies and destroying any remaining illusions about the classless rhetoric of neoliberal "modernization."

In Peru, while the international financial institutions continue to lavish praise on Fujimori for his relentless commitment to neoliberal reforms, more than half the population subsists below the poverty line and less than one in ten Peruvians has stable, full-time employment, despite a sustained period of economic growth.[8] Urgently needed social projects have been abandoned as the informal economy grows apace. By April 1996, Prime Minister Dante Cordova and more than half of the Cabinet had stepped down from their posts in protest over Fujimori's failure to proceed with his commitments to create more jobs and tackle the poverty issue.[9]

Determined as ever to brook no opposition to his neoliberal policy agenda, Fujimori has kept up the pace of "reforms." Having already privatized approximately 173 of the 183 state-run companies that were operating in 1990,[10] the government announced in May 1996 that an irreversible decision had been taken to sell off the state oil company Petroperu and all remaining public enterprises by 1998. This—despite a public opinion poll taken that same month that showed almost 70 percent of the population opposing the policy and an even greater majority demanding a referendum on the issue. To eliminate the referendum option, the government rammed an amendment through the Congress to block any such bid.[11]

In August 1996 in Argentina, with the labor movement now in more or less open revolt against the Menem regime over its austerity policies and the accompanying large-scale unemployment, the newly appointed economics minister, Roque Fernandez, a University of Chicago-trained monetarist, announced a further package of measures that included an increase in fuel and gas prices, cuts in industrial and export promotion incentives, and the elimination of export subsidies and tax concessions for manufacturers and importers of capital goods. He also declared that no general strike, such as the one organized by the General Confederation of Workers, or CGT, earlier that month, would weaken the government's resolve to push through stronger spending cuts and higher taxes to deal with the main priority: the growing fiscal deficit. In late September, the CGT staged another highly effective general strike, supported by the country's two other umbrella organizations, to protest the regime's economic policies. Menem denounced the strike, reiterating his determination to proceed with the neoliberal economic program.[12]

According to the National Statistics Institution (INDEC), the pattern of income distribution has become more skewed than ever during Menem's hold on political power.[13] The Argentine Center for Macroeconomic Studies estimates that 45 percent of the working-age population are currently without jobs or underemployed or do not earn enough to meet basic subsistence needs.[14] Meanwhile, graft and corruption charges are threatening to engulf the regime. Some cabinet ministers have been publicly accused of engaging in illicit activities for private financial gain, including corrupt involvement in the privatization of government services.[15]

The successful passage of at least five major legislative proposals to facilitate the hiring and firing of workers, and generally give capital greater power over labor, has been a hallmark of Menem's two administrations. Employers have also been the major beneficiaries of every collective agreement since 1991: More than 90 percent of the clauses have involved cost-cutting initiatives, changing job requirements, lowering wages, extending working hours, and binding employees to increase productivity. In late 1996, Menem signaled his intention to submit a new package of labor "reforms" to Congress, ostensibly to solve the unemployment problem. Described as *"flexibilizacion,"* the legislation seeks to further strip workers of hard-won gains and increase their vulnerability to capital's profit-making requirements. The two key features that have provoked powerful trade union resistance are the proposals that would eliminate the current rules on severance pay and those that would abolish the principle that new collective agreements cannot be negotiated "downward," meaning that benefits gained in previous agreements cannot be removed.[16]

The transition from Perez to Caldera in Venezuela witnessed a rerun of the gap between campaign promises and the new regime's policies. Confronted with an economy in recession, a ballooning deficit, and surging inflation, Caldera quickly sidelined his election commitments to antipoverty, social reform measures in favor of "going to the IMF." With over 70 percent of families living below the poverty line and close to 50 percent of the economically active population eking out a living in the informal economy,[17] the prescribed remedy was another round of neoliberal "adjustment" measures to "stabilize" the economy. Price controls were eliminated, gasoline costs increased, and in July 1996, an approving IMF released a $1.5 billion standby credit in return for another round of austerity measures. As the year drew to an end, the socioeconomic circumstances of close to three-fourths of Venezuela's populace could only be described as catastrophic. Unemployment among the lower and middle classes ran into the millions. Meanwhile, the neoliberal solution had pushed the crime rate to new heights: Drug trafficking remained the most profitable business sector, but car theft had pushed petroleum from second to third place.[18]

Campaigning for the presidency of Bolivia in late 1993, Gonzalo Lozada, a mining magnate and principal architect of the country's 1985 stabilization program, told voters he would continue the Paz Zamora regime's economic restructuring program while simultaneously addressing a raft of social concerns (including the lack of access of half the population to potable water and sewer systems) that he accused his predecessors of neglecting. Once in office, however, neoliberal economic policies assumed priority status, generating a level of popular discontent that led the government to declare a state of siege, suspend all constitutional rights, and assume extraordinary powers in April 1995. Against a background of wage stagnation, escalating unemployment, and nationwide demonstrations by workers protesting against downsizing and other deflationary economic measures, Lozada received yet another loan from the IMF under the enhanced SAP in April 1996 to support his neoliberal "reforms."[19] Among the latter was a highly unpopular decision to privatize selected public enterprises, including the state petroleum company Bolivian Petroleum Company (YPFB). Neither opposition political parties nor the trade union movement was able to prevent Senate approval of the YPFB partial privatization bill in May.

Populist rhetoric and a commitment to social reforms were also instrumental in Fernando Cardoso's election as Brazil's new president in 1995. And, like other third-wave regimes, the Cardoso government quickly became preoccupied with an economic stabilization program that, in turn, triggered growing popular opposition. Workers in both the public and private sectors embarked on a series of strikes over government plans to downsize the bureaucracy and over inadequate minimum-wage increases. But the key issue was the neoliberal regime's failure to address the unemployment problem. The trade union's statistical department, DIESSE, calculated that as of April 1996 more than 2 million people were unemployed in five of the country's major cities: São Paulo (where industrial recession had pushed the rate up to almost 16 percent), Porto Alegre, Belo Horizonte, Curitiba and Brasilia. According to the national statistical institute, IBGE, unemployment increased by more than 39 percent between mid-1995 and mid-1996. This largely explains the results of two public opinion polls in May (1996) that revealed that Cardoso's popularity had crashed to 25 percent from a high of 68 percent.[20]

As was the case with his predecessor, an important factor contributing to Cardoso's eroding political base has been the sustained popular (and parliamentary) opposition to efforts to accelerate the privatization process. The limited contraction in the overall weight of the state sector between 1990 and 1995 is partly explained by this fact: State firms accounted for 60.4 percent of the assets of the top 500 companies in 1995, a decline of only 7.4 percent, and accounted for 30.5 percent of the turnover of the top 500 companies in 1995, a fall of just 7.1 percent. The focus of nationalist opposition was the government's sale of the mining conglomerate (CVRD), one of the top ten publicly traded companies in Latin America, one with an enviable operating reputation.[21]

In Mexico, the third-wave neoliberal regime of Ernesto Zedillo has been no more successful than that of Salinas or de la Madrid in improving the socioeconomic conditions of the mass of the population—whether in the areas of jobs, wages, prices, or public services. To meet the strict economic and fiscal conditions imposed by Washington and the IMF in return for a multibillion-dollar financial bailout following the post-December 1994 economic crisis, Zedillo introduced a new austerity plan that included budget cuts, increases in food and electricity prices, and a rise in the value-added tax. These measures, together with a devaluation of the peso, further impoverished the working and middle classes. Between the onset of the crisis and mid-1996, a combination of price jumps for basic goods and a decline in real wage levels of more than 50 percent had thrown an additional 5 million Mexicans below the poverty line.[22] In common with a number of other neoliberal regimes, however, Zedillo has been forced to backtrack, at least temporarily, on the pace and scope of his privatization ambitions. In October 1996, he was forced to bow to widespread pressures from trade unions, opposition political parties, and even sectors of the governing PRI, and revise his plans to sell off all of the state-owned petrochemical industry (PEMEX).[23]

The shift toward a more militarized version of the neoliberal approach during the second-wave regimes has become more marked with the advent of the third-wave presidents. In February 1996, for example, Caldera used the Venezuelan military to savagely put down street protests in Caracas and kept it on alert to crush any antigovernment opposition getting out of hand. In April, Brazilian police opened fire on landless peasants occupying uncultivated property in the state of Pará, resulting in at least 19 deaths. Weeks later, President Cardoso warned that future land occupations would be treated as a national security issue and the armed forces would be used to evict squatters.[24] Nor has Argentina's Menem been reluctant to fill the streets of Buenos Aires with soldiers and tanks to block peaceful demonstrators taking part in general strikes. Last, but not least, Zedillo's method for dealing with the socioeconomic conditions that created the basis for the emergence of the Zapatista guerrillas in Chiapas has been to militarize a broad swath of southern Mexico.

Popular support for virtually all the third-wave neoliberal presidents has collapsed or declined significantly since they entered office. Barometro Iberoamericano, a survey conducted jointly by fourteen political firms in late 1996, revealed the extent of regional hostility toward these proponents of the free market agenda. Menem (79 percent), Lozada (63 percent), and Caldera (60 percent) received the highest disapproval ratings, but even the most "popular" of the group, Alberto Fujimori, had experienced a 15 percent fall in his approval rating (to 58 percent) over the preceding twelve months.[25]

Unlike the first- and second-wave social protest movements that participated in antiregime actions that were typically sporadic, sectoral, and defensive, the third wave of liberal politicians confronts organized popular power with a social revolutionary perspective. In Mexico, the Zapatista guerrillas revealed the depth of the socioeconomic crisis and posed a fundamental challenge to the national political system; in Brazil, the Landless Workers Movement, or MST, currently occupies rural properties in twenty-two of the country's twenty-six states, in an aggressive response to government inaction over agrarian reform;[26] in Bolivia, the Chaparé coca growers played a leading role in opposing the 1996 agrarian legislation, which included a 50 percent reduction in land tax and other concessions to property holders.[27]

These and other movements across the continent not only illustrate a new type of revolutionary democratic opposition to neoliberal electoral politics but have also been successful in attracting important sectors of the downwardly mobile lower middle class that have previously been hesitant about, if not hostile to, radical politics and direct action and that represent a prime base of electoral support for the neoliberal regimes. In Mexico, the debtors' organization of small and medium farmers (Barzon) and businesspeople and professionals have developed links with the Zapatistas; in Brazil, sectors of national industry and commerce have expressed support for the landless rural workers' demands for agrarian reform; in Bolivia, small and medium-size business groups have expressed support for the coca farmers; in Paraguay, professionals, journalists, and teachers articulate the interests of peasant movements.

The degree of middle-class alienation in the big cities varies. Deep-seated prejudices toward radical movements of the poor and a continued belief in old discredited liberal-democratic models of social consensus momentarily block any rapid shift to the Left. Nevertheless, as Center-Left pragmatists fail to prevent the fall of the middle class into poverty, there is a perceptible questioning of electoral politics and the viability of the neoliberal model— hastening the move, especially among affected public sector employees, toward extraparliamentary politics. As the neoliberal cycle plays itself out, the electorate is becoming increasingly distrustful of the political class and its capacity to define a new political-economic project.

The duality of neoliberal politics—populist electoral campaigns and austerity free market regimes—has bred general cynicism toward all politicians. At the same time, the class perspective toward politics has gained ascendancy in the social movements, challenging a basic tenet of neoliberal doctrine that there are "no alternatives." The social movements are increasingly moving toward defining an alternative political project—moving from protest against neoliberal policies toward the politics of social transformation. In Brazil, the MST is debating a program that goes beyond agrarian reform to self-managed socialism. In Bolivia, the coca farmers have organized a new political movement, the Alliance for the Sovereignty of the People, which incorporates the autonomy of the Indian nation, social ownership, and free market production of coca. In Paraguay, the National Peasant Federation has openly defined a Socialist program in which rural co-operatives and public owner-ship are counterposed against Stroessner-style "statism" and the Wasmosy government's liberalism. The division between "social movement" and "pol-itics" is coming to an end. The political definitions of the social movements are taking place without looking to external oracles and encompass search-ing debates and the exploration of new terrains of discussion.

From Critics to Celebrants: Entrenching the Neoliberal Agenda

In analyzing the contemporary Latin American political cycle, it is important to address *why* the apparent voter opposition to neoliberalism translates into the election of successor regimes that espouse the same policies.

First, as has been observed in virtually every case, neoliberals do *not* cam-paign for political office on their program; they do *not* promise to lower salaries, dismantle the welfare state, reduce pensions, or increase prices of es-sential food items and basic social services. On the contrary, neoliberals dis-guise themselves as populists, flay the incumbent neoliberals, and promise to change course. In the quest for the presidency, populist and nationalist slo-gans predominate; candidates promise to address the problems of poverty and unemployment; proponents of the free market doctrine are vigorously denounced. But once in office, the reformist commitments are subordinated to IMF-style "adjustment" and "stabilization" programs as severe as any the outgoing neoliberal regimes were denounced for—all to the accompaniment of dismantled social welfare systems, the elimination of laws protecting la-bor, downward wage spirals, rising unemployment, the growth of the infor-mal economy, and greater impoverishment of populations.

Electoral campaign programs are inversely related to postelection politics. Neoliberalism has debased the electoral process as much as it has marginal-ized the legislature in the postelectoral period. Under neoliberalism, elec-toral politics has become meaningless as a method of providing meaningful choices to the electorate, in which voter expectations are correlated to elec-toral outcomes. The result calls into question the whole issue of representa-tive government. Electoral nonrepresentativeness is a result of the funda-mentally elitist character of neoliberalism: Its socioeconomic policy is incompatible with free elections. Under military rule, neoliberal measures could be announced openly and imposed. Under civilian rule, they must be disguised and then imposed via the fiction of the electoral mandate. The pseudolegitimacy of neoliberal regimes rests on the false assumption that the government is "freely elected." But politicians are legitimately elected only as representatives of a publicly defended position. Stripped of political context, the electoral process loses its legitimacy, as would any other instance of political fraud. To the extent that neoliberal electoral campaigns are manipulated to secure voting outcomes diametrically opposed to those supported by the majority of the electorate, it is a violation not only of trust but of the very notion of representative government.

The neoliberal cycle—the reproduction of neoliberal regimes—is thus based on their practitioners' capacity to distort the electoral process through conscious deception; it deepens the gap between voter preferences and the practices of the political class, between electoral processes and policy outcomes.

The second reason public opposition to neoliberalism translates into the election of neoliberals is the political power of economic groups organized "outside" the electoral process. The main determinants of political decisions are not voter preferences but are embedded in the socioeconomic structures in which elected politicians operate. The latter, committed to working within existing capitalist property relations, international circuits, and financial networks, automatically seek to accommodate their policies to the basic economic interests of this configuration. The key capitalist actors—international and national, productive and financial—base their investment decisions on the perpetuation of the neoliberal model. The result is that capitalist politicians who attempt to "regulate" or change the rules of investing to accommodate the social interests of the majority of voters inevitably provoke capital flight, declining investment, and reductions of external financial flows. The elected politicians, anticipating a possible crisis of "investor confidence," move swiftly to repudiate their campaign promises and implement the "other," hidden agenda.

In today's executive-centered political system linked to the neoliberal, free market model, there is little or no institutional space for countervailing social forces proposing alternatives to a capitalist strategy. The ease with which "reformist" or "popularist" politicians repudiate their campaign rhetoric suggests that organized social forces or institutions capable of holding them to political accountability, at least via the electoral process, are very weak.

The third reason that neoliberalism reproduces itself despite widespread electoral opposition can be found in the accommodationist behavior of Center-Left politicians. Despite electoral mandates to change, an ideology that purports to oppose neoliberalism, and a prior political trajectory of opposition, the Center-Left quickly adapts to the neoliberal power configuration.

History (social background and struggles) does not influence Center-Left political behavior as much as immediate contextual factors do; ideological commitments are less important than narrow political interests; electoral mandates are not as relevant as self-enrichment. Contextual factors, political interests, and self-enrichment have taken on such prominence in today's world because they resonate with the dominant ethos of the time. Center-

Left politicians denounce neoliberalism in the abstract: In practice, they are strongly attracted to the ethic of quick and easy fortunes made through public-private transactions. This process is facilitated and legitimated by the privatization discourse. For the petty bourgeois (and not a few ex-workers), upward social mobility through politics has been a staple practice. In the past, this opportunism has been controlled to some degree or checked by strong class institutions (which held leaders accountable) and sanctioned by stern moral prescriptions. Today, majoritarian popular discontent is not institutionalized; class ethics have been eroded. As a result, Center-Left politicians are free to drift across the political and social map redefining the terms for "opposing neoliberalism." Such terms are sufficiently vague as to allow various forms of procapitalist "modernization" stratagems to surface that are hardly popular "alternatives."

The reproduction of neoliberalism can also be analyzed in terms of institutional continuities between the military regimes and the new electoral system. The debates on "transitions" from dictatorship to democracy have typically ignored or falsified a key element: the continuity of socioeconomic power, state institutions, and the development "model." The electoral regimes were neither able nor willing to confront the rigid policy parameters established by international and domestic capital. To do so would call into question the very origins of the "political pact" that allowed electoral politicians to emerge from obscurity. This historical legacy and recognition of the policy boundaries has become part of the revived electoral political culture. Transgressors of the "political pact" face the prospect of a crisis of investor confidence and, beyond that, the threat of a return of military rule. Under neoliberal hegemony, the new rules of the electoral game allow opposition parties free rein to attack neoliberalism in *pursuit* of government office but insist on "responsibility" for accelerating the model *after gaining* office. Freedom, in the market democracy sense, involves talking to the people during electoral campaigns and working for the rich when in power.

Impoverishing Societies:
The Crisis Multiplier in Neoliberalism

The fundamental problem of neoliberalism is that it is not able to create a stable predictable policy with any foreseeable takeoff into sustained growth and incremental benefits that would allow for long-term consolidation. Although regimes espousing this approach have revealed an uncanny capacity to reproduce themselves, this has invariably led to a further radicalization of the "adjustment" and "stabilization" measures accompanied by a slow, but sure, growth of sociopolitical opposition movements challenging their rule and their "model."

The basic question that proponents of the "model" must answer is this: Why does neoliberalism enter into a deeper crisis with each new wave of "adjustments" rather than into an economic "takeoff" and prosperity? The key to understanding the SAP is reconceptualizing it in terms of a political and class strategy, because its prime effect is to alter the terrain of social struggle and reconcentrate political power, as well as to widen the wealth gap between rich and poor. The discourse of socioeconomic development is a peripheral consideration. SAPs are preceded by "stabilization" measures that are political in character, establishing the terrain for the more profound "adjustments" that follow.

The typical stabilization measures create barriers that make popular resistance to the SAP much more difficult. Stabilization induces an economic crisis that forces the working and middle classes to concentrate on the struggle for existence. It also weakens popular movements by targeting bastions of organized labor, notably public sector, mining, and petroleum unions. In such an environment, labor leaders may be quickly outflanked and intimidated into accommodation. In Argentina, Brazil, and Venezuela, where trade unions administer multimillion-dollar health and welfare budgets, those in charge are disinclined to mobilize political opposition to adjustment as their organizational and monetary resources are put in jeopardy by stabilization.

Rather than assume the economic rationale of the SAP, it is more relevant to stress the political logic undergirding stabilization policies and their socioeconomic consequences. The neoliberal policies have little to do with economic development. Privatization or the sell off of public assets adds little to new productive facilities. At best, additional investments may occur, but most of the original inflow of resources is counterbalanced by outflow through larger remittances to the home office. Capitalizing privatized enterprises is accompanied by a greater decapitalization of the economy, creating balance-of-payment problems, not solutions.

Trade liberalization, the unilateral elimination or drastic reduction of tariffs, has not usually created "competitive" enterprises. It has led to a massive number of bankruptcies, the dominance of the market by a small number of large enterprises, and heavy dependence on foreign imports. Between 1986 and 1994, exports failed to keep pace with imports, transforming the region's large positive trade balance into an $18 billion deficit.[28] The "opening of trade" assumes that the shock of competition will spur enterprises to catch up technologically, upgrade their labor force, and discover overseas markets in a time frame and global context that far exceeds the capacity of any country or firm at a comparable stage of development. The application of open trade policies, when done independently of the historical specificities and capabilities of a country, reflects the fact that the policy originated in doctrinal belief systems rather than in any historical or empirically situated context.

The liberalization of financial flows has not contributed to new investment capital in large-scale, long-term productive activities. Most new financial flows have been directed at short-term high-interest bonds and government notes to strengthen foreign reserves, meet debt payments, or balance external accounts. In 1990, portfolio investments accounted for a mere 3.7 percent of all foreign investment in Latin America; during 1993 to 1995, that figure jumped to between 42 percent and 62 percent.[29] Financial deregulation is frequently associated with the growth of speculator capital: easy entry and quick exit. These speculative practices are imitated by local investors, who take advantage of deregulation to move their capital to and from overseas accounts on the basis of shifts in interest rates that are integral to the "opening," increasing the costs of borrowing for local producers and stifling entrepreneurial behavior by shifting earnings from profits to interest payments. As a result of increased indebtedness to banks, productive capital usually exerts pressure to lower salaries and reduce social payments to labor. Many employers subcontract to the so-called informal sector or divert capital from slow-maturing productive investments into high turnover commercial activity or lucrative interest-bearing government bonds. In other words, the neoliberal strategy has more to do with concentrating private wealth and increasing foreign and monopoly ownership than with stimulating entrepreneurial skills, productive investment, or well-paid employment.

Even less convincing is the neoliberal argument that downsizing social-sector budgets helps employers and investors by eliminating excessive costs that hinder accumulation and growth. Cuts in social programs undermine labor productivity and lead to an increased turnover of workers and the loss of expertise associated with stable employment. The strategy encourages labor-intensive investments, which in turn weakens the incentive for research and development that creates new technological innovations. The growth of neoliberalism has spawned a vast army of "informal" employees (those stripped of social benefits) who have no future and frequently engage in drug and contraband activities. In Brazil, for example, the "informal" economy accounted for almost 30 percent of the monies circulating in the country's financial system in 1992, most of which is related to drug trafficking, illegal financial activities, corruption, and smuggling.[30] Higher profits that do accrue are not likely to be invested in depressed domestic markets with large numbers of low-income workers and consumers, hence, the interest in overseas markets (Mercosur, NAFTA) and speculative global investments.

Neoliberalism is premised on the notion of prioritizing external debt payments over and above any domestic development. The argument is that overseas investor and creditor confidence is central to securing strategic inflows of capital to rebuild the economy. In practice, the obligation to make full, prompt debt payments has led to the massive deterioration of the physical infrastructure: Roads, transport systems, educational, and health facilities have deteriorated, leaving only private facilities for the elite. The transport/market "grids" that linked productive sectors have been replaced by a central "spoke" system linking productive enclaves to export-central cities directed toward overseas markets. Enclave development may result in high export growth statistics and adequate debt payment performance, but it leaves the bulk of the provincial economies in shambles. The deterioration of the infrastructural shell, related to cutbacks in state capital investment in communication and transportation, discourages productive investment, particularly outside of the capital cities. The decline of public education and the expansion of elite private education is also linked to a specialized economy catering to overseas markets and speculative services. Social cuts enlarge the role of enclave-based capital. Speculator capital and foreign debt holders preside over a stagnant economy populated by an impoverished labor force.

The opening to foreign capital (particularly the elimination of protected strategic sectors) through deregulation, tax incentives, and free trade zones induces investment in export production with little value added (assembly plants, mining, forestry, fishing, agriculture). The elimination or lowering of multinational corporate taxation results in declining state revenues and increased taxation on local business and wage earners. The attempt to compensate for declining corporate revenues through social cuts fuels social unrest, which in turn dampens the climate for long-term, large-scale productive investment. Neoliberalism creates an investment culture in which perpetual low labor and social costs are a specified condition for new or sustained investment. The lowering of labor costs is not merely an enticement for entry capital but a built-in and assumed condition for "normal" capitalist investment.

Thus, working-class sacrifice is not a short-term precondition for general prosperity but a long-term structural condition for concentrating income. With declining internal markets, high rates of business and agricultural bankruptcy, greater import dependency, and high, fixed money costs (due to debt payments, external imbalances, and flight capital), neoliberal regimes confront domestic budget deficits and a need to seek external borrowing. To secure external financial support, however, they must apply a new SAP, which in turn recreates the conditions for a new crisis. The process continues in a spiral that constantly keeps wages declining and social conditions deteriorating, while those classes in the state and private sector linked to the new circuits grow richer. Foreign ownership of basic resources multiplies, while high profits and interests continue on an upward spiral, creating a new class of super-rich billionaires.

Conclusion

Neoliberalism is, in essence, about the "adjustment" cycle: a downward spiral for the working and middle class and an upward spiral for the multinational corporations, bankers, and domestic ruling classes linked to the state and external circuits. The dialectics of adjustment are expressed in a highly polarized class structure. As salaries decline and domestic resources are taken over by foreign capital, public officials and the political class cannot accumulate wealth through "normal paths." Neoliberalism then becomes an attractive doctrine for facilitating corrupt practices, including commissions and partnerships for the public officials presiding over the privatization process, financial "rewards" from local capitalists for trade and resource concessions, and support for probusiness labor agreements.

The "new ethics" of private enrichment undermines public virtue and converts most conventional electoral politicians into neoliberals. Exiting from the public sector means appropriating the greatest amount of wealth in the shortest time—before the private sector takes it all. In turn, state corruption facilitates the accumulation of private wealth, which becomes the basis for partnerships with those in the private sector who benefit from the sell-off of public enterprises. Given such behavior, a political reading of SAP provides a more appropriate framework for understanding neoliberalism than its purported treatment as an economic strategy.

The neoliberal electoral cycle and the socioeconomic spiral continually intersect, each time around producing more "radical" conditions for social and political action. A rupture in these cycles, as has been shown here, is not structurally predetermined but rather depends on the conscious political intervention of the growing pool of downwardly mobile classes. The politics of "opposition" have been deflected at each point of neoliberal crisis because a systemic (socialist) alternative has been absent. The process of movement beyond neoliberalism has begun, not only in the "social sense" but also politically. As this analysis suggests, the new sociopolitical movements have their greatest chance of success outside of the electoral framework because of the tight constraints and limitations within which the electoral process operates. The break with neoliberalism is likely to take place in the extraparliamentary arena by political forces that move beyond the pragmatism of the Center-Left.

Notes

1. A 1996 study by the United Nations Economic Commission for Latin America concluded poverty, unemployment, and various other social problems plaguing the region had either worsened or remained unchanged during the last decade of market reforms. See Gabriel Escobar, "Latin America's Poor Not Helped by Reforms," *Washington Post*, April 13, 1996, p. A15. Another recent U.N. study observed, somewhat ironically, that during "a period of economic recovery" (1985–1990), the incidence of poverty in Latin America rose from 23 percent to 28 percent. United Nations Development Program, *Human Development Report 1996* (New York: Oxford University Press, 1996), p. 60.

2. On the Belaunde and Garcia presidencies, see James D. Rudolph, *Peru: The Evolution of a Crisis* (Westport, Conn.: Praeger, 1992).

3. "Brazil's Democracy in the Balance," *Washington Report on the Hemisphere,* December 7, 1988, p. 4.

4. "No End to Perez's Misfortunes in Sight," *Washington Report on the Hemisphere,* June 17, 1992, p. 5.

5. "Menem Speeds Reform for Argentine Vote," *Washington Report on the Hemisphere,* June 25, 1993, p. 1.

6. "Menem's Second Term off to a Rocky Start," *Washington Report on the Hemisphere,* August 18, 1995, p. 4.

7. Guillermo Rochabrun, "Deciphering the Enigmas of Alberto Fujimori," *NACLA Report on the Americas,* July/August 1996, p. 17.

8. Manuel Castillo Ochoa, "Fujimori and the Business Class," in Rochabrun, "Deciphering the Enigmas of Alberto Fujimori," p. 27.

9. "Free Markets Spur Political Upheaval," *Washington Report on the Hemisphere,* April 12, 1996, p. 6.

10. Ochoa, "Fujimori and the Business Class," p. 27.

11. "Region Begins New Privatization Drive," *Latin American Regional Reports: Andean Group,* May 23, 1996, p. 4.

12. "Economic Problems in Argentina," *Washington Report on the Hemisphere,* September 21, 1996, pp. 1, 6; "Menem Toughs It Out," *Latin American Monitor: Southern Cone,* October 1996, p. 4; "Menem Unmoved by General Strike," *Latin American Weekly Report,* October 10, 1996, p. 458.

13. "Official: Incomes Pattern Is Worse," *Latin American Weekly Report,* February 1, 1996, p. 47.

14. Howard LaFranchi, "Argentines Dig Up Dirt That May Bury Reforms," *Christian Science Monitor* (International Weekly Edition), December 13–19, 1996, p. 6.

15. Ibid.

16. "Argentina's New Labour Squeeze," *Latin American Regional Reports: Southern Cone,* October 17, 1996, pp. 4–5.

17. "Trying to Count the Unemployed," *Latin American Regional Reports: Andean Group,* June 29, 1995, p. 7.

18. "Venezuela's Weak Financial Structure," *Washington Report on the Hemisphere,* October 16, 1995, pp. 1, 6; "Gas and Gunpowder," *Washington Report on the Hemisphere,* November 30, 1996, p. 4.

19. "IMF Approves Second Annual Loan," *Latin American Monitor: Andean Group,* May 1996, p. 12.

20. "Cardoso Tries to Placate His Critics," *Latin American Regional Reports: Brazil,* June 6, 1996, p. 6; "Two Million Jobs Lost in Seven Years," *Latin American Regional Reports: Brazil,* July 11, 1996, p. 2.

21. "How Much Is Still in State Hands?" *Latin American Regional Reports: Brazil,* September 19, 1996, pp. 4–5; Jack Epstein, "Brazil Asks: Is Mine Sale a Sell-Off—Or Sell-Out?" *Christian Science Monitor* (International Weekly Edition), January 3–9, 1997, p. 7.

22. "The Uncertain Road to Mexican Recovery," *Washington Report on the Hemisphere,* May 16, 1996, p. 4; "Land Lessons from Chiapas," *Washington Report on the Hemisphere,* October 9, 1996, p. 5.

23. "Opposition Forces Zedillo to Curtail, But Not Cancel, the Petrochemical Sell-Off," *Latin American Weekly Report,* October 24, 1996, p. 481

24. "Cardoso Threatens to Halt Invasions," *Latin American Regional Reports: Brazil,* July 11, 1996, p. 2.

25. "Joint Union Protest Highlights Discontent," *Latin American Weekly Report,* October 24, 1996, pp. 486–487.

26. "Brazil's Landless Movement Wins Support in Cities," *NACLA Report on the Americas,* November/December 1996, p. 1. Also see "MST Goes Back to Direct Action," *Latin American Weekly Report,* September 19, 1996, pp. 428–429.

27. "Agrarian Law Forced Through Congress," *Latin American Weekly Report,* October 24, 1996, p. 482.

28. Duncan Green, *Silent Revolution: The Rise of Market Economies in Latin America* (London: Cassell/Latin American Bureau, 1995), p. 80.

29. "FDI Flows, But 'Lumpy,'" *Latin American Weekly Report,* October 10, 1996, pp. 462–463.

30. "Multibillion-Dollar Underground Economy Exposed," *Latin American Monitor: Brazil,* September 1996, p. 5.

PART THREE

The United States and Latin America

The debates, struggles, and opposition to neoliberalism confront a formidable adversary in the U.S. government. Among the leading advocates and promoters of neoliberalism are members of the executive branch of the U.S. government, their appointees in the international financial agencies and senior executives of the multinational corporations, and banks, who work closely with the U.S. government. The relation between the U.S. elite and their counterparts in Latin America is viewed as the major obstacle to social change and democratization of the economy by the major opposition groups in Latin America, particularly by the extraparliamentary Left. The reason is the large-scale extraction of wealth from Latin America to the United States to the detriment of labor and the peasantry; the growth of debt payment that leads to social cuts; and the free market policies that lead to the growth of U.S. agribusiness firms at the expense of Latin American peasants and landless workers.

8

Liberalization and U.S. Global Strategy

WITH TODD CAVALUZZI

There are a number of explanations for the liberalization policies that have been applied in Latin America. One school argues that there is a nationalist-populist policy cycle that begins with state intervention, nationalization, and protectionism, then consolidates an "import-substitution" development strategy, and finally enters into crisis because of growing state and trade deficits, macroeconomic imbalances, and declining competitiveness, leading to the initiation of the "liberal revolution." Another line of argument focuses on the growth during the 1970s of a class of transnational Latin capitalists, linked to the world market and benefiting from state-sponsored export strategies, who became the central nucleus defining the strategy of liberalization. A third school emphasizes the role of the foreign debt and the leverage and influence of the World Bank and the IMF in imposing the liberal agenda as a condition for refinancing the debt. Others emphasize class conflict and the changing relationship of class forces, both internally and externally. According to this line of inquiry, a coalition made up of the national bourgeoisie, the working class, and the peasantry, which formed the basis of the import-substitution strategy, broke apart as a result of a "squeeze" on profits and state resources, leading to a new coalition of military regimes linked to an export bourgeoisie in partnership with MNCs. Parallel to this internal shift, the collapse of Eastern European socialism eliminated an alternative source of funding and markets, forcing Latin regimes to adapt to the demands of the remaining global powers—the advanced capitalist countries.

There is no doubt that all of these suppositions provide us with a partial explanation. The import-substitution model did enter into crisis—through it is not clear that it had exhausted its economic potential. The possibility of "deepening substitution," of moving from consumer to durable goods to capital goods production and investment in high technologies, was at least a theoretical possibility. What is clear is that *politically*, the social coalition had

149

reached an end—with the class issues that divided labor and capital creating difficulties in sustaining a common policy. Although the liberal transformation is thus in part a *product* of class conflict, that does not explain the particular economic policies adopted, particularly those unfavorable to national capital.

The second line of reasoning, the growth and hegemony of a "new" capitalist class linked to overseas circuits and thus a determinant force in bringing about the liberal transformation does refine the previous argument by identifying a particular segment of capital linked to export markets and overseas financial institutions: a social stratum that straddles both the "internal" and "international" economy. The problem with this argument is that this segment is *determinant* of *domestic* policy but *dependent* on *external* institutions, both political and economic for its economic strategy to succeed. Moreover, the "transnational capitalist" explanation may explain shifts in *country* policies, but it fails to explain the *regional* transformation—liberalization has taken place on a continentwide basis.

The argument is made that the class struggle and the fall of Eastern European socialism may have reinforced and accelerated the liberal transformation, but the latter *preceded* the collapse of the Berlin Wall by at least a decade. One could just as easily argue that the liberal transformation caused the demise of socialism as much as that the latter brought about the ascent of the former.

The explanatory paradigm in which the IMF and World Bank play a decisive role in the liberalization process certainly is a powerful one: Their regional reach, the uniformity of their prescriptions, the powerful leverage they exercise, and the high correlation between their prescriptions and regime implementation of their policies suggest that they indeed had a major hand in engineering the liberalization process.

Nevertheless, one is left with several questions. If the World Bank and IMF are important actors, the internal composition of these institutions reflects the principal donor countries, primarily the United States, Germany, and Japan. However, the policy impact of liberalization in Latin American has not had a uniform effect on all three central powers. The IMF and World Bank strategies are themselves shaped and given substance by the competing economic superpowers.

In this context, liberalization in Latin America should be examined not merely as an outcome of local ruling segments or the effects of MNCs and international financial institutions but rather as being shaped by the strategic economic needs of the United States. The primary fact in the post-Communist world is the increasing competition for dominance of world markets by the United States, Germany, and Japan. Each economic superpower has carved out regions of domination from which to reach out to undercut competitors. Over the past two decades, the United States has lost its competitive advantage in a number of product areas (automobiles, electronics, and so forth). As a result, the United States has been piling up a huge trade deficit both with Japan (and other Asian countries) and to a lesser degree with Germany. The reduction of U.S. troops in Europe and Japan means that NATO and other military alliances are less effective as levers for U.S. policymakers. Threats of "commercial war" are two-edged swords that can adversely affect U.S. exporters and importers (and low-wage domestic consumers of cheap foreign imports). The line of least resistance and the one most congenial and compatible with historic U.S. policies (Monroe Doctrine, Panamerican Union, Alliance for Progress, and so on) is a regional bloc strategy in which the United States as the major hegemonic power can extract trade, investment, interest, and royalty surpluses from Latin America. From this vantage point, Latin America (and Canada) are strategic sources for the accumulation and transfer of profits, interest, and royalty payments to the United States to compensate for the negative transfers to other regions. The U.S. trade surpluses with the Latin American countries serves to compensate for the negative trade balances with Asia and Western Europe. Low-cost production in Latin America (cheap labor in Mexico and the Caribbean) allows U.S. producers to compete overseas and in the U.S. market with global competitors.

In this context, the liberalization of Latin America was essential to providing U.S. capital with access to markets and earnings to remain globally competitive. Thus, liberalization is intimately linked to U.S. strategic global interests. This policy is a product of a consistent continentwide push by the United States from the early 1970s on. Liberalization was pursued via the IMF and World Bank through U.S. representatives: Latin dictators who promoted liberalization were financed and supported; electoral transitions were brokered by Washington on condition that the new electoral regimes deepen the liberalization process. In a word, liberalization as a regional strategy is part and parcel of U.S. strategic global policy: Insofar as liberalization "works," it has worked primarily for the benefit of U.S. MNCs and banks, but most important, for the U.S. political economy as a whole. Liberalized Latin American economies provide strategic benefits to the United States in balancing its external accounts. The following section analyzes the different forms, or types of return, by which the United States has benefited from its hegemonic relation—through MNC investments, bank loans, and royalties.

Profits, Rents, and Interests: Three Ways to Skin a Cat

Royalty and License Payments

The U.S. battle to include "intellectual property" clauses in GATT is based on the fact that royalties and license fee payments have become increasingly

TABLE 8.1   Royalties and License Fee Payments to the United States from Latin America, 1962–1993 (in million US$)

Year	Average Payment per Year	Total Payment
1962–1971	−2.6	−26.0
1972–1981	−24.2	−242.0
1982–1991	−39.5	−395.0
1992–1993	−189.5	−379.0

Source: U.S. Department of Commerce, Bureau of Economic Analysis, *Royalties and License Fees Payments* (CD-ROM) (June 29, 1994). Available from National Trade Data Bank, U.S. Department of Commerce, Bureau of Economic Analysis: U.S. International Transactions: Latin America and Other Western Hemisphere-Direct Investment Payments.

important to the U.S. balance of payments (see Table 8.1). Between 1972 and the first quarter of 1994, royalty and fee payments totaled $1.06 billion. Between the 1960s and the 1990s, royalty and license payments skyrocketed: In 1962–1971, average payments per year were $2.6 million; in 1972–1981, they grew to $24.2 million; in 1982–1991, to $39.5 million; and during 1992–1993, the yearly average was $189.5 million. Royalty and license payments are a form of *rent* that is not based on either investing in productive facilities or financing production. Royalty and licensing payments withdraw income without adding value.

The growing importance of "rentier income" to U.S. external accounts is evident when we compare U.S. earnings from investments to payments for royalty and licenses. In 1962–1971, total license and royalty payments ($26 million) were one-third of total profits from direct investment ($76 million); in 1972–1981, the royalty and license ($242 million) to profits ($4,174 million) ratio declined to 6 percent; in 1982–1991, royalty payments amounted to $395 million, whereas direct investment to Latin America resulted in a $374 million loss. Between 1992 and 1993, the net royalty and license payments almost six times greater than profit remittances.

Direct Investment Profits

In the twenty-year period between 1962 and 1981, U.S. multinational corporations remitted $4.25 billion to the United States. This was the boom period of the Latin American economies. Particularly between 1972 and 1981, U.S. corporations benefited from the first wave of liberalization and the huge influx of overseas financing (see Table 8.2).

However, with the onset of the world recession in 1982, the debt crises and the SAPs caused the Latin market to shrink; consumer spending declined, and most economies in the region went into a tailspin. The negative

TABLE 8.2   Direct Investment Payments to the United States from Latin America, 1962–1993 (in million US$)[a]

Year	Average Payment per Year	Total Payment
1962–1971	–7.6	–76.0
1972–1981	–417.4	–4,174.0
1982–1991	37.4	374.0
1992–1993	–32.0	–64.0

[a]Direct investment payments to the United States are made up of profits remitted, nonremitted profits, and reinvestments, as well as distributed earnings.

Source: U.S. Department of Commerce, Bureau of Economic Analysis, *Direct Investment Payments* (CD-ROM) (June 29, 1994). Available from National Trade Data Bank, U.S. Department of Commerce, Bureau of Economic Analysis: U.S. International Transactions: Latin America and Other Western Hemisphere-Direct Investment Payments (for 1993 annual data, contact USDOC B.E.A. Howard Murad).

effects of massive channeling of resources to meet debt led to a precipitous decline in direct investment payments to the United States. Between 1982 and 1991, there was a net loss of $374 million. As will be shown below, there is an inverse relationship between interest payments and profit remittances: As the banks extracted vast sums of interest and principal payments, profits from productive investments declined. Nonetheless, the debt crises provided leverage for the IMF and World Bank to push for the privatization of public enterprises—many of which were purchased by U.S. multinationals. As the limited economic recovery took place, U.S. profit remittance also recovered. Between 1992 and the first quarter of 1994, $150 million in profits was remitted—an improvement over the dismal performance of the 1980s, but far below the levels of 1972–1981. The debt crises and SAPs not only had an adverse impact on the Latin American economies but a substantial negative impact on the profit payments of U.S. multinational corporations.

Interest Payments

The principal source of private payments from overseas economic activities has been interest payments. The growing liberalization of financial circuits and the conversion of the United States into a "financier state," or creditor to Latin American private and public investors, led to heightened debt burdens. Spiraling interest rates led to a massive increase of interest payments to the United States (see Table 8.3). Interest payments from Latin America to the United States were an important counterbalance to the U.S. deficit with Japan and Germany. Thus, while the United States was a creditor to Latin

TABLE 8.3   Interest on U.S. Bank Loans and Other Payments to Latin America, 1962–1993 (in million US$)[a]

Year	Average Payment per Year	Total Payment
1962–1971	–198.2	–1,982.0
1972–1981	–2,769.3	–27,693.0
1982–1991	–17,360.4	–173,604.0
1992–1993	–14,608.0	–29,216.0

[a]These payments are made up of approximately 90 percent interest payments to private U.S. banks, with the other 10 percent being made up of foreign securities, private corporate bonds, and stock dividends.

Source: U.S. Department of Commerce, Bureau of Economic Analysis, *Other Private Payments* (CD-ROM) (June 29, 1994). Available from National Trade Data Bank, U.S. Department of Commerce, Bureau of Economic Analysis: U.S. International Transactions: Latin America and Other Western Hemisphere-Direct Investment Payments (for 1993 annual data, contact USDOC B.E.A. Howard Murad).

America, it was a debtor to the rest of the advanced capitalist countries. The total interest payments transferred from Latin America to the United States in 1972–1992 amounted to over $230 billion, of which $202 billion was transferred between 1982 and the first quarter of 1994. These vast transfers had a very negative impact on Latin American growth, imports, and domestic demand—but they provided the United States with a sizable source of income to compensate for its deficits with Japan and Germany. "Liberalization" has the effect of increasing interest and rent payments to the United States at the expense of the growth of productive assets. Liberal economic policies increased outflows of interest payments while facilitating the sale of licensing and patent agreements. Privatization opened public enterprises to buyouts and revived the prospects for the return of profit payments.

The flows of payments to the United States show a spectacular overall increase with the deepening of liberalization—particularly in interest and rent payments. It is no wonder that "free market" policies have become the keystone of U.S. policy, and that is one reason U.S. policymakers are willing to support "free market" electoral regimes against military coups.

U.S.–Latin American Trade

Examining the U.S. trade surplus with Latin America reveals another dimension of the asymmetrical U.S.–Latin American relationship and the underlying reason for U.S. support for "free trade agreements."

From the 1960s to the beginning of the 1980s "debt crises," the United States had a substantial trade surplus with Latin America. In 1962–1971, the U.S. average annual trade surplus amounted to $4,246 million; in

TABLE 8.4   Cumulative U.S. Trade Surpluses and Deficits by Decade with Latin America, Japan, Germany, and the EEC, 1962–1993 (in million US$)

Year	*Latin America*	*Japan*	*Germany*	*EEC*
1962–1971	4,246	–8,795	–2,730	13,892
1972–1981	43,445	–75,468	–13,838	47,310
1982–1991	–17,250	–432,373	90,103	–84,130
1992–1993	8,481	–109,356	–17,242	5,761

Sources: Unless otherwise noted, all data are derived from U.N. Department of Economic and Social Development, *1992 International Trade Statistics Yearbook* (E/F.94.17.3, vol. 1) (New York: 1993), data gathered from Special Table B in 1964–1993 editions.

For Latin America: U.S. Department of Commerce, Bureau of Economic Analysis, *Balance on Merchandise Trade* (CD-ROM) (June 29, 1994). Available from National Trade Data Bank, U.S. Department of Commerce, Bureau of Economic Analysis: U.S. International Transactions: Latin America and Other Western Hemisphere: Balance on Merchandise Trade; U.S. Department of Commerce, *Final 1993 Merchandise Trade Tables* (Internet) (December 1993). Available from Internet-Economic Bulletin Board (UMich): Foreign Trade. Final 1993 Merchandise Trade Tables.

For Japan: U.S. Department of Commerce, International Trade Administration, *U.S. Total Trade Balance with Individual Countries, 1980–1993* (Internet) (June 29, 1994). Available from Internet-National Trade Data Bank: USDOC International Trade Administration: U.S. Foreign Trade Highlights. U.S. Total Trade Balances with Individual Countries, 1980–1993; "U.S. Balances on International Transactions, by Area and Selected Country: 1990 to 1992," no. 1330, p. 796. In *Statistical Abstract of the United States, 1993,* 113th ed. (Washington, D.C.: GPO, 1993).

For the EEC: U.S. Department of Commerce, *Final 1993 Merchandise Trade Tables* (Internet) (December 1993). Available from Internet-Economic Bulletin Board (UMich): Foreign Trade. Final 1993 Merchandise Trade Tables; U.S. Department of Commerce, Bureau of Economic Analysis, *Balance on Merchandise Trade* (CD-ROM) (June 29, 1994). Available from National Trade Data Bank, U.S. Department of Commerce, Bureau of Economic Analysis: U.S. International Transactions: European Communities: Balance on Merchandise Trade.

For Germany: Organization for Economic Cooperation and Development, *Monthly Statistics of Foreign Trade, Series A* (Paris: OECD, 1994).

1972–1981, the annual trade surplus grew to $43,445 million. The surplus turned to a trade deficit beginning in 1983 and continued until 1989. The average yearly deficit between 1982 and 1991 amounted to $1,725 billion. (See Table 8.4.)

With the "economic recovery," the United States once again began to accumulate a trade surplus between 1992 and 1993, an annual surplus of $2.2 billion. The trade surplus of the United States grew during the first decade of liberalization (1970–1982). With the debt crises and the structural adjustment programs, U.S. exports to Latin America declined while imports increased as part of the Latin American "export strategy" designed by the IMF to accumulate income to pay the bankers. Nonetheless, if we examine the long-term effects of SAPs, these policies have opened new opportunities for the United States to reenter and penetrate Latin American markets. If we compare the four years prior to the debt crises (1979–1982) to the years after the adjustments (1990–1993), we observe that the consequence of deeper liberalization has been to increase U.S. trade surpluses beyond their historic high points. Although the debt crises and SAPs did result in temporary loss of markets in the long run, the structural changes leading to the elimination of protective barriers have led to greater U.S. penetration and takeover of Latin markets.

If we compare the U.S. balance of trade with Latin America and with Japan in the period between 1970 and 1982, we observe that the U.S. favorable balance in Latin America compensates in part for the deficits with Japan (see Table 8.5). During the debt crisis years (1983–1989), the U.S. deficit with Latin America was only a fraction of the deficit with Japan. With the economic recovery in Latin America, the U.S. surplus reemerges, but it is only a fraction of the deficit with Japan and barely covers the trade deficit with Germany.

The U.S. loss of trade competitiveness in relation to Japan and Europe was *temporarily* papered over by the exploitation of favorable trade relations with Latin America. However, the U.S. gains through "liberalization" have sufficiently undermined the Latin productive capacity to the point where the surplus from a weak trading region fails to compensate for the deficits with strong trading partners.

Latin America: The Cumulative Balance Sheet

If we add the three sources of U.S. income from Latin America (rent, trade interest, and profit) and compare that to the trade deficits that the United States has with Japan and Germany, we can begin to understand the strategic importance of Latin America to U.S. global politics (see Table 8.6).

The contribution of Latin America to the U.S. global position can be best understood by looking at the *combined returns* from trade, investments, loans, and licensing agreements. The data reveal a steady upward movement (the reverse of the U.S. relation with Asia and Europe). During 1962–1971, the cumulative return amounted to roughly $6.5 billion; between 1972 and 1981, the cumulative return was a little more than $75.5 billion and between 1982 and 1991, about $156.4 billion; between 1992 and 1993, the cumulative returns were roughly $38.1 billion (see Table 8.6). The cumulative returns to the United States are of strategic importance in reducing the global deficit and compensating for loss of competitiveness in other regions.

TABLE 8.5   U.S. Balances of Trade, 1962–1993 (in million US$)

Year	Latin America	Japan	Germany	EEC
1962	100	0	100	1140
1963	−140	320	82	2300
1964	370	130	121	2380
1965	200	−440	150	1780
1966	280	−660	−230	1360
1967	310	−380	−250	1190
1968	590	−1200	−1008	290
1969	710	−1560	−486	940
1970	1240	−1405	−389	1992
1971	1120	−3600	−819	520
1972	1039	−4042	−1438	−877
1973	1069	−1378	−1562	712
1974	1643	−2366	−1442	2672
1975	5126	−1839	−215	6127
1976	3478	−5860	30	6804
1977	1701	−9507	−1376	2448
1978	2675	−12453	−3182	976
1979	4420	−9271	−2704	5028
1980	8920	−11173	−844	15859
1981	13374	−17579	−1105	7561
1982	3540	−16243	−2683	4051
1983	−11685	−22094	−3958	−2223
1984	−11569	−37887	−7912	−10176
1985	−8657	−44507	−11189	−18638
1986	−2908	−58403	−14563	−23530
1987	−850	−57328	−15322	−25517
1988	1077	−54204	−12172	−12682
1989	−1070	−50964	−7951	−2652
1990	5758	−44763	−9442	−2859
1991	9114	−45980	−4913	10096
1992	6200	−50002	−7592	6728
1993	2281	−59354	−9649	−967

Sources: Unless otherwise noted, all data are derived from U.N. Department of Economic and Social Development, *1992 International Trade Statistics Yearbook* (E/F.94.17.3, vol. 1) (New York: 1993), data gathered from Special Table B in 1964–1993 editions.

For Latin America 1992: U.S. Department of Commerce, Bureau of Economic Analysis, *Balance on Merchandise Trade* (CD-ROM) (June 29, 1994). Available from National Trade Data Bank, U.S. Department of Commerce, Bureau of Economic Analysis: U.S. International Transactions: Latin America and Other Western Hemisphere: Balance on Merchandise Trade.

(continues)

TABLE 8.5   *(continued)*
***

For Latin America 1993: U.S. Department of Commerce, *Final 1993 Merchandise Trade Tables* (Internet) (December 1993). Available from Internet-Economic Bulletin Board (UMich): Foreign Trade. Final 1993 Merchandise Trade Tables.

For Japan 1992: "U.S. Balances on International Transactions, by Area and Selected Country: 1990 to 1992," no. 1330, p. 796. In *Statistical Abstract of the United States, 1993,* 113th ed. (Washington, D.C.: GPO, 1993).

For Japan 1993: U.S. Department of Commerce, International Trade Administration, *U.S. Total Trade Balances with Individual Countries, 1980–1993* (Internet) (June 29, 1994). Available from Internet-National Trade Data Bank: USDOC International Trade Administration: U.S. Foreign Trade Highlights. U.S. Total Trade Balances with Individual Countries, 1980–1993.

For the EEC 1992: U.S. Department of Commerce, Bureau of Economic Analysis, *Balance on Merchandise Trade* (CD-ROM) (June 29, 1994). Available from National Trade Data Bank, U.S. Department of Commerce, Bureau of Economic Analysis: U.S. International Transactions: European Communities: Balance on Merchandise Trade.

For the EEC 1993: U.S. Department of Commerce, *Final 1993 Merchandise Trade Tables* (Internet) (December 1993). Available from Internet-Economic Bulletin Board (UMich): Foreign Trade. Final 1993 Merchandise Trade Tables.

For Germany: Organization for Economic Cooperation and Development, *Monthly Statistics of Foreign Trade, Series A* (Paris: OECD, 1994).

Without the growing exploitation of Latin America, the decline of the United States would be more marked, and the unfavorable impact on its global position more pronounced.

Between 1962 and 1971, U.S. income from Latin America amounted to three-fourths of its trade deficit with Japan and was 50 percent greater than its trade deficit with Germany. In the following decade, between 1972 and 1981, U.S. income from Latin America matched the cumulative trade deficit with Japan. In the past decade, between 1982 and 1991, while the U.S. doubled its earnings from Latin America, its cumulative trade deficit with Japan increased almost five and a half times, and its deficit with Germany increased sevenfold. The same pattern seems to hold for the present decade. The liberalization of Latin America has augmented the surplus appropriated by the United States, thereby in part compensating for its growing trade deficits with Japan and Germany. The growing exploitation of Latin America is matched by the declining trading position of the United States vis-à-vis its main competitors in the world market. As Table 8.6 indicates, Latin America has been of strategic importance to the United States in balancing its trade accounts and disguising its declining global position.

TABLE 8.6   Cumulative Income from Latin America Compared to Trade Deficits with Japan and Germany by Decade, 1962–1993 (in million US$)

	1962–1971	1972–1981	1982–1991	1992–1993
Income from Latin America	6,330	75,554	156,375	38,140
Balance of trade with Japan	–8,795	–75,468	–432,373	–109,356
Balance of trade with Germany	–2,730	–13,838	–90,103	–17,242

Sources: For Latin America 1962–1991: U.S. Department of Commerce, Bureau of Economic Analysis, *Royalties and License Fees Payments* (CD-ROM) (June 29, 1994). Available from National Trade Data Bank, U.S. Department of Commerce, Bureau of Economic Analysis: U.S. International Transactions: Latin America and Other Western Hemisphere-Direct Investment Payments (for 1993 annual data, contact USDOC B.E.A. Howard Murad); U.S. Department of Commerce, Bureau of Economic Analysis, *Direct Investment Payments* (CD-ROM) (June 29, 1994). Available from National Trade Data Bank, U.S. Department of Commerce, Bureau of Economic Analysis: U.S. International Transactions: Latin America and Other Western Hemisphere-Direct Investment Payments (for 1993 annual data, contact USDOC B.E.A. Howard Murad); U.S. Department of Commerce, Bureau of Economic Analysis, *Other Private Payments* (CD-ROM) (June 29, 1994). Available from National Trade Data Bank, U.S. Department of Commerce, Bureau of Economic Analysis: U.S. International Transactions: Latin America and Other Western Hemisphere-Direct Investment Payments (for 1993 annual data, contact USDOC B.E.A. Howard Murad); U.N. Department of Economic and Social Development, *1992 International Trade Statistics Yearbook* (E/F.94.17.3, vol. 1) (New York: 1993).

For Latin America 1992–1993: U.S. Department of Commerce, Bureau of Economic Analysis, *Royalties and License Fees Payments* (CD-ROM) (June 29, 1994). Available from National Trade Data Bank, U.S. Department of Commerce, Bureau of Economic Analysis: U.S. International Transactions: Latin America and Other Western Hemisphere-Direct Investment Payments (for 1993 annual data, contact USDOC B.E.A. Howard Murad); U.S. Department of Commerce, Bureau of Economic Analysis, *Direct Investment Payments* (CD-ROM) (June 29, 1994). Available from National Trade Data Bank, U.S. Department of Commerce, Bureau of Economic Analysis: U.S. International Transactions: Latin America and Other Western Hemisphere-Direct Investment Payments (for 1993 annual data, contact USDOC B.E.A. Howard Murad); U.S. Department of Commerce, Bureau of Economic Analysis, *Other Private Payments* (CD-ROM) (June 29, 1994). Available from National Trade Data Bank, U.S. Department of Commerce, Bureau of Economic Analysis: U.S. International Transactions: Latin America and Other Western Hemisphere-Direct Investment Payments (for 1993 annual data, contact USDOC B.E.A. Howard Murad); U.S. Department of Commerce, Bureau of Economic Analysis, *Balance on Merchandise Trade* (CD-ROM) (June 29, 1994). Available from National Trade Data Bank, U.S. Department of Commerce, Bureau of Economic Analysis: U.S. International Transactions: Latin America and Other Western Hemisphere: Balance on Merchandise Trade; U.S. Department of

(continues)

TABLE 8.6   *(continued)*

Commerce, Final 1993 Merchandise Trade Tables (Internet) (December 1993). Available from Internet-Economic Bulletin Board (UMich): Foreign Trade. Final 1993 Merchandise Trade Tables.

For Japan 1962–1991: U.N. Department of Economic and Social Development, *1992 International Trade Statistics Yearbook* (E/F. 94.17.3, vol. 1) (New York: 1993).

For Japan 1992–1993: "U.S. Balances on International Transactions, by Area and Selected Country: 1990 to 1992," no. 1330, p. 796. In *Statistical Abstract of the United States, 1993*, 113th ed. (Washington, D.C.: GPO, 1993); U.S. Department of Commerce, International Trade Administration, U.S. Total Trade Balances with Individual Countries, 1980–1993 (Internet) (June 29, 1994). Available from Internet-National Trade Data Bank: USDOC International Trade Administration: U.S. Foreign Trade Highlights. U.S. Total Trade Balances with Individual Countries, 1980–1993.

For Germany 1962–1993: Organization for Economic Cooperation and Development, *Monthly Statistics of Foreign Trade, Series A* (Paris: OECD, 1994).

Latin American Billionaires

Parallel to the heightened U.S. exploitation of Latin America, the free market policies have led to a profound polarization of Latin American societies and the growth of a new class of super-rich Latin American billionaires.[1] This class is a direct product of the liberalization process: In 1987, there were fewer than 6 billionaires; by 1990 there were 8, in 1991, there were 20 and by 1994, there were 41. Most of the super-rich were millionaires prior to free market liberalization; most became billionaires with the buyout of public enterprises during the late 1980s and 1990s. Essentially, this class of billionaires, with their vast network of media outlets and allies in the state apparatus, control economic policy and electoral processes. In Mexico through the PRI, in Brazil through the corrupt political class, in Chile through the Concertación, and in Argentina, Venezuela, and Columbia through the traditional major two parties, the super-rich have gained valuable mining concessions, telecommunication systems, and tourist and manufacturing assets.

There are now more Latin American billionaires (41) than there were in most parts of the world in 1987, when Europe had 36, Japan and Asia had a combined 40, the Middle East and Africa had 8, and Latin America had almost as many as the United States, with its 49. The great concentration of wealth in a small group of families is one of the most significant "success" stories in Latin America, for these groups have truly entered the top floor of the "First World" in every sense of the word. It is they who have not only benefited from liberalization—at the expense of the massive impoverishment of the majority—but who, through their links with the liberal electoral regimes, have been the major backers of neoliberal policies.

The process of economic concentration of wealth occurring in Latin America is part of a global process—a product of the "neoliberal counterrevolution." Between 1987 and 1994, the number of super-rich billionaires has increased from 49 to 120 in the United States, from 40 to 86 in Asia Pacific, from 36 to 91 in Europe, and from 8 to 14 in the Middle East and Africa. The decline of welfare programs and the privatization process have been instrumental in polarizing the world into a small group of very rich business families and hundreds of millions of marginalized temporary workers. The notion of center-periphery does not capture the super-rich classes North and South, linked through a multiplicity of investments, financial and trade circuits, and licensing and pattern agreements. The integration of the super-rich into the global marketplace and their capacity to direct and regulate the nation-state to finance and subsidize their international links is the most significant fact of global politics. Globalism is the program of the super-rich.

The parallel growth of the billionaire class in Latin America and heightened U.S. exploitation are dual outcomes of the neoliberal counterrevolution. This is most evident in the countries that have advanced furthest on the path of neoliberal politics: Mexico has 24 billionaires and has been the main source of trade interest, royalties, and profit income for the United States; followed by Brazil with 6 billionaires; Argentina, Chile and Columbia with 3 each; and Venezuela with 2. The basic reason for growing poverty and declining health services and educational institutions is the diversion of public resources to the private sector and within the private sector to the very rich. *"Neoliberalism" is in essence a euphemism for the reconcentration of income through the international regulation of state policy.* Income is transferred upward and outward—leaving the poor to struggle in marginal "microenterprises," informal employment, and handouts from projects sponsored by nongovernmental organizations.

The importance of the liberalization and privatization policy for the concentration of wealth and the emergence of the super-rich in Latin America can be glimpsed by looking at the brief biographies published in *Forbes* magazine of a sample of six Mexican billionaires.[2]

The Peralta family, worth $2.5 billion, is involved in a major joint venture with Bell-Atlantic of the United States, which has invested $1 billion in a cellular phone company.

The Guitron family enterprises are traded on the U.S. stock exchange, and they have climbed to billionaire status thanks to the fortune they made through investment in BANACCI, the financial conglomerate that arose from the 1992 privatization of the Banco Nacional de Mexico.

The Salinas Pliego family, worth $2 billion, was enriched through the purchase of the government-owned Television Azteca for $645 million in a joint venture with the U.S. General Electric–owned National Broadcasting Company (NBC) for programming.

Jorge Larrea Ortega and family also invested in and profited enormously from the privatization of BANACCI. He bought the state owned La Cananea copper mine for $500 million and now his Grupo Industrial Mineria Mexico is Mexico's biggest mining company, producing 90 percent of the country's copper, gold, silver, and zinc in partnership with ASARCO of the United States and Belgian Union Miniere, with revenues of $1 billion per year.

The Franco family, valued at $1 billion, became billionaires thanks to a $400 million investment in the privatization of Telefonos de Mexico and, in 1992, a $200 million investment in BANACCI.

The Cosío Ariño family also became billionaires with their investment in the privatization of the Banco Nacional de Mexico. In 1991, with the privatization of the state-owned Mexican telephone industry, the Cosío Ariño clan got 5 percent of preferred voting stock for $50 million, which in 1994 was valued at $400 million.

This sample of Mexican billionaires illustrates the way in which state policy (neoliberal privatization) favors the concentration of private wealth *and* the growing joint exploitation of minerals and penetration of markets by Mexican billionaires and U.S. multinational corporations.

Conclusion

Liberalization and structural adjustment policies have played a strategic role in opening up Latin America to U.S. exploitation and in providing a major source of income to compensate for U.S. declining competitiveness in other regions. At the same time, liberalization has created a new class of Latin billionaires, who increasingly dominate politics and the economy and are major partners with U.S. banks and multinationals. The result is reshaping the regional economic structure with greater integration at the top and increasing disintegration at the subnational level. The neoliberal policies have also polarized the class structure, bringing about the emergence of a new class of Latin billionaires with major investments in the United States, as well as joint ventures in Latin America with U.S. conglomerates. The very rich are indeed an integral part of the First World. On the other side is the growth of an impoverished labor force faced with declining state social expenditures, chronically low-paid employment, and landless peasants deprived of influence in politics and economy. The majority are paying the price for the admission of the super-rich into the First World.

Liberalization as the ideology of the hegemonic power in this hemisphere has become an instrument of global competition—and should be viewed as part of strategic economic goals. In any case, liberalization has not and is not merely a "development strategy" elaborated to facilitate Latin American integration into the world market. Nor is it an inevitable product of some immanent "globalization process." Rather, liberalization is a product of U.S. economic policymakers, bankers, and multinational corporations allied with Latin American transnational capitalists. It is specific class and state interests (not world-system imperatives) that dictate the new liberal political economy. In this sense, reversing liberalization must begin at the national level within the class structure and move upward and outward.

Notes

1. The data are drawn from *Forbes*, July 18, 1994, pp. 135, 152, 153.
2. *Forbes*, July 18, 1994, pp. 186–190.

9

Clinton's Cuba Policy

WITH MORRIS MORLEY

The Clinton administration's policy toward Cuba needs to be placed in a historical and political context in order to be properly evaluated. Liberal and conservative commentators have seized on particular policies at different moments, concluding that Clinton is "opening up" relations with Cuba or that the administration is "caving in" to the right-wing Cuban-American lobby. Others insist that the White House has no policy, that it wavers according to electoral calculations ("winning Florida" in 1996) or to short term pressures from Cuban lobbyists. The argument made here is that Clinton has a policy that is consistent in its general outlines with both his global and domestic policies, even as his tactical moves vary from circumstance to circumstance. In this perspective, the important point is the overall historical and political context in which Clinton's Cuba policy takes place and the political *dynamics* that it unleashes. The critical issues are to identify and evaluate the *major policies undertaken* as they affect the Cuban economy and the U.S. domestic political climate.

Policymaking in Historical Context

The broad thrust of the Clinton administration's policy toward Cuba has combined increased pressures and restrictions on trade, aid, travel, and cultural exchanges with stepped-up diplomatic and propaganda efforts to topple the Fidel Castro regime. In evaluating the policy approach, this chapter highlights the way in which Clinton has not only sought to extend and deepen the actions pursued by his Republican predecessors but also to reverse longstanding policies and substitute new policies that invoke earlier periods (e.g., the early 1970s) when American hostility toward the revolution was at least as intense, if not more so, than during the Reagan-Bush era.

For more than three decades, Washington's trade embargo and economic blockade strategy has been a centerpiece of U.S. policy toward Cuba. During the 1992 presidential election campaign, the Democratic candidate Bill Clinton not only signaled his complete support for continuing this strategy but also his determination to further tighten pressures on the Cuban economy. This manifested itself most strikingly in Clinton's relentless and uncritical support for the Cuban Democracy Act (CDA), the so-called Torricelli Bill, which exhumed embargo provisions revoked by the Ford administration in 1975 relating to foreign shipping and U.S. overseas subsidiaries' trade with Cuba. Clinton endorsed the CDA in a celebrated fund-raising speech to Cuban-Americans in Miami in April 1992, where he criticized the Bush administration, which was demanding the harshest concessions from Havana for normalizing bilateral relations since the early 1960s, for being insufficiently tough on Castro: "I think this administration has missed a big opportunity to put the hammer down on Fidel Castro and Cuba."[1]

The Bush White House, which had been at least as zealous as the Reaganites in prosecuting the bilateral, regional, and global economic war against Cuba, was initially reluctant to support the CDA for precisely the reasons given by Gerald Ford and Henry Kissinger for dropping the earlier law: the problems certain to reemerge with European, Canadian, and Latin American allies over the attempt to block subsidiary trade with Cuba. As the State Department's Robert Gelbard told a congressional committee hearing on the CDA, the previous legislation "was found to be completely ineffective. What it ended up producing was not support for our policy but more opposition for our policy and implicitly more support for Castro."[2] But ultimately, electoral considerations overrode Bush's concern about the CDA's likely effect on relations with allies, leading him to endorse what one European Community (EC) official succinctly called an "extraterritorial application of U.S. law."[3]

America's allies around the world attacked the bill, especially its prohibitions on overseas subsidiaries of U.S. corporations from trading with Cuba and on vessels loading or unloading cargo at U.S. ports if they entered Cuban harbors within the previous 180 days. The EC, France, the United Kingdom, Canada, and Mexico publicly denounced this latest example of Washington's support for the doctrine of extraterritoriality, terming it an affront to national sovereignty and a contravention of international law. "The United States," observed a Canadian embassy official, "is the only country that . . . tries to stretch its long arm across the borders."[4] The governments of Canada and the United Kingdom were so aggrieved that they issued executive orders blocking any application of the CDA on their territories. Presidential candidate Clinton's response to this universal condemnation of the proposed legislation was to simply reaffirm his support for it. In early October, he wrote to the congressional sponsors of the legislation to express his pleasure at their successful navigation of it through both Houses, also emphasizing the "important opportunity to increase pressure on Castro" provided by the collapse of the Soviet Union.[5]

Once in office, Clinton's vigorous promotion of the CDA prefigured an aggressive and hostile policy toward Cuba. "[It was] very hard to envision [any normalization of U.S.-Cuban relations] taking place," Secretary of State designate Warren Christopher told the Senate Foreign Relations Committee during nomination hearings, "with Castro still in place." Therefore, the new administration intended to "maintain the embargo to keep the pressure on the Castro regime."[6] Testifying on Capitol Hill in mid-July, Deputy Assistant Secretary Robert Gelbard described "our comprehensive trade embargo" as the "cornerstone of our policy."[7]

Apart from the CDA, efforts to tighten the economic sanctions against the Caribbean island during Clinton's first eighteen months in office ranged from pressures to dissuade countries from trading with Cuba, to discouraging investment by Western corporations, to various initiatives to limit the Castro government's access to hard currency, to travel restrictions on Cuban citizens visiting the United States. In September 1993, for instance, American embassies were directed to inform host governments that Washington strongly opposed any foreign investment in Cuban enterprises formerly owned by U.S. nationals.[8] That same month, in order to constrict access to tourist dollars, the Clinton White House banned the sale of package tours to exiles visiting Cuba and prevented U.S. travel agencies from issuing telephone credit cards that would permit calls to Cuba through Canadian facilities.[9] Dismissing rumors that the administration "intends to soften its [Cuba] policy," Assistant Secretary of State for Inter-American Affairs Alexander Watson told a luncheon sponsored by the right-wing Cuban-American National Foundation (CANF) in late October that there would be no letup in the government's efforts to break "the hammerlock of the Castro regime."[10] In the following months, this included denying visas to Cuban diplomats, artists, and intellectuals who had been allowed to visit the United States during the Reagan-Bush era.[11] The other side of this coin was the opposition to U.S. tourist and business travel to Cuba. One such initiative in this area was the exclusion of Cuba from a February 1994 State Department proposal to relax travel restrictions to embargoed countries.

Meanwhile, the White House attempted whenever and wherever possible to limit Cuba's ability to accumulate badly needed American dollars to fund critical imports in a period of economic crisis. In March 1994, the administration rejected a bid by four U.S. telephone companies to improve communications links with the island on the grounds that the former's agreement to pay Cuba a $4.85 fee for its share of collect calls to the United States was excessive.[12]

Throughout this period, the Cuban economy was also severely buffeted by the success of the CDA in diminishing trade between the island and overseas subsidiaries of American corporations. Such trade declined from $718 million in 1991 to $336 million in 1992 to almost zero ($1.6 million) in 1993.[13] Responding to hostile questioning from conservative congressmen on the House Foreign Affairs Committee in mid-1994, Secretary of State Warren Christopher insisted that one only had to look at the administration's support for the CDA to counter accusations of "softness" in Cuba policy: "We're proceeding to carry out the Cuban Democracy Act, which is one of the most severe sets of sanctions that there is on the books anyplace."[14]

In August 1994, responding to criticism from Congress and the Cuban-American community, unhappy over the new "tougher" immigration policy measures in the absence of new harsher measures against the Castro regime, Clinton announced additional economic and travel sanctions to increase the pressure on Havana. First, he blocked all cash remittances from the United States to Cuba, imposed strict limits on family gift packages, and directed that the Treasury Department approve all future humanitarian aid. Second, all charter flights to the island were eliminated; only those carrying legal immigrants between Miami and Havana were allowed to continue. Third, the president signaled a more active use of radio and television broadcasts, including a plan to use American military aircraft to augment Radio Martí by beaming radio and television broadcasts to the island. Fifth, under the new travel restrictions, those individuals wishing to visit relatives in Cuba, as well as academics, were now required to apply for specific licenses from the Treasury Department; henceforth, only government officials and journalists were eligible to visit Cuba under the general license category.[15]

Clinton's economic warfare against Cuba has involved a two-pronged attack: on the one hand, multiple efforts to tighten and extend preexisting policies, thus affirming his continuity with Reagan-Bush efforts to destabilize the revolutionary regime; on the other, the implementation of new policies that went beyond those of his predecessors and whose cumulative effect has been to even more severely obstruct the possibilities for Cuban economic revival.

Like Reagan and Bush, Clinton has also contested Cuba's reintegration into the inter-American community every step of the way: from pressuring countries not to renew political (e.g., Chile) or trade (e.g., Honduras) ties with the Castro regime to opposing Cuban membership in the Organization of American States (OAS). When Chile restored full diplomatic relations with Cuba in April 1995, Washington even invoked the threat of economic sanctions. A State Department official commented that Chile's decision "won't make things easier" for the Frei government's application to join NAFTA.[16]

Finally, most revealing of Clinton's hostility toward Cuba relative to that of his predecessors has been a willingness to contemplate the most extreme kind of measures to force political changes, up to and including a naval blockade of the island, which was last taken up by the Kennedy administration in the context of superpower confrontation over the placement of Soviet missiles in Cuba. Discussing the August economic sanctions, White House chief of staff Leon Panetta would not rule out even more dramatic initiatives in the future to gain U.S. policy objectives: A U.S. naval blockade is "obviously one of the options that we would look at in the future as we see whether or not Castro begins to make some legitimate movements towards democracy."[17]

But the extremist nature of Clinton's policies is perhaps most obvious if we consider them within the historical context in which they are taking place. At a global level, despite the CDA, European and Canadian companies continue to trade with Cuba, participate in joint ventures, and sign mineral exploration contracts; Dutch and German banks have financed investments in the sugar and mining sectors; France increased its export credits in 1995 and has renewed a $120 million government guarantee to support wheat-for-sugar countertrade deals; British trade missions have visited Cuba to discuss development financing and investment opportunities; and even Boris Yeltsin's Russia has expanded economic, trade, and scientific ties with Havana since 1993.[18] Speaking for most of America's allies, French president François Mitterand called the embargo "primitive" and described U.S. economic hostility toward Cuba as "stupid."[19]

At a regional level, Clinton's policy toward Cuba has left the United States more isolated than ever. Not only have almost all hemispheric governments renewed diplomatic relations with Havana, but Latin public and private investment has begun to flow into the Cuban economy and trade between Cuba and the rest of Latin America has increased appreciably. In mid-1994, over strong U.S. opposition, the Mexican government invested $1.4 billion to purchase 49 percent of Cuba's telephone system, and even before political ties were normalized, Chilean private investment in the island economy was close to $40 million.[20] The growth in overall trade between Cuba and its neighbors has been particularly dramatic and offers a devastating rebuff to White House efforts to maintain a regional economic "iron curtain" around the island: In 1990, Cuba conducted only 5 percent of its total trade with Latin America; by 1994, the figure had risen to 35 percent.[21]

During 1993 and 1994, the Caribbean Community (CARICOM) established a joint CARICOM-Cuba trade commission to oversee trade and cooperation and, despite U.S. objections, welcomed Cuba as a founding member of a new regional trade bloc, the Association of Caribbean States. At the OAS, retiring secretary general João Baena Soares echoed growing regional sentiment when he called for Cuba's readmission to organization: "Cuba is a part of the hemisphere, and the 1990s are no longer the 1960s."[22] Although Clinton acknowledged "a policy difference" over Cuba between the United

States and most Latin governments, his regional isolation policy seemed set in concrete as he refused to invite Fidel Castro to a Summit of the Americas meeting of heads of state in Miami in December 1994.[23]

Today, Washington is almost totally isolated in its efforts to maintain and, where possible, tighten the regional and global political-economic blockade of Cuba. There is no more striking illustration of this than the increase in worldwide opposition to the U.S. trade embargo since Clinton entered the White House. In 1992, 59 countries voted for a United Nations General Assembly resolution calling for an end to the embargo, with 71 countries abstaining and only 3 voting no. When the resolution was resubmitted in 1993, 88 countries voted in favor; in October 1994, 101 member states voted in support of the anti-embargo resolution, the number of abstentions fell to 48, with 4 countries (including the United States) opposing the resolution.

Ironically, the Clinton administration even concedes that the minimum rationale for its hostile posture toward the Cuban Revolution no longer exists. The current policies are totally divorced from the "national security" rhetoric of previous decades that justified policy on the basis of Cuba's export of revolution in Latin America and its military links to the Soviet Union. In January 1994, Assistant Secretary of State Alexander Watson stated that communism no longer posed a threat to the region: "In national security . . . there's no external threat, really to the hemisphere."[24] In the same statement, however, he indicated that the United States still remained opposed to Cuba's readmission to the OAS. Nor did the Defense Department perceive Cuba as posing any kind of security problems for Washington. Although Secretary of Defense William Perry said the administration was "not happy" about the Russian intelligence listing post at Lourdes to monitor U.S. compliance with arms control agreements, it was not considered "a national security threat."[25] A September 1995 Pentagon report on U.S. security interests in Latin America restated the agency's belief that Cuba posed no military threat to the dominant regional power.[26] But if the "national security" argument for maintaining an aggressive U.S. policy toward Cuba is anachronistic, the Clinton White House has offered no indication of a willingness to seriously rethink the existing approach. Looked at historically, the intensity and scope of Clinton's anti-Cuba policies are fundamentally more extreme versions of past imperial state policies—absent the earlier rationales that provided the justification for White House efforts to overthrow the revolutionary regime.

Making Cuba Policy: The Political Context

Clinton's policy approach toward Cuba operates essentially within the same political framework that shaped Reagan-Bush policy: the pursuit of an isolation strategy designed to provoke severe hardships among the Cuban population, leading to a civilian-military uprising that topples the Castro government from power. This strategy categorically dismisses any consideration of measures that would ease the economic embargo and contests Cuba's efforts to increase its economic relations in the world market.

Mirroring the attitude of its Republican predecessors, the Clinton administration has refused to respond in a reciprocal fashion to the major shifts in Cuban foreign and domestic policies that have occurred since the late 1980s. Cuba's termination of support for Third World revolution, the severing of its large-scale military ties with the Soviet Union, its continually expanding diplomatic and economic ties with the capitalist world, the opening of the economy to market forces, and the aggressive courting of foreign investors have not constituted, as far as the State Department is concerned, the kinds of "fundamental changes" deemed necessary to justify any significant shift in Washington's policy.[27] Deputy Secretary of State Gelbard told a House subcommittee in mid-1993 that Cuba "continues to resist real reform."[28] Commenting on the Castro government's decision to legalize the dollar and its willingness to resume diplomatic talks, President Clinton said this simply meant that the embargo was working and that it was important to "keep the pressure up."[29]

Following a September agreement to repatriate 1,500 Cubans currently held in American jails, a *Washington Post* correspondent reported that despite some support within the middle levels of the State Department for "engagement" with Havana, including consideration of a possible limited easing of the embargo policy, administration officials made it clear that these sentiments were not shared by senior policymakers.[30] Clinton forcefully articulated the White House stance at a December press conference when questioned about Cuba's efforts to reach a modus vivendi with the United States: "I see no indication that the nation, or that the leadership, the Castro government, is willing to make the kind of changes that we would expect before we change our policy."[31]

Although Secretary of State Warren Christopher stated on more than one occasion that the administration was ready to respond "in a carefully calibrated way" to Cuban economic and political reforms, this was invariably accompanied by assertions that the United States would not negotiate broader issues of dispute between the two countries or loosen the trade embargo. To do so, as Undersecretary of State Peter Tarnoff put it, would be to "delay, not hasten, reform."[32]

Thus, Washington chose to markedly downplay the accelerated opening up of the Cuban economy to market forces since 1990: the more than $500 million in foreign investment that flowed into the island economy between mid-1991 and mid-1994 from Europe, Canada, Latin America, and Israel to participate in almost 150 joint ventures in tourism, mining, agro-industry, manufacturing, telecommunications, and consumer products; the growth of hundreds of enterprises that are self-financing in their foreign trade and the establishment of more than 160 domestic and foreign trading companies; and the decisions during the latter half of 1994 to partially privatize the telephone system, allow foreign investment in the key sugar industry, and authorize the opening of free markets for industrial and consumer goods.[33] Secretary Christopher passed judgment on these developments in testimony before the House International Relations Committee in January 1995: "We have emphasized that we want to see both market reform and political reform in Cuba. We haven't yet seen an adequate response, *or even the glimmerings of a response*" (emphasis added).[34]

During 1993–1994, Cuba also expressed a willingness to negotiate compensation for nationalized U.S. properties, signed an immigration agreement with Washington, made the dollar legal currency, reduced its demand for a $4.85 surcharge on operator-assisted calls between the two countries to $1, invited the United Nations High Commissioner for Human Rights to visit the island, and announced that it would sign the 1967 Treaty of Tlatelolco banning nuclear arms in the hemisphere. Foreign Minister Roberto Robaina even held discussions with Miami-based Cuban opponents of the revolutionary regime. But the White House refused to budge. A State Department official put the official line bluntly: "Everything they've done recently are things we've been advocating. That's good, but our question is, what's next?"[35]

In adopting the posture it does, Clinton policy operates with the same logic that drove the Reagan-Bush White House. Cuban liberalization and reforms are either minimized or dismissed, or they are not viewed as "good faith" moves that could provide the basis for bilateral negotiations over broader issues. Instead, they are more often taken as expressions of weakness and demonstrations of the effectiveness of a hostile, "extremist" policy approach. Moreover, as administration officials are quick to note, "Politically, you can never be too tough on Castro."[36] Or as another observed, "There is no downside to being tough."[37] Even the newly appointed chairman of the Democratic National Committee, liberal senator Christopher Dodd, while sympathetic to the idea of easing bilateral tensions through increased "dialogue" with the Cubans, rejected any move to tamper with the embargo. "The first action," he insisted, "has to begin with Mr. Castro."[38]

Politically, Clinton's extremist policies must also be understood in terms of his attempt to compete with, and imitate, the Republicans in order to establish his credentials and expand his support among right-wing constituencies for the 1996 election. These efforts focused principally on Florida, the state with the largest Cuban-American community, where victory in the 1996 presidential election was seen as vital to Clinton's winning a second term in the White House. As Wayne Smith noted, "Clinton won Dade

County, where the majority of Cuban-Americans live. . . . He lost in the northern counties where few Cuban-Americans live and lost over issues that had nothing to with Cuba.[39] Nevertheless, Clinton's policy toward Cuba has been fueled by a determination to maximize support among the most conservative elements of the exile community. His success in so doing has allowed some of the most extreme anti-Castro Cubans in the United States to exert a significant influence over policymaking toward the island government.

During the 1992 presidential election campaign, Clinton anointed Jorge Mas Canosa, a Bay of Pigs veteran, private fund-raiser for the Nicaraguan Contras, and chairman of the right-wing group CANF, as *the* representative of the Cuban exile community and allowed him disproportionate influence over the direction of Cuba policy during the campaign and after Clinton entered the White House. Beginning with an April 1992 speech by the Democratic candidate to over 300 wealthy Cuban-Americans in Miami, organized by Mas Canosa, which raised almost $300,000 for Clinton's candidacy, hundreds of thousands of dollars flowed into the Democratic Party campaign coffers from Mas business associates and other Cuban exiles over the following months.[40] Mas Canosa's role in shaping the administration's Cuba policy was initially revealed when he effectively vetoed the president's first choice for assistant secretary of state for Inter-American Affairs, the Cuban-American lawyer Mario Baeza, arguing that he could not be trusted to maintain a hard line against Castro. The successful appointee, Alexander Watson, received Mas's benediction.[41] Clinton's willingness to allow Mas and his supporters to exert a powerful hold over Cuba policy continued through 1994, in return for ongoing financial donations and the hope of electoral success in Florida in 1996. In a March 1994 speech to rightist Cuban-Americans in Miami, Clinton expressed his gratitude to the gathering after obtaining pledges of more than $3.5 million for the Democratic National Committee in no uncertain terms: "This is an amazing dinner. It reminds me of why we got into this is the first place."[42]

Mas Canosa's role in the making of Cuba policy reached new heights at the time of the August 1994 refugee crisis. From June through August, the Coast Guard had intercepted over 23,000 Cubans attempting to reach U.S. shores by boat.[43] Animated partly by a desire to avoid another 1980 Mariel boat lift (when 125,000 Cubans had come to Florida in a five-month period) and to accommodate the rising national anti-immigration mood, as well as seeking to exploit the possibility of developing a viable social constituency inside Cuba through whom the United States could pursue its own political agenda, the Clinton White House imposed a ban on Cuban refugees entering the United States.[44] Mas Canosa was one of five Miami civil and political figures invited by Florida governor Lawton Chiles to discuss the crisis in a meeting with the president. During the conference, Mas

Canosa forcefully argued for a number of retaliatory measures against Castro, including a naval blockade of the island. Although Clinton refused to consider this latter option, he did agree to keep it on the agenda for possible future use and acceded to the exile leader's other major demands. Among them was a presidential "pledge that the United States would undertake no talks with Cuba" over nonmigration issues.[45]

Intent on placating the most virulent segments of the anti-Castro exile community in order to consolidate their support for the refugee ban, the White House rejected Castro's request for broad-ranging bilateral talks, agreeing only to resume low-level diplomacy to resolve this latest migration problem.[46] The president also announced new economic sanctions, eliminating current airline services between Miami and Havana for family members and banning cash remittances from U.S. residents to their relatives in Cuba. And in a particularly important concession to Mas Canosa, Clinton stated that Radio and TV Martí broadcasts into Cuba would be expanded. In a 1994 memorandum to U.S. Information Agency director Joseph Duffey, one senior research analyst at Radio Martí described it as Mas Canosa's "private broadcasting system in Cuba."[47] The White House has consistently sought, in Vice President Al Gore's words, to "turn up the volume" on both stations as part of its broader strategy for eliminating Castro's hold on political power.[48] The combined funding request for fiscal year 1995 totaled almost $28 million; an equally supportive Congress eventually cut only $3 million from the executive funding request.[49] Reflecting on Mas Canosa's lobbying success in high places, one involved administration official put it this way: "[He] has his hooks into a number of strategically placed White House officials."[50]

On September 9, 1994, a new migration agreement was finally signed but only after Cuba relented to Washington's pressure to drop its demands for a revocation of the August economic sanctions and restrictions on Radio and TV Martí broadcasts from Florida to the Caribbean island. Under the accord, the United States agreed to accept a minimum of 20,000 legal immigrants annually from Cuba, and the Castro government promised to vigorously enforce measures to prevent boat people from leaving from its shores.[51]

Despite recommendations from middle-level State Department officials supporting limited modifications of the embargo and greater engagement with Castro, administration policy through 1994 remained hostage to extremist Cuban-Americans in Miami, their supporters in Congress, and Clinton's electoral objectives in Florida, hence the refusal to respond to Cuba's opening to the market and foreign policy concessions in favor of continuing the politics of hostility in the hope that the Castro regime would eventually become amenable to the kinds of economic and political changes Washington desired. Essentially, Clinton's posture mirrored and prolonged the Bush approach: If the external pressure was maintained, the changes would occur, and Castro would be overthrown.

During the first half of 1995, however, support for a limited policy shift began to take hold among some senior State Department and National Security Council (NSC) officials who participated in a major review of Cuba policy. The report's conclusions questioned the efficacy of the current strategy and recommended consideration of new approaches on the ground that the emphasis on economic warfare had failed to produce the desired political reforms. Over the opposition of the State Department's Bureau of Inter-American Affairs, which remained wedded to a policy of minimal cooperation with Havana and opposed an easing of sanctions, Clinton's senior advisers recommended that the president ease those economic sanctions adopted in August 1994 relating to travel and cash remittances. The idea was to test Castro's willingness to make the kinds of reforms that Washington was demanding as a precondition for a fundamental improvement in bilateral ties. Amid a hostile response by leading right-wing Republicans on Capitol Hill, the White House stressed that although very limited changes were under consideration, there would be no weakening of the trade blockade. Clinton's spokesman Michael McCurry sought to ameliorate the fury of the anti-Castro rightists in Congress: "There is no review or change in our view that the embargo of Cuba is an effective tool."[52]

Nonetheless, Undersecretary of State Peter Tarnoff and NSC official Morton Halperin, both of whom played prominent roles in the policy review, continued searching for a "wedge" to at least move Cuba policy off dead center.[53] The renewed White House attention to the migration issue, following a late March meeting between Clinton and Florida senator Bob Graham who had just visited the Cuba refugee camp at Guantanamo, provided the opportunity. Graham described the situation as a "tinderbox" and was convinced that "it couldn't last through the summer without the strong potential of a riot." He also conveyed the Pentagon's similar concern over the very real likelihood of a major "civil disturbance" unless a short-term solution was found and its added unhappiness over the $1-million-a-day cost of maintaining the camp.[54] These warnings, together with the fear of a possible new boat flotilla of refugees leaving the island, triggered "serious alarm bells" in a White House already preoccupied with the 1996 election and cognizant of the growing domestic anti-immigration sentiment. Senior policymakers quickly agreed that this potential crisis had to be gotten "off the screen" as quickly as possible. As an official recalled: "The word was: Solve it. Make it go away with the least amount of turmoil."[55] Only serious negotiations with Havana could achieve such an outcome.

Having decided that the concerns of the Pentagon and anti-immigration sentiment outweighed the political costs of offending its extreme right-wing Cuban-American supporters, the administration agreed to secret talks with the Castro government. Those State Department officials, including Coordinator of Cuban Affairs Dennis Hays, who opposed any improvement in bilateral relations were not even told of the decision. In late April, the U.S. negotiator Peter Tarnoff and Cuba's Ricardo Alarcón reached an agreement, and a week later, President Clinton announced an end to the decades-long special treatment afforded those fleeing the island. The current residents at Guantanamo would be the last group automatically paroled into the United States.[56]

A furious Mas Canosa who, on this occasion, was kept out of the policy-making loop, withdrew a pledge of $45 million that private sponsors had earmarked for resettling up to 15,000 Guantanamo refugees. But Clinton actions did not reflect any disposition to sever the close relationship he had cultivated with the rightist Cuban-American community in Havana; it had more to do with other factors, including White House–commissioned polls showing that among white and Hispanic voters in Florida, there was more support for an anti-immigration stance than new "get tough" measures against Fidel Castro.

Although the importance of domestic factors in shaping Cuba policy should be conceded, it is still the case that Clinton's actions were not primarily the result of "electoral opportunism" but stemmed more from particular ideological and strategic political outlooks. His hard-line policy toward the Cuban Revolution is best understood as part of these basic commitments and those established by preceding Democratic administrations in confronting dissident Central American–Caribbean states. These basic commitments range from the promotion of low-wage nonunion industrial expansion in Arkansas during Clinton's governorships to the wholehearted support of NAFTA and the neoliberal governments throughout Latin America—whose major beneficiaries have been U.S. multinational corporations and banks. Clinton is squarely in the tradition of earlier Democratic White House interventions from the Dominican Republic in 1965 (direct) to Nicaragua in 1978–1979 (indirect).

Clinton's Haiti policy of forcible intervention to replace recalcitrant clients, prevent the accession to power of a mass popular movement advocating radical socioeconomic changes, reconstitute the state in the image of U.S. interests, and convert an elected populist president into a "free marketeer" also speaks directly to the administration's Cuba strategy. The consistent refusal to negotiate "broader questions" has been part of an effort to force the Castro government to not only adopt free market economic policies but also to change its political system, thus undermining the Cuban revolutionary state. Essentially, what motivates past and current White House policy toward the "revolution on its doorstep" is the drive to homogenize Latin America, politically and economically—to eliminate any regional alternative dominant political-economic model. For Clinton, like Bush and Reagan before him, Cuba has been perceived as the most visible obstacle to promoting this outcome, hence the determined commitment to policies that would enable him to preside over the fall of a Communist regime.

Bilateral Relations in a Changing International Environment

The post–Cold War international environment has had a contradictory effect on Washington and Havana: Whereas the former has *deepened* its adversarial posture, the latter has systematically *reversed* what American policymakers previously described as "obstacles" to improved bilateral ties. None of the major global or regional shifts since the late 1980s have produced a softening in the U.S. policy of hostility toward the Cuban Revolution. On the contrary, Washington has tightened the economic noose, heightened ideological warfare, and sought to "run down" the Cuban economy to eliminate a competitive regional alternative to its highly polarized free market model.

The first major change in the international environment that impacted on Clinton policy toward Cuba was the collapse of the Soviet Union. This triggered a White House belief that Cuba was the next Communist "domino," leading it to take a more active role to translate this wish into reality. Misreading the historical differences between the origins and evolution of the Cuban Revolution and the disintegrating states of Eastern Europe, Bush, and subsequently Clinton, acted as if there were no differences—in their assumption that the same degree of political illegitimacy existed in both cases—and that the right mix of coercion and ideological warfare would soon bring Castro's regime to its knees. This perception was strengthened by a prediction of the imminent collapse of a Cuban economy that had been so economically dependent on the Soviet bloc, hence the move toward a tightening of the economic screws rather than a tempering or relaxation of the existing policy approach. White House and State Department officials saw the new context as an opportunity to go for the jugular rather than accommodate a weakened and relatively more isolated Cuba.

As noted, the United States perceived the post-Soviet context as an invitation to escalate its pressure on the Cuban Revolution. But Havana's response moved in the opposite direction: Cuba moderated its policies toward the capitalist world, North and South, including all manner of overtures to Washington, the Cuban exile community, and American business interests and began to accelerate the gradual shift toward an export-based strategy begun in the latter half of the 1980s.

The problem in the bilateral relationship was the dialectic: Cuban concessions were interpreted as "weakness" gained due to U.S. intransigence rather than seen as pragmatic decisions in a new and changing global order, hence the asymmetrical overtures: Positive initiatives on one side were met with increased hostility on the other.

The second major change in the international environment that has influenced U.S. policy toward Cuba has been the intensified economic competition among the dominant capitalist powers. Each has sought to consolidate hegemony in an economic region (Germany in Europe, Japan in Asia, the United States in Latin America). Washington's determination to tighten its hold ("integration") on Latin America has been reinforced by the fact that it is the only major region where it has a favorable external account to compensate for its trade deficits elsewhere. And given the relatively more precarious internal political situations in the hemisphere (compared to Europe and Asia), the United States has revealed itself less tolerant than its leading capitalist competitors of exceptions to market hegemony. Thus, whereas Havana views greater integration into Latin America as a means of greater assimilation into stable market relations, for the White House, "integration" means the continued "exclusion" of Cuba from the inter-American community.

Global superpower competition, however, not only exposes U.S. market weakness but also opens up new market opportunities for Cuba. Neither its European or Asian competitors have participated in the U.S. quest to isolate Cuba. For them, Washington's Cuba policy symbolized the continued ascendancy of Cold War politics in an era in which the principal battlefield was the world market. For Europe and Japan, Cuba has always been merely a minor trading partner; for Washington, it was an alternative to regional regimes' nurturing U.S. global trade imbalances.

The third major change that shaped U.S. policy toward Cuba in the 1990s derived from the electoral transitions ("from dictatorship to democracy") that swept Latin America in the preceding decade. During the 1980s, beginning in the Reagan presidency, the United States shifted from supporting authoritarian military rulers against "totalitarian" Communist threats to "brokering" redemocratization processes. The reasons for this policy shift were, in most cases, a fear that military regimes, weakened by the economic crises, the loss of elite support, and growing popular-social mobilization within which a resurgent Left often played a leading role, would collapse and be replaced by mass-based civilian governments opposed to the "free markets" that were the symbol of dictatorial rule. Washington opted to oversee "transitions" that produced promarket electoral regimes opposed to radical social reforms. The experience of the "early" transitions in Peru (1980) and Argentina (1983) confirmed a perception that it was not only possible but politically and propagandistically advantageous to promote an electoral transition under a given set of assumptions that preserved the "old" state, socioeconomic system, and (neoliberal) economic strategy.

Thus, what originated as Washington's "adaptation" to practical exigencies for political and social change emanating from Latin America was soon transformed by the United States into a new political strategy for preserving the status quo. The electoral regimes would provide legitimacy to the payment of debts incurred by the military regime, corrupt political figures absconding with funds, and the rich illegally transferring billions abroad. More important, Washington argued that "free trade markets and democracy" were interlinked and hence any regime that resisted the demands of the bankers and the multinationals was undermining democracy. This argument overlooked the fact that the free markets had their origins in the dictatorships and had been sustained by military-dominated or dependent electoral regimes that had granted amnesties from prosecution for human rights abuses committed by their autocratic predecessors during the 1980s.

Once the formula ("democracy and free markets") was in place and the rules for electoral transitions were firmly established, Washington proceeded to encourage, promote, and support "democratization" on a global level as the most effective lever for breaking down barriers to markets, privatizing public enterprises, and attacking one-party collectivist states. The "electoralist shift" of U.S. policy thus had a two-edged slant: It allowed support for the most retrograde socioeconomic electoral regimes (e.g., Guatemala, El Salvador) while simultaneously legitimating efforts to run roughshod over national and international law to undermine and disintegrate adversaries (the Nicaraguan Contras, according to Reagan and Bush officials, were fighting for "democracy").

The "moral authority" that the United States manipulated through its support of electoral transitions in Latin America was exploited to legitimate its hostile posture toward Cuba. The electoral regimes' methods of political rule and socioeconomic policies were secondary concerns. Only "elections" dictated support or opposition to a particular regime. Illegal embargoes, violations of third-country trading rights, and intervention in the internal affairs of sovereign states were set aside: "Democracy" displaced self-determination in Latin America. Thus, as the political transitions took place, the United States hardened its propaganda posture toward Cuba. As the Cold War policy justifications receded—clearly Cuba could no longer be described as a Soviet "outpost" in the hemisphere—Washington relied increasingly on the electoral transition argument. Cuba was the exception, and, therefore, it could not be included in regional organizations, meetings, or trading groups. The paradox, however, was that while Washington promoted electoral transitions to facilitate and guarantee market access, the new civilian regimes resumed diplomatic and economic relations with Cuba, thus undercutting the continuing Bush-Clinton efforts to isolate the Caribbean island within the inter-American system.

The fourth major shift in the global context affecting U.S.-Cuban relations has been the decline in the nonalignment movement (NAM). Because the latter functioned as a broad forum of Third World countries who were more less independent of the two Cold War superpowers, it provided a source of support for the Cuban Revolution that reached far beyond the Soviet orbit. Successive U.S. governments exhibited hostility toward the NAM, except on those occasions when countries became affiliated with the movement after having broken relations with the Soviet Union. The reasons for Washington's stance toward the NAM were varied. Broadly speaking, though, they centered on the idea that South-South and multilateral relations would weaken U.S. leverage over the Third World.

Today, bilateral relations and North-South ties have largely replaced the nonaligned movement, strengthening the bargaining position of the West in general and the United States in particular. This is evident in debt negotiations, the increasing intrusiveness of the World Bank and IMF in setting Third World development (free market) agendas, and in the spread of Western-funded NGO projects to replace comprehensive Third World social programs.

The NAM's demise has allowed Washington to fix the framework of U.S.-Cuban discussions in terms much more favorable to itself and to limit the alternative outlets for Havana to gain a hearing. Moreover, it has strengthened U.S. hegemony over the Third World, has increased the spread of neoliberal ideology, and has made North-South relations central to development policies, forcing the Cubans to turn toward the North more than would be to their advantage. As their former allies in NAM resort to neoliberal policies and compete for foreign investment, the pressures increase on Cuba to do likewise, as interregional ties become more and more limited.

What is particularly striking about the adversarial nature of Clinton policy toward Cuba in the new global environment, however, is the extent to which such a posture contradicts larger U.S. policy goals. There are at least four basic contradictions, discussed below, in Washington's policy toward the Caribbean island.

Free Trade

U.S. multinational corporations in the 1990s depend more than ever on foreign markets for a growing proportion of their profits. This trend reinforced Washington's determination to provide "global leadership" in the post–Cold War era: to open markets and new investment locales. The prime ideological instrument in this drive was the free trade doctrine. The United States has taken the position in every global and regional forum that free trade is the cornerstone of its foreign economic policy, yet this doctrine conflicts with the restrictive trade practices supported by the White House and the Congress to obstruct and limit world trade with Cuba. This policy inconsistency has encouraged rivals to view Washington's embrace of free trade as a self-serving policy to be used only when it serves U.S. political interests. In a period of heightened intercapitalist competition, the Clinton administration's response to Cuba's "opening to the world market" undermines its claim to leadership in the era of "free trade." In part, Washington's anti-free-trade policy regarding Cuba stems from an effort to appease the Cuban-American National Foundation in Florida in order to secure the "Cuban vote" in that populous state. Thus, conjunctural electoral considerations threaten to undermine the logic of the free trade doctrine, not only weakening the latter but also demonstrating a lack of global leadership on Clinton's part, as he willingly truckles to a small parochial group of right-wing extremists.

Intercapitalist Competition

A vigorous advocate of a level playing field for all of the world's trading partners, the White House attempts to interfere and limit trade relations between Cuba and Western competitor countries. Moreover, it seeks to extend its policies to subsidiaries of U.S. multinationals based in third countries. The so-called doctrine of extraterritoriality violates the sovereignty of competing capitalist countries and is clearly directed at undermining the authority and trade laws of competition. Such an imperial doctrine, though, has failed comprehensively to bully major trading partners and allies to do Washington's bidding.

Ideological Warfare

Washington continues to pursue an unrelenting ideological war against Cuba. Whether in the mass media or through Radio Martí or in international forums, Cuba remains embedded in U.S. Cold War rhetoric. Today, the more Cuba moves away from the fixed points on the U.S. ideological map, the more intense the Clinton administration's rhetorical onslaught becomes. This is occurring notwithstanding the realities of Cuban economic liberalization: European, Asian, Latin America, Canadian, and other governments around the world have not only recognized and responded to the market openings and the shifts in foreign investment rules but have encouraged hundreds of millions of dollars in investment in the Cuban economy by their overseas capitalist classes. Thus, the United States pursues a phantom ideological war: Its totalitarian imagery fails to evoke any allied support because it rings false in the ears of participants in a mixed economy. U.S. ideological arguments lacking credibility are thus self-limiting: They are so remote from current realities and practices that they produce the self-isolation of the United States rather than evoking support. Rather than the United States playing to the liberalization in Cuba, thus deepening changes, its hostility allows other countries and social actors a more active role. Driven by the perverse notion that the more Cuba changes, the more dangerous and subtle its threat, Washington has contributed to allowing the revolutionary leadership to limit the market changes—to proceed with liberalization while retaining revolutionary gains in health, education, and culture.

The Mercantilist Versus the National Security State

Since the early 1990s, the United States has been desperately trying to maintain and improve its global competitiveness on the new battlefield of the world market, where weapons systems and ideological bluff do not gain market shares. Increasingly, foreign policy institutions are being recycled to gain markets, sell products, and exploit public enterprise sell-offs. Washington is in the process of trying to reconvert the imperial state from a national security to a mercantilist state; to recycle its imperial institutions from an ideological-military to an economic-commercial focus. Yet the retention of a basically ideological and military posture in relations with Cuba serves to preserve and nurture those forces resisting this shift to a mercantilist state: The search for "threats" from the past linger on in the rhetoric of those nostalgic right-wing figures who currently hold influential posts within the executive and legislative branches of the U.S. government. This tension within the state, between the mercantilist and the national security elements, is played out in the Cuba policy sphere: On the one hand, travel and trade restrictions satisfy the nostalgic; on the other, there is a lack of rigid implementation and enforcement of these measures, accommodating the activists in the mercantilist wing of the state. Hence, the gap between the radical rhetoric and the limited will to pursue specific policies that undermine the larger commercial relationships.

Conclusion: The Dynamics of Cuba Policy

One direct consequence of Clinton's hard-line policy toward Cuba has been to create a favorable political climate for domestic right-wing forces to pursue their own, more extreme, agendas regarding the Caribbean island. The Republican congressional victories in the 1994 midterm elections resulted in two of the most anti-Castro legislators assuming the chairmanship of key foreign policy committees. Senator Jesse Helms took over the running of that chamber's Committee on Foreign Relations; in the House, Representative Dan Burton became head of the Western Hemisphere Affairs Subcommittee of the Committee on International Relations.

In February 1995, Helms and Burton cosponsored the Cuban Liberty and Democratic Solidarity [Libertad] Act, whose objective was to severely punish foreign governments, foreign corporations, and global lending institutions pursuing economic relations with Cuba. The key provisions of the bill were quite specific and not subject to interpretation: The former American owners of nationalized properties were granted the right to sue foreigners who invested in these enterprises in U.S. courts; any foreign business executive who owned such properties or profited from them in other ways would be denied visas to enter the United States (an attempt to halt the growth of joint ventures and other kinds of foreign investment); countries buying sugar or molasses from Cuba or trading in these sweeteners would lose their preferential trade rights in the American market; U.S. contributions to the World Bank and the IMF would be reduced by the amount of aid either may decide to grant Castro's government in the future; and U.S. economic assistance to Russia would be withheld equal to the amount Moscow provides Havana in payment for the electronic intelligence facility it maintains at Lourdes to monitor Washington's compliance with international arms control agreements (approximately $200 million).

European, Canadian and Latin American governments denounced the bill because of its extraterritorial reach and its contravention of world trade rules. In a letter to congressional leaders, the European Union described the key features of the legislation as "objectionable" and "illegitimate" and warned that their implementation was likely "to cause grave and damaging effects to EU-US relations."[57] The Canadian trade minister Roy McClaren attacked the bill on the grounds that it undermined Washington's NAFTA and World Trade Organization obligations. The ban on sugar and molasses imports raised particular concern in Ottawa because it threatened almost $1 billion in bilateral trade.[58] The Rio Group of foreign ministers condemned the bill as contrary to "universally recognized free trade practices."[59]

Confronted by this worldwide opposition, the administration informed the House International Relations Committee that it would oppose the legislation because key sections "would anger allies of the United States and force Washington to violate international agreements."[60] During House and Senate hearings on the bill, senior State Department officials Peter Tarnoff and Alexander Watson, while reaffirming Clinton's strong support for the trade embargo as "the best leverage the U.S. has to promote change in Cuba," detailed White House misgivings over those provisions that were likely "to cause disputes with our allies" and appeared to infringe on the president's constitutional responsibilities in the foreign policy area.[61]

Although the Clinton White House continued to place the onus for improved relations on "far-reaching political and economic reform" by the Castro government,[62] in 1995, some commentators discerned a "new approach" in administration decisions, pronouncements, and policy implementation. These included the policy shift on Cuban refugees; opposition to the Helms-Burton bill in its original form; statements about the possible relaxation of the economic sanctions; the failure to rigorously enforce particular travel ban laws despite the harsh official rhetoric; and the October presidential announcement of plans to increase person-to-person exchanges and ease restrictions on Cuban-Americans visiting the island or sending dollars to relatives living there.

To interpret these developments as amounting to a "new approach," how-ever, ignores the right-wing framework within which Clinton policy toward Cuba has been made—and which his more "liberal" advisers are burdened with. From the perspective of an administration whose initial "get tough" measures established the foundation block for an even more extreme policy approach adopted by the political Right, the current "relaxation" proposals cannot be interpreted as a fundamental shift in American policy. It is more appropriate to describe them as a return to policies of the Reagan-Bush era.

To the extent that any policy shift has taken place, it has been the success of the State Department liberals in persuading President Clinton to adopt a two-track approach based on increased educational, artistic, academic, and religious exchanges between the two countries while keeping the economic embargo in place. But the justification offered for selective political, ideolog-ical, and cultural openings reflects the persistence of a bureaucratic consen-sus regarding the fundamental strategic goal: overthrowing the Castro lead-ership. Administration liberals convinced the White House that it was precisely these kinds of contacts that played an invaluable role in hastening the collapse of the Communist-ruled regimes of Eastern Europe.[63]

Any disagreements that may have surfaced over Cuba policy are confined to the most effective methods of achieving the larger consensual objective. The "liberal" U.S. policymakers, observed Fidel Castro in a recent speech, are no less determined than the hard-line domestic rightists "to penetrate us, weaken us, create all kinds of counterrevolutionary organizations to destabi-lize the country." Foreign Minister Roberto Robaina was even more pointed and cutting: "They are not debating whether to cut off our heads . . . but how they will do it, with a knife or with a razor.[64]

Yet, insofar as the Clinton White House pursues a politics of hostility to-ward Cuba against a background of changes in the global environment fa-vorable to capitalism, it limits U.S. ability to benefit from the new advanta-geous circumstances; it contradicts and undermines both Washington's ideological and economic aspirations (free trade) and its efforts to recycle the U.S. state (from "national security" to mercantilist). Moreover, the "two-track policy" of cultural-ideological openings combined with eco-nomic pressures that proved successful in Eastern Europe is unlikely to achieve its destabilizing goals in Cuba because of the rigid ideological blink-ers imposed by parochial electoral concerns and the appeals of a heterodox market-welfare model of development on the rest of Latin America.

Notes

1. Quoted in Larry Rohter, "Clinton Sees Opportunity to Break G.O.P. Grip on Cuban-Americans," *New York Times,* October 31, 1992, p. 6.

2. U.S. Congress, House, Committee on Foreign Affairs, *Consideration of the Cuban Democracy Act of 1992,* 102d Cong., 1st sess., March 18, 25; April 2, 8; May

21; June 4, 5, 1992 (Washington, D.C.: Government Printing Office, 1993), p. 403. Gelbard was deputy assistant secretary of state for inter-American affairs in the Bush administration.

3. Quoted in *CubaInfo,* April 30, 1993, pp. 2–3. On the role that the doctrine of extraterritoriality has played in U.S. economic policy toward the Cuban Revolution between 1959 and 1982, see Michael Krinsky and David Golove, eds., *United States Economic Measures Against Cuba* (Northampton, Mass.: Aletheia Press, 1993), especially pp. 107–134.

4. Quoted in *CubaInfo,* October 2, 1992, p. 2.

5. Quoted in ibid., p. 3.

6. U.S. Congress, Senate, Committee on Foreign Relations, *Nomination of Warren M. Christopher to Be Secretary of State,* 103d Cong., 1st sess., January 13 and 14, 1993 (Washington, D.C.: Government Printing Office, 1993), pp. 33, 140.

7. Quoted in National Security Archive, *United States Policy Toward Cuba: The Clinton Administration's First Year—A Chronology* (Washington, D.C.: National Security Archive, 1994).

8. See ibid.

9. Daniel Williams, "U.S. Rejects Cuba's Demand That Exiles Buy Tour Packages," *Washington Post,* September 17, 1993, p. A2.

10. Quoted in Tom Carter, "Cuban Relations Won't Warm Soon, State Official Says," *Washington Times,* October 27, 1993, p. A12. Also see National Security Archive, *United States Policy Toward Cuba.*

11. See, for example, "Blockaded Minds," *Nation,* July 25–August 1, 1994, p. 112.

12. See *CubaInfo,* March 17, 1994, p. 1.

13. Mark Sullivan, *Cuba: Issues for Congress* (Issue Brief), September 6, 1994 (Library of Congress: Congressional Research Service), p. 7.

14. Quoted in *CubaInfo,* August 5, 1994, p. 1.

15. Douglas Jehl, "President Moves to Punish Castro for Cuban Exodus," *New York Times,* August 21, 1994, p. 1; *CubaInfo,* September 22, 1994, p. 11.

16. Quoted in *CubaInfo,* April 27, 1995, p. 7. On U.S. pressure on Honduras not to trade with Cuba, see *CubaInfo,* November 5, 1993, p. 5.

17. Quoted in Ann Devroy, "Panetta Hints at Blockade of Cuba," *Washington Post,* August 22, 1994, p. A11.

18. See *CubaInfo,* September 24, 1993, p. 7; December 14, 1994, pp. 9–10; January 12, 1995, p. 6; February 23, 1995, p. 6; Economist Intelligence Unit, *Quarterly Economic Review of Cuba,* first quarter 1995, p. 12; *Latin American Monitor: Caribbean,* March 1995, p. 6.

19. Quoted in Charles Trueheart, "U.S. Hard-line Stance on Cuba Draws Icy Reviews from Trading Partners," *Washington Post,* September 10, 1994, p. A18; *CubaInfo,* February , 1995, p. 4.

20. *CubaInfo,* April 27, 1995, p. 7. Also see James Brooke, "Latin America Now Ignores U.S. Lead in Isolating Cuba," *New York Times,* July 8, 1995, pp. 1, 5.

21. *Latin American Monitor: Caribbean,* May 1995, p. 6.

22. Quoted in *CubaInfo,* April 8, 1994, p. 6.

23. Quoted in ibid., December 15, 1994, p. 2.

24. Quoted in ibid., January 28, 1994, p. 1.

25. Quoted in ibid., February 7, 1995, p. 2.

26. See ibid., September 14, 1995, p. 1.

27. Quoted in Douglas Farah, "U.S.-Cuban Ties: Slight Warming But Both Sides Doubt Massive Shift," *Washington Post*, July 31, 1993, p. A18.

28. Quoted in *CubaInfo*, August 6, 1993, p. 1.

29. Quoted in ibid., September 4, 1993, p. 2.

30. Thomas W. Lippman, "U.S.-Cuba Accord Limited to Convicts," *Washington Post*, October 2, 1993, p. A14.

31. Quoted in Daniel Williams, "U.S. Stands Its Ground on Cuba," *Washington Post*, December 21, 1993, p. A11.

32. Christopher and Gelbard quoted in Tom Kenworthy, "U.S. Rejects Expansion of Talks with Castro," *Washington Post*, August 29, 1994, p. A14. Also see statement by Christopher quoted in *CubaInfo*, December 15, 1994, p. 5.

33. "Cuba: How Foreign Firms Fare," *Business Latin America*, August 22, 1994, p. 2; Andrew Zimbalist, "Dateline Cuba: Hanging On In Havana," *Foreign Policy*, no. 92 (Fall 1993), p. 193.

34. Quoted in *CubaInfo*, February 7, 1995, p. 3.

35. Quoted in *Miami Herald*, September 25, 1994, p. 24A.

36. Quoted in Daniel Williams, "U.S. Stands Its Ground on Cuba," p. A11.

37. Quoted in Williams, "U.S. Rejects Cuba's Demand That Exiles Buy Tour Packages, p. A2.

38. Quoted in *CubaInfo*, February 7, 1995, p. 7.

39. Wayne S. Smith, *Our Cuba Diplomacy* (Washington, D.C.: Center for International Policy, October 1994), p. 3.

40. See Ann Louise Bardarch, "Our Man in Miami," *New Republic*, October 3, 1994, pp. 20–21.

41. See John M. Goshko, "Controversy Erupts on Latin American Post," *Washington Post*, January 23, 1993, p. A4.

42. Quoted in David Corn, "Cuban Gold," *Nation*, October 3, 1994, p. 334.

43. Congressional Research Service, Report to Congress, *Cuban and Haitian Asylum Seekers: Recent Trends*, September 1, 1994.

44. See Jim Mann, "White House Pressure Tactics Aimed at Castro," *Los Angeles Times*, August 21, 1994, p. A24; Steven Greenhouse, "Untidy Policy Pays Off in Cuba Crisis," *New York Times*, September 11, 1994, p. 8.

45. R. W. Apple Jr., "Castro vs. Clinton," *New York Times*, August 26, 1994, p. 12. Also see Jon Nordheimer, "Cuban Group Forges Link to Clinton," *New York Times*, August 26, 1994, p. 12.

46. See Daniel Williams and John F. Harris, "U.S. Shuns High-Level Talks with Cuba; Raft Rescue Costing Millions," *Washington Post*, August 26, 1994, p. A22.

47. Quoted in Peter Kornbluh and Jon Elliston, "Will Congress Kill TV Martí?" *Nation* August 22–29, 1994, p. 195.

48. Quoted in *CubaInfo*, May 21, 1993, p. 2.

49. Sullivan, *Cuba: Issues for Congress*, p. 13.

50. Quoted in Peter Kornbluh, "Cuba, No Mas," *Nation*, May 29, 1995, p. 745.

51. See Robert Suro, "U.S., Cuba Agree on Stemming Raft Tide," *Washington Post*, September 10, 1994, pp. A1, A18.

52. Quoted in Daniel Williams, "Continued Cuba Sanctions Pressed by GOP Leaders," *Washington Post,* March 8, 1995, p. A22. Also see Daniel Williams and Ann Devroy, "Clinton May Ease Sanctions on Cuba," *Washington Post,* May 7, 1995, p. A7; Steven Greenhouse, "Clinton Opposes Move to Toughen Embargo on Cuba," *New York Times,* May 5, 1995, p. 8.

53. U.S. official, quoted in Ann Devroy and Daniel Williams, "'Serious Alarm Bells' Led to Talks with Cuba," *Washington Post,* May 5, 1995, p. A4.

54. Quoted in Steven Greenhouse, "How the Clinton Administration Reversed U.S. Policy on Cuban Refugees, *New York Times,* May 21, 1995, p. 8; Devroy and Williams, "'Serious Alarm Bells' Led to Talks with Cuba," p. A4. The "civil disturbance" quote was by the chief of the Atlantic Command, General John J. Sheehan.

55. Quoted in ibid., p. A4.

56. Steven Greenhouse, "U.S. Will Return Refugees to Cuba in Policy Switch," *New York Times,* May 3, 1995, pp. 1, 14.

57. Quoted in *CubaInfo,* April 6, 1995, pp. 2–3. Also see the statement by German foreign minister Klaus Kinkel in *CubaInfo,* May 18, 1995, p. 8.

58. Clyde H. Farnesworth, "Congress Move on Cuba Irks Canada and Mexico," *New York Times,* May 23, 1995, p. 3; *CubaInfo,* April 27, 1995, p. 1.

59. Quoted in ibid., June 8, 1995, p. 3.

60. Quoted from a letter written by the State Department chief liaison with Congress, Wendy Sherman, in Greenhouse, "Clinton Opposes Move to Toughen Embargo on Cuba," p. 1.

61. Quoted in U.S. Department of State, *Dispatch,* May 29, 1995, pp. 446–449; *CubaInfo,* April 6, 1995, p. 3, and June 8, 1995, p. 3.

62. Quoted in Mireya Navarro, "Castro Confers with Exiled Foe," *New York Times,* June 28, 1995, p. 1.

63. See Steven Greenhouse, "To Undercut Castro, U.S. Plans Links with Cubans," *New York Times,* June 12, 1995, p. 9.

64. Castro and Robaina quoted in Tim Golden, "Cuban Leadership Shows Little Hope of Closer U.S. Ties," *New York Times,* August 7, 1995, pp. 1, 3.

10

Mexico and the United States: Cures That Kill the Patient

On January 15, 1997, President Clinton announced that Mexico had repaid all of the $12.5 billion it had borrowed from Washington to stave off financial collapse and bail out Wall Street speculators. The *New York Times* (January 16, 1997) reported that "the repayment of the loan—three years ahead of schedule—was marked by a celebration at the White House today presided over by Mr. Clinton and Treasury Secretary Rubin." In Mexico, President Zedillo celebrated the occasion, declaring that his government had made a "bold step toward the economic recovery of Mexico." According to Zedillo, "The early retirement of the debt demonstrated the coherence and responsibility the Mexican people and Government have shown in these times."

While Clinton, Robert Rubin, and Zedillo claimed the debt repayment was a reflection of the successful recovery of the Mexican economy, Guillermo Ortiz, the Mexican finance minister, clarified the issue by stating that Mexico raised the money for the final payment to the U.S. Treasury by selling bonds to investors in Europe, Asia, and the United States. Hence, the net debt stays the same, and although the rates of interest decline (the U.S. Treasury pocketed a profit of half a billion on the loan), the payment of the debt was not the result of any boom in the economy.

The deeper social, economic, and political consequences for the Mexican workers and farmers of paying the debt three years in advance were not discussed at Clinton's celebration. The transfer of debt payments overseas has depressed the Mexican economy via exorbitant interest rates (between 35 percent and 75 percent annually) that undermine industrial and agricultural producers. Widespread and severe domestic indebtedness, a precarious financial system dependent on state subsidies, and a growing rate of bankruptcy are some of the immediate consequences that afflict the private sector of the Mexican economy. However, the high interest rates attract the return of overseas speculative capital, which makes short-term investments in government bonds and in bargain price purchases of mineral concessions. On the Mexican side, local investors feel the whole financial system is insecure and have been investing heavily in the United States. The subsidiaries of overseas U.S. banks and enterprises also ship most of their profits out, thus draining valuable and scarce earnings out of productive investment in Mexico.

On the social front, the minimum wage and general wages and salaries continue to plummet; the rate of inflation continues to exceed the annual salary adjustments that the government imposes through the state-controlled Mexican Labor Confederation (CTM); and the bulk of agricultural producers, farmers, and peasants suffer from declining income, unequal competition (from the United States and Canada), and lack of credit.

On the political front, although the state political party, the PRI, continues to engage in electoral fraud, political assassinations, and vote buying through "poverty programs," it is losing its political stranglehold on the country.

Making Mexico Safe for Wall Street— and Unsafe for Mexicans

It should be clear that in analyzing any country today in the so-called free market era, it is important to specify the impact that policies have on *different social classes* and *sectors of the economy*. Thus, such terms as "macroeconomic indicators" and increases in the stock market are meaningless in themselves unless the analyst tells us who benefits and who pays the cost, as well as specifying the long-term, large-scale structural effects on class relations, income distribution, and development of productive forces. For example, this past year the biggest increases in stock prices occurred in countries going through very severe socioeconomic crises. Among what stock speculators and investment brokers refer to as "emergent markets," Russia's stocks grew by 156 percent, Venezuela's by 132 percent, Hungary's by 95 percent, and Poland's by 71 percent. Among the top five performers, China, with a growth of 89 percent, was the only country to experience sustained growth. What all these countries have in common is a severe unemployment or underemployment problem, a precipitous decline in overall living standards, the auctioning off of lucrative public enterprises to private overseas investors, and an opening of their raw materials to foreign exploitation. Brazil, with a 30 percent increase in the stock index, Argentina with 19 percent, and Mexico with 16 percent also provided lucrative returns to overseas and local speculators. The liberalization of the markets in both Russia and Venezuela, which attracts foreign capital, is also responsible for the growth of poverty, encompassing 70 percent of the Venezuelan and over two-thirds of the Russian population. In the case of Mexico, the 16 percent increase for bettors in the stock market was accompanied by further decline in wages. The government fixed wage adjustment for 1996 was at least 10 percent below the actual rate of inflation.

Further evidence of the lucrative profiteering for U.S. speculators in Latin America was revealed by a study by a New Jersey–based research group that found that Latin American funds performed better than all other U.S.-managed international equity funds. The study revealed that the average Latin American fund returned 27 percent in 1996, putting it ahead of U.S. equity funds that averaged only 19 percent. The biggest profiteers among the funds have taken advantage of the privatization of publicly owned mineral resources, energy, precious and industrial metals, timber, and real estate. One of the most lucrative fields for speculators in Latin America was debt funds (the buying and selling of public overseas debt), returning 42 percent. The strongest bond funds in the world had heavy exposure in Latin America with the top-performer GMO Emerging Country Debt, returning 66 percent—containing a 10 percent weighing in Mexico and a 32 percent weighing in the rest of Latin America.

The consequences of the high returns to U.S. speculators, however, are largely negative, even for many Mexican investors and businesspeople. In order to attract foreign capital with high interest rates, the Mexican government has forced huge increases in the cost of borrowing for Mexican businessmen. The result is large-scale poverty, declining incomes, and the depression of the internal market; the growing political and social discontent that accompanies the stagnant market has generated widespread insecurity among large and small Mexican investors, causing them to ship their money across the border, thus further undermining any economic recovery. Mexican deposits in U.S. banks have more than doubled since 1994—rising from $12.2 billion to $26.3 billion by July 1996, according to the U.S. Federal Reserve. Thus, while saving deposits in Mexico declined by 4 percent in 1996, Mexican deposits in the United States increased by 8 percent in the first half of 1997. The amount of deposits that accumulated in the first seven months of 1996 in U.S. banks is around one-third of the potential savings that the national private sector deposited in Mexico at the same time. This outflow does not include the Mexican share of the approximate $45 billion that has been estimated as having been transferred by U.S. subsidiaries to the tax paradises in the Bahamas and the Cayman and Virgin Islands. Clearly, the Mexican government's early payment of its external debt obligation has not created a secure and favorable climate for Mexican savers. Thus, the flight of Mexican capital becomes a further pretext for greater overseas indebtedness, which encourages the continuance of excessive interest rates, further undercutting local production and encouraging greater capital flight. The Mexican regime's policy of an "open economy" that liberalizes capital flows has had a boomerang effect by increasing debt *outflows* and encouraging local capital flight. This undermines any basis for financing the recovery of the productive economy, while enhancing financial and speculative returns.

Faltering Investment and Rising Unemployment

The influx of so-called portfolio investments of overseas speculators does not create jobs for the 65 percent of the Mexican labor force that is underemployed or unemployed (in the so-called informal sector). And the state's tight control over wages ensures that the 60 percent of the labor force working and living in poverty will not benefit from any dubious projections of economic growth. The Mexican Confederation of Chambers of Industries (Concamin) listed six major obstacles to the government's plans to overcome unemployment: the weak stimulus of the internal market for private investors; the persistent debt among families and firms; the persistent low private consumption levels; and the unbalancing of external accounts via the import of inputs by expanding industries. The private sector expects low levels of real investment, and there is little likelihood that whatever growth occurs will not be jeopardized by political and social conflict. Such conflict is inevitable, given the persistence of record-high unemployment and deepening rural poverty generated by the free market policies.

Meeting Foreign Obligations and the Minimum Wage

Mexican minimum wage levels are among the lowest in the semi-industrialized world and have suffered severe deterioration as the Mexican government seeks to attract more foreign investment on the basis of cheap labor.

As of January 1, 1997, the general minimum wage ranged (by regions) between $3.40 and $2.90 a day. Even among skilled workers and professionals, minimum salaries do not allow for minimum living conditions. For example, the minimum wage for truck drivers in the higher-paid regions is $5.00 a day; certified nurses have a minimum of $5.50; auto mechanics $5.00. In the countryside, agricultural workers average about $2.50 a day, if and when they receive full payment. While salaries and wages have continued to decline, basic food prices have been skyrocketing, thanks to free market deregulation. Between 1996 and mid-1997, the consumption of basic food items has declined 29 percent. Over the same period, nominal salaries increased 38 percent, but inflation increased by 66 percent. Basic food items like beans increased by 240 percent, tortillas by 86 percent, wheat flour by 305 percent, and cooking oil by 70 percent.

In January of 1997 in Guasave Sinaloa, over 3,000 agricultural workers, most from southern Mexico, went on strike and fought the police, demanding the end of a 4-peso weekly deduction to fund the government-controlled CTM union and an increase in salary to 25 pesos a day ($3.20). The strike paralyzed the export of 40,000 boxes of vegetables—mostly tomatoes. Faced with the threat of rotting fruit and the militancy of the workers, the owners accepted the 70-cent-per-day raise. As one striking farm worker put it, "We live like animals; they transport us like them and nobody cares if we are killed in an accident; there's nobody to defend us."

As malnutrition stalks the land, the Mexican agricultural economy shows all the signs of deformed growth characteristic of the free market. Overall, the agricultural sector grew a mere 1.5 percent, which still failed to compensate for the 3.5 percent decline in 1995. The net balance between agricultural food exports and imports was negative—to the tune of $1.5 billion in 1996.

The basic problem is the basic inequality of trade between Mexico and its North American neighbors. Mexican farmers suffer from lack of financing and high rates of interest. In addition, the infrastructure is inadequate, and the commercial networks are inferior to those of their U.S. and Canadian competitors. These material conditions make it impossible for Mexican producers to compete within the framework of the free trade agreement. In the specific area of corn production, Mexico's average output is about 2 tons a hectare, whereas the U.S. output currently runs to 7 tons, with projections to increase output to 17 tons. But the aggregate figures hide basic socioeconomic differences: Although 5 percent of the large corn producers in Mexico grow over 5 tons per hectare, there are 1.5 million small farmers producing for subsistence. In 1996, the ranks of the "subsistence producers" were swelled by the addition of 300,000 corn farmers who were so heavily in debt and lacking in capital financing that they were unable to incur new loans to upgrade production to become competitive. Although government financing rose slightly (by .3 percent), moving to 31.3 billion pesos in 1997 from 26 billion in 1996 (in nominal terms, not corrected for inflation), the great bulk of the financing goes to the large agribusiness firms. For example, the regime's main development promotional agency, Alianza para el Campo, has twenty-two programs designed to increase income and output, but they reached only 10 percent of the producers. The overall impact in the agricultural sector was negligible. The result is deeper social polarization between those big farm exporters who are linked to the state and the small producers who are excluded from the government's subsidy programs. Because of its commitment to meeting external debt payments and because of gross corruption of agricultural officials who pocket funds destined for the agro sector, there is growing social protest in rural areas. One typical example of peasant protest occurred early in 1997 in the state of Chiapas. In January, over 350 police attacked thousands of peasants in the La Frailesca zone who were blocking highways protesting the government's failure to carry out previous agreements signed in November 1996. The original agreement stipulated that the peasants would accept depressed corn prices, and in exchange, the government would implement a Program of Temporary Rural Employment that would supposedly fund 3 million person hours of work. The peasants thought that the added income from this work would compensate for lost income from depressed prices. The prices stayed low, but the jobs never materialized. The peasants took to the streets, the PRI sent in the police, and scores of peasants were injured and jailed. But the government was able to save money and pay its debt to the U.S. two years early.

The problems of Mexican agriculture go far deeper than the impoverishment of the poor peasant. Middle-size farm owners and even many owners of larger farms are suffering from the squeeze of high interest rates and declining international prices. The size of the rural debt continues to increase, and the number of farmers who cannot meet debt payments is growing. In 1996, over 20.9 billion pesos in loans were far in arrears, compared to 17.4 billion in 1995. The total internal public debt in Mexico amounted to 13 percent of the gross domestic product.

To avoid foreclosures, Mexican debtors have organized a nationwide movement called Barzon, which claims 2 million members and demands government relief, lower interest rates, postponement of payments, and an end to foreclosures. Organized protesters have effectively blocked bank takeovers of farms in many states. Moreover, Barzon leaders recently met with Zapatista leaders in Chiapas and have announced support in some states for oppositionist left-wing candidates.

Finance and the State

Although Mexican government officials constantly proclaim that the chances of a repeat of the financial crash of 1994 are "remote," the economic fundamentals to provoke a new crash are still in place. The government is obsessed with keeping the current financial system afloat, no matter what its cost to the rest of the economy. This reflects the regime's increasing dependence on overseas financial flows and the fragility of this external relationship. Today, Mexico does not seek external finance to produce; rather it "produces" to sustain the financial markets. In 1996, the Mexican government's bailout of banks and large-scale debt holders exceeded 8 percent of the GNP, a bill that taxpayers will be paying for the next twenty-nine years. With ballooning external debt payments in the tens of billions coming due in 1997 and Mexican savings and subsidiary profits flowing outward, the government is intent on maintaining the free market economy. President Zedillo's only solution is to apply new and more severe "adjustments," or downward pressures on the already low wages, to privatize social security funds, and to increase the exploitation of nonrenewable resources (oil, metals, forests, and so on) to at-

tract speculative capital from overseas "money funds." There is a direct relation between the decreasing income available to Mexicans and the increasing
dependence on money flow via narcotics traffic. Corruption and drugs have
permeated all levels of government—while social rebellion grows in the
southern states and electoral protest spreads in the northern and central regions of Mexico.

The Decline of the Party-State:
Political Consequences of the Free Market

The party-state dictatorship that has been dictating Mexican politics for the
greater part of this century is being challenged on three fronts: electorally in
most of the country, by social movements in a wide range of social sectors,
and by at least three guerrilla movements in the South. In the electoral field,
political analysts project the combined vote of the conservative PAN and
Center-Left PRD to total close to 55 percent, with the PRI hovering around
31 percent. In 1997, nearly 50 million Mexicans voted for state governors,
municipal officials, and federal deputies. The PRI lost the mayor's office in
Mexico City to the PRD and suffered defeats in numerous other states and
cities. The elections of 1996 were a time of triumph for the PAN, which increased its vote in the municipal elections by 27 percent; the PRD advanced
by 4 percent, while the PRI declined by 15 percent. Between 1992 and
1997, the PAN has gained 15 million new voters and will likely win elections
in the most populous northern and central states, if there is a minimum of
transparency. This is a big "if," as the government has launched a multibil-
lion-peso "poverty" program that is a faintly disguised vote-buying campaign.

The party-state's trade union arm, the CTM, concedes that workers have
lost over three-fourths of their purchasing power since 1982. In response, it
launched a government-financed "beans and rice" giveaway program aimed
at the poorest villagers and urban squatters, coinciding with the electoral
campaign. The Zedillo government can be expected to continue to give free
rein to the PRI paramilitary forces responsible for killing an average of two
PRD leaders or activists a week—since Zedillo's inauguration—and none of
the assassins have been arrested.

Despite coercion, corruption, and fraud, the opposition has made significant inroads, even at the local level. The PAN has demonstrated strong electoral support in the northern industrial zones, in the agroindustrial central-
western region, and in the State of Mexico, including the capital. The
Center-Left PRD has its electoral support in the industrial and middle sectors of the State of Mexico and particularly in the agricultural South. Despite
its decay and the violent internal struggles for power and control over narco-

traffic (including numerous murders), the party-state still has a vast apparatus that penetrates every village, neighborhood, and sector of the economy, a vast range of print and electronic media, and billions of pesos in taxpayers' money and oil revenues to spend on the elections. As in the past, the U.S. government continues to back the PRI, and the U.S. mass media continue their support for the Zedillo regime that controls and runs the party-state.

Washington is not too perturbed by the decline of the PRI, since the PAN shares the neoliberal program promoted by the PRI. In fact, the PAN would deepen the process of globalization and liberalization, if and when it took power. Lacking a majority, the PAN formed a coalition with the PRI in Congress rather than with the PRD, despite the fact that the latter's leadership offered to be a partner in a coalition.

The electoral opposition is led by the PAN, but the picture changes dramatically when we look at the social movements. In the countryside, particularly in Oaxaca, Chiapas, Guerrero, and Tabasco, as well as among the Indian communities and particularly in a number of important trade unions (transport, teachers, university, electrical, and communication workers) the left wing of the PRD and the radical Left have been gaining influence. Through direct action, occupying municipal buildings, blocking highways, making land occupations, and conducting urban marches and strikes, the extraparliamentary Left has sharply undercut the PRI's stranglehold over workers, peasants, and neighborhood organizations.

Many Mexicans who are disgusted with the electoral fraud of the PRI prefer to engage in direct action rather than vote in elections in which the outcome is decided by the local PRI bosses. The problem is not the size or scope of these social movements but their dispersed and localized nature. This is beginning to change. The debtor organization Barzon, which was organized by middle-class farmers and professionals; the new national coordinating organization set up by Indian organizations in June 1997 in Chiapas; and the efforts by the Zapatistas to establish a new inclusive political movement, a new National Zapatista Liberation Front (FZLN), all speak to the growth of a national challenge to the PRI.

Another source of opposition is found in the newly emerging guerrilla movements in the South: the EZLN, or the Zapatistas, with their powerful political appeals throughout the country, despite their limited geographic sway; the People's Revolutionary Army with its key cadres in some of the more radicalized and impoverished southern rural states. Other smaller armed groups have also manifested signs of activity. Although the government has militarized the regions of conflict, its unrelenting pursuit of the free market doctrine ensures that social violence will continue, particularly as the agricultural policies continue the enrichment of 10 percent of the agro-exporters, deepen the indebtedness of the 30 percent who are middle-sized farmers, while impoverishing the other 60 percent, mostly peasantry and landless laborers.

What the United States and foreign investors fear most is the breakdown of the party-state, the loosening of controls over civil society, and the mass eruption of the social demands of the tens of millions whose declining living standards have financed the opening of the market and the payment of the interest on the foreign debt. In this context, Washington favors a "peaceful, negotiated" transfer of power to the PAN, and the consolidation of a new police-military-judiciary structure that can continue to enforce the rules of the free market.

Conclusion

The Mexican Government's success in attracting the return of overseas lenders to Mexico following the 1994 debacle has its counterpoint in the impoverishment of the Mexican middle class and the severe pauperization of the lower class. The Clinton administration's White House celebration of the early payback of the bailout loan has its Mexican side in the proliferation of guerrilla groups and social mobilization in the countryside. The 34 percent loss of purchasing power of salaried workers since 1994 is the other side of the coin that on its face shows exorbitant returns amassed by the managers of U.S. money funds. While the privatization process was proceeding full steam ahead in 1996, salaries remained 78 percent below what they were in 1982 when the current crisis emerged. The conditions for foreign capital inflows are precisely those that create massive poverty and social discontent, which in turn encourage the outflow of Mexican savings. By making foreign debt payments the number one priority, the government has made the recovery of Mexican living standards its lowest priority. Whether through ballots or bullets, Mexico in 1998 is ripe for political change.

11

Globaloney and the State

Globalization began in the fifteenth century with the growth of capitalism and its overseas expansion: The first pattern of globalization is seen in the conquest and exploitation of Asia, Africa, and Latin America and the white colony settlements in North America and Australia. In other words, *globalization was, from the beginning, associated with imperialism:* The global linkage was based on European accumulation—exploitation of the Third World for accumulation in the First World. The imperial origins of globalization define the impetus, nature of the networks, and the "dynamic" of the process. From the beginning, class configurations and state institutions in the Third World were essential in opening the countries to exploitation and in assuring raw materials, controlled labor, administrative cadres, and a reliable army to facilitate the "deepening of globalization." The greater the articulation in the Eurocentric global economy, the greater the disarticulation of the domestic, indigenous economy. The global empires (Spain and Portugal) were initially built around exploiting domestic economies to finance overseas conquest and private accumulation.

The second pattern of globalization was built around *inter-imperial trade.* The exchanges within Europe and then later with the United States (today with Japan) have created a series of regional groupings linked together via "regional" hegemons. In this context, globalization involves competition and collaboration: struggles between nationally based multinationals over market shares as well as collaboration in order to jointly exploit markets.

Third, globalization involves *international trade* (as distinct from pillage, extractive investments, and loans). International exchanges of commodities link markets and classes in social hierarchies that give globalization its class character as an arena for class and trade conflict.

In summary, globalization is not a new phenomenon: It is a new name that subsumes diverse sociopolitical and economic processes. The imperial historical origins have remained embedded in a matrix in which new states and actors compete for privileged access to networks and state support. The principal agencies today, the multinational corporations, fulfill the roles played earlier by the trading companies: integrating and appropriating resources and exploiting cheap labor. Today, the imperial states extract domestic resources (from employees and taxpayers) to finance overseas expansion. Hence, in the North and South, labor is exploited: Past projects in the North finance current expansion in the South.

Cyclical Patterns of Globalization

The globalization process rooted in the past has not been a linear process of ever-increasing world integration. Economies, North and South, have alternated between the global and national or regional markets over the past five hundred years. In the twentieth century, globalization was intense until 1914, followed by a prolonged period of shifting to national development from the late 1920s to the mid-1940s, followed by an increasing and uneven effort from the 1950s to the 1970s to return to globalization. The overthrow of nationalist and Socialist regimes and the increased competitiveness of Asian capitalism in the 1980s has led to the current period of globalization, a phase that is itself today under increasing attack from within most countries, North and South. Thus, globalization is not the "ultimate" phase of capitalism but rather a product of state policies linked to international economic institutions. Globalization is a cyclical phenomenon that alternates with periods of national development. Cyclical patterns are largely a function of internal class and state forces and general conditions affecting the process of capitalist accumulation. The ascendancy of globalism is largely the product of capitalist forces *defeating* endogenous working-class, peasant, and small-business political forces, capturing the state, depressing living standards, and creating state incentives that promote export strategies (of commoditized capital) described as globalization. The decline of globalization is the product of the worldwide crisis of capitalism (such as in the 1930s) and the rise of national and social revolutionary movements that subordinate external exchanges to internal development (here we are clearly *not* describing "autarchy"). The rise of globalization is intimately related to the growth of class conflict and the squeeze of profits during the limited globalization period associated with the "welfare state." The crisis of declining profits associated with rising popular power is the source of the demise of "national development." The success of capital in undermining popular power, dismantling the welfare state, and converting the state into an instrument of overseas expansion is the underlying condition for globalization, not technological changes, new information systems, or world market imperatives. Technology and new information systems are just as compatible with national-statist models as neoliberal systems, as the Asian capitalists have demonstrated.

In summary, globalization is not a *new* phenomenon, nor is it the culmination of history. Historically, it has its cycle of rise, consolidation, and decay. To understand globalization, it must be viewed as a sociopolitical outcome. This requires an analysis of its social agents. An understanding of globalization first requires a critical discussion of what is not the "driving force" behind it. Three basic arguments center on "the advances of technology," or the so-called Third Scientific Revolution, and on the "imperatives of the world market," also referred to as the "logic of capital."

The argument that globalization is the result of the technological or information revolution has several basic weaknesses. The new computer-driven technologies *facilitate* information flows, increase the velocity of transfers and movements of capital, and provide the communication networks that eases plant relocations. But "technology" does not determine the location of investment, research, or design. The rates of profit determine how information will be utilized. The *type* of economic activity (whether it is financial speculation or productive investments) and location is a function of sociopolitical decisions and the state's capacity to execute them. Politics is in command of technology. The new technologies *facilitate* and *provide resources* for sociopolitical decisions made by whichever social class or economic institution is in control of the state.

The argument that world market imperatives make globalization inevitable overlooks the viability and dynamism inherent in local and regional markets. The competing demands between classes linked to different "markets" means that the turn to the "world market" is not the result of "imperatives" but the result of the superior political-military organization of social classes (multinational corporations) linked to "global markets." The imperatives do not emanate from an abstract world market but from the boardroom of the MNCs and in the government ministries linked to them.

In addition, the whole issue of the influence of the market varies with its relation to other *social considerations* and other *competing demands*. Classes, particular workers, peasants, and public employees can shape the scope and depth of "market"-driven forces—as has been true throughout history. Under the hegemony of the popular classes, the market (meaning the capitalists who produce and sell commodities for profit) can be subordinated to serve social interests, in the short run.

The very language of the ideologists of globalization is shot through with a kind of anthropomorphism that obscures its essential nature. For example, the very notion that "the market demands" is nonsense. The market does nothing of the sort. Only specific people organized in classes (like corporate executives) and economic institutions (directors of the IMF) demand—in the name of the market—economic policies favorable to their interests. The "market" is a symbol or code word for capitalists and the "world market" for capitalists linked to multinational corporations and banks. The basic question related to the behavior of markets is essentially a political question ultimately resolved by state policy. The relative importance of producing for social classes in the domestic market or the world market, the question of how open or closed an economy will be in relation to the market (how to insert in the market), when to enter markets, and which markets to enter—all these issues are in great part influenced by political decisionmakers.

There is no single set of commands emanating from a single source, as the globalization theorists would have it. The globalization, or the production and exchange in the world market, is a particular command emanating from a specific set of classes (exporters, financiers, and so on) dictating a particular type of insertion ("free markets").

Finally, the notion that "globalization is the result of the logic of capitalism" is both asocial and ahistorical—and it is a very abstract notion. First, it obscures the multiple actors (different capitals, role of workers, and so forth) and multiple states that intervene and shape the "movements" (or logic) of capital. Second, the "logic of capital" approach fails to explain the periods of "involution" of capital, the crises that cause capital to go "overseas" or to "return" to the domestic economy. Third, it fails to explain the different degrees of insertion of capital in the world economy at different times.

The logic of capital is a linear conception of capital moving upward and outward without any sense of its rise and decline. Nor does it locate "the logic" in relation to the role of politics, ideology, and state policy in setting the parameters and conditions for capital accumulation. To understand the "real," or historical, process of globalization requires an analysis of the *state* and its relation to capital, both in the imperial and the Third World countries.

The Sociopolitical Agents of Globalization

The main protagonists of globalization are *ascending* imperial countries—meaning countries whose principal economic institutions are "world competitive" and thus have nothing to lose and everything to gain from open markets. Ascending imperial countries favor *unrestricted* globalization. They tend to open their economies as well as demand the openness of others (Germany, Japan). Second groups of countries favoring unrestricted globalization are "clients" of the ascending imperial countries who "specialize" in exports of agro-mineral, forestry, and maritime primary goods that provide high profits and inputs for the growth of imperial centers (Chile).

Declining imperial countries combine *restrictive and selective globalization,* pursuing openness where they still retain a superior competitive position while imposing state import constraints in sectors where they have lost competitiveness (United States). Ascending developing countries with diversified industrial bases combine globalization as a formula for export while *re-taining strong state regulation* that controls inflows of foreign capital and imports that may hinder weak or newly emerging economic sectors. Thus, while almost all countries pay lip service to the globalization discourse, there are varying interpretations of its meaning and application, according to their location in the imperial cycle (ascending or descending) and their relation to imperial centers (as client or ascending developing country).

The central role of the state in the current phase of globalization is illustrated by its essential activity in reconstructing the capitalist system at the end of World War II. The starting point for globalization is the reconstruction of Western Europe and Japan through the Marshall Plan and the subsequent military alliances (NATO, SEATO, and so forth). State-to-state economic policies and military alliances, largely at the initiative of the U.S. imperial state, provided the "shell" for overseas expansion of the multinational corporations. U.S. and European military and CIA intervention in the Third World (Indochina, Korea, Vietnam, the Congo, Santo Domingo, Indonesia, Guatemala, Brazil, and others) were extensions of state policy, securing the region for multinational expansion. Imperial state-brokered "transitions" from colonies to independence were designed to guarantee state access and widen opportunities for multinationals (Kenya, Nigeria, Jamaica, Malaysia, and so forth).

The imperial state also played the principal role in opening the world economy through the creation of supposedly "international" economic institutions like the World Bank, the IMF, and GATT. These institutions were controlled by appointees of the respective imperial states, initially predominantly by the United States. Their function was to displace national markets and local producers and undermine popular social legislation to facilitate the entry of multinationals and the primacy of domestic export elites producing for the markets of the imperial countries.

In a word, the *imperial state* played a basic role in the economic *reconstruction* of the major corporate-dominated economies, provided a military-political *shell* for its expansion, and intervened to preserve and deepen its presence, while it financed "international" lending agencies established to open new markets and investment sites. Far from being antistatist, multinational capital demands an "activist state," but one that dismantles the welfare state in favor of *globalization*. Under the impetus of export and multinational capital, the imperial state subsidizes and finances global expansion while facilitating internal exploitation to accumulate capital for export. As empire grows, the domestic society declines.

A similar activist role is evident in the role of the state in the Third World. There is a dialectical relation between the state role in the "domestic economy" and in the process of globalization. By pursuing policies of lowering wages, implementing social cuts in the budget, and transferring pensions to private capital, the *Third World states reconcentrate income upward for overseas expansion* (globalization, or "capital relocation"). This process is most clearly evident in the current neoliberal phase of capitalism with the so-called structural adjustment policies. Designed by Third World states in collaboration with the IMF and World Bank, they increase the "upward" flows of income and the availability of national public property for privatization to multinationals and the wealthy domestic elites.

In summary, the imperial and Third World states are essential elements in establishing the *initial conditions* for the movements of capital and elaborating incentives and policies (privatization, free trade) facilitating its continued *expansion,* while shifting the burden for the periodic *crises* onto the shoulders of wage and salaried earners. In no case do the multinationals create their own universe or "transcend" the existing state structures.

But the question remains: How and why does the "state" play its role in globalization?

Class Conflict, the State, and Globalization

The current phase of globalization is rooted in the change in the correlation of class forces within the state, society, and workplace. The eclipse of trade unions and left-wing parties, in part the result of repression in the 1970s (Chile, Argentina, Brazil, Indonesia, Uruguay, and so on) and of co-optation (trade unions in the United States, Western Europe, and elsewhere) and the right turn of Social Democratic and Communist parties, allowed for high rates of accumulation while depressing labor costs, thus encouraging globalization. Once the globalization process took hold, there was a *feedback* effect: Overseas investments in cheap labor undermined labor's role as a countervailing force. As the trade unions and labor movements were fragmented, this further encouraged capital to intensify exploitation and export capital in a continuing spiral.

The first generation of globalizers in the United States and England in the North and in Chile and Mexico in the South evoked imitators and the creation of a "second generation" that reproduces the process. Today, Germany and Japan are relocating capital abroad (Eastern Europe, Southeast Asia) and the rest of Latin America "follows" the "free market" model.

The beginning of globalization is located, in the case of Chile, in the change in state power, from Allende to Pinochet. This change in the state is accompanied by changes in the rules of regulation—based on social actors oriented toward the "world market." State intervention is directed at controlling and defining the social activities of civil society, establishing new parameters for political economic debate. State subsidies to exporters and the public subsidies of private bank losses are accompanied by massive state-directed redistribution of income upward and outward. Neoliberal statism becomes the controlling ideology dictating the terms of the so-called transition to electoral politics. The consolidation of globalist politics is found in the electoral process: The elected presidents deepen and extend the neoliberal doctrine in alliance with the local and foreign multinationals and the international banks, with the tacit or overt support of the military.

Contradictions of Globalization

The emergence of globalized capitalism is a contradictory phenomenon. As MNCs grow overseas, they absorb a growing proportion of local resources, while the fiscal bases to sustain the state that supports the MNCs declines. The result is an increase in taxes on wage or salary workers relative to multinational corporations and deeper social cuts to finance the export economy. Hence, globalization is accompanied by domestic decay.

Under the fiscal pressures imposed by capital movements, the state sells off more and more of its public resources: forests, mining regions, natural reserves, maritime resources. In the Third World among the indebted declining economies, there are no longer any public constraints as the "state regulators" are largely allies of the MNCs. The greater the external integration, the greater the exploitation of domestic resources to fuel expansion overseas. External *linkages* between Third World capitalists and the MNCs requires vast amounts of capital accumulated by cheap labor and pillage of the natural resources. For the economic elite, the price of "entering" the First World is expensive, and the quickest road is via unlimited exploitation of nonrenewable resources.

Conclusion

The growing contradiction between globalization and decay of the domestic economy in the North and the contradiction between growing elite integration in the world market and the pillage of domestic resources and labor in the South is creating the basis for a new kind of internationalism built around common opposition to the state- and class-control and directing of globalization. In both instances, the struggle to recreate "national economies" and domestic markets serving popular classes passes through several channels, taking state power and redirecting national resources and information systems toward the popular classes.

Majority movements that oppose NAFTA exist today in the United States and Mexico. In Europe, the Maastricht agreement is under severe attack, as the French workers demonstrated in their rejection of Jacques Chirac's attack on social welfare. At the same time that defensive struggles emerge in favor of the welfare state, the deepening crisis of globalization is generating reactionary solutions—channeling middle-class and working-class discontent onto the most oppressed classes: immigrant workers, women, and minorities.

There is a profound division between progressive forces trying to rebuild a powerful popular democratic welfare state and reactionary globalists attacking the state. Globalization has given rise to social movements that attempt to link the state to comprehensive national programs that can protect the environment and induce long-term, large-scale social transformation.

12

Beyond the Free Market: The Resurgence of the Left

The current phase of neoliberal ascendancy is rooted in changes in the correlation of class forces within the state, society, and workplace. The eclipse of trade unions and left-wing parties, in part the result of repression beginning in the mid-1960s and continuing to the mid-1970s (Argentina, Chile, Brazil, Indonesia, Uruguay, and so on), the co-optation of trade union bureaucrats (in Argentina, Mexico, Venezuela, and elsewhere), the conversion of Social Democratic parties to liberalism (Chile and Bolivia, for example), and the right turn of intellectuals allowed for high rates of accumulation by depressing labor costs and thus encouraging greater flows of capital and goods across national boundaries. In the 1980s, with the end of the Cold War, the collapse of the ex-Soviet Union into mafia-run ministates and bankrupt economies, the incorporation of China into the world economy, and the retreat of Third World revolutionary movements from the anti-imperialist struggle, the external opportunities for Latin American countries seeking alternative trading and investment partners dried up. In the new international context, even the language of politics changed: Imperialism became "globalization," and Latin American dependence on creditors was called "interdependency." Investments in cheap labor undermined the trade union's role as a countervailing force. The fragmentation of the trade unions and divisions in the labor movements encouraged local and overseas investors to intensify exploitation and accumulate capital. State intervention directed at controlling and defining the sociopolitical activities of popular sectors in civil society and establishing narrow parameters for political and economic debate increased. Big business may be oriented toward the "world market," but neoliberal statism has become the practice: State subsidies to exporters and government bailouts of private bank losses have been accompanied by massive state-directed redistribution of income upward and outward, justified on the basis of "international competitiveness."

This analysis emphasizes the sociopolitical agencies and struggles as determining factors in the ascendancy of capitalism in the 1980s and 1990s. From the perspective of social action theory in a world historical context, the movements of capital in Latin America rest on a particular history of political victories and defeats. The resurgence of the "free market" and the neoliberal project is the effect of political and social changes in the balance of power between labor and capital. The ascendancy of free market regimes in Latin America since the 1980s has not led to the development of productive forces: Speculator capitalism is supreme, and industrial capitalism has become a subordinate force. The reasons for the decline of the revolutionary Left in the 1980s are not to be found in any successful transformation of capitalism (the 1980s was referred to as the Lost Decade) and are not due to the moral superiority of capitalism. The triumph was in many instances the product of long and sustained Western (particularly involving the United States) political-military warfare, state terror, and political exclusion directed against revolutionary regimes and movements. The physical liquidation of over 250,000 Indians, peasants, workers, and professionals in Central America was a result of U.S.-backed military regimes or authoritarian civilian regimes. Hundreds of thousands of activists were jailed, killed, or exiled in Brazil (1964), Bolivia (1971), Chile (1973), Uruguay (1974), Argentina (1976). All these events played a major role in reversing the post–Cuban Revolution upsurge in Latin America and in securing the condition for the ascendancy of neoliberalism.

The very terms of "success" of the neoliberal model have created the conditions for the resurgence of radical, extraparliamentary, sociopolitical movements. The declining incomes of wage and salary workers, the firing of tens of thousands of public sector employees, the impoverishment of the provinces, and the ruination of millions of small producers and peasants have propelled the growth of radical movements that see the closed system of free markets for the rich as their main enemy.

This understanding of neoliberalism and its opposition is based on interaction between class and state in a world historical context. It should be emphasized that history is not predetermined by existing economic institutions but is influenced by class, national, and social struggles that intervene and transform the economic structures. Social action theory emphasizes the role of class relations, state intervention, repression, class conflict and organization, and ideology and its decay—rather than "global structural factors"—in shaping the conditions for the dominance and decay of neoliberalism.

Neoliberalism in Latin America is a highly contradictory phenomenon. As multinational corporations expand, they absorb a growing proportion of local resources through the process of state subsidies, buyouts, and loans, while the fiscal bases to sustain the economy and state decline. The result is a sharp decline in social services and resources for local producers relative to multinational corporations. The deeper social cuts to finance the export economy are accompanied by domestic decay.

What is occurring in Latin America has some similarities to the privatization processes that took place in the mid-nineteenth century: large-scale growth of capital accompanied by the expulsion of indigenous peasants and the growth of low-paying jobs, poverty, crime, and human suffering. Today, the official number of the unemployed and underemployed in the countries of Latin America stands at over 50 percent of the labor force, and in some countries (Peru, Venezuela, Bolivia), the figure is close to 80 percent. It is indicative of the nature as well as the severity of the effects of neoliberalism that there has been a mass exodus out of the countryside and into the sprawling urban slums. At the same time, the principle of profit maximization, which nowadays goes completely unchecked under the pretext of operating in a "global market," threatens the world with an ecological disaster. The tropical forests, which have experienced a decline of more than 40 percent during the last twenty-five years or so, are disappearing at a rate of 30,000 to 37,000 square miles every year as multinational timber companies are having a field day under free trade, free market legislation.

Indeed, the ecological effects of globalized capitalism are catastrophic. Under the financial pressures imposed by capital lenders, the Latin American neoliberal state sells off more and more of its public resources—forests, mines, natural reserves, maritime resources. The greater the external integration, the greater the exploitation of domestic resources to fuel overseas capital flows and the greater the depredation of the environment. External linkages between Latin America's neoliberal regimes and the multinationals require vast amounts of capital; in a neoliberal setting, cheap labor and pillage of the natural resources are the chosen means available for capital accumulation. For the economic elite, the price of "integration" into the world economy is expensive, and the quickest road is via unlimited exploitation of nonrenewable resources. This is the lesson of Brazil, Chile, Mexico, and so many other Latin American nations. In this sense, colonial-style exploitation is making a comeback.

The growing contradiction between neoliberal "globalism" and decay of the domestic economy and society in Latin America and the contradiction between growing elite integration in the world market and the pillage of domestic resources and labor are creating the basis for a new kind of revolutionary politics built around common opposition to the neoliberal state and globalized capitalism. Major oppositional movements exist today throughout Latin America. Radical political activity among peasants and workers is resurfacing once again in an effort to counter the devastating consequences of the neoliberal project.

In order to effectively counter the new wave of liberalization, rural urban coalitions are being built. The state is viewed as a potential resource and lever for change. The new radicalism views the state as an agency to redistribute resources to the popular sectors of civil society. Social movements working for radical change reject the sharp distinctions between state and civil society. They perceive how the neoliberal capitalists thrive on exploiting the state (and the masses of working taxpayers). They reject the ideology of classless "identity politics" in favor of integrating the struggle for gender, race, and ethnic equality into a class struggle perspective. The challenge to the neoliberal ideology grows from alternatives that work from productive forms of social organization, not populist handouts from a paternalist state. Within this context, the national economy is seen as the starting point for any political confrontation with the forces of neoliberal capitalists and their international allies. The rhetoric of globalization, which serves to reduce wage levels toward the lowest international levels while encouraging the import of the products of low-wage labor, is challenged by a strategy that channels earnings into developing the domestic market. Measures ranging from capital controls to socialization of the means of production and worker self-management are part of the new alternatives. The strengthening of the local economy leads to the reconstruction of a labor force capable of fighting on a level playing field.

Index

Printed in the United States
by Baker & Taylor Publisher Services